Culture Wise
TURKEY

The Essential Guide to Culture, Customs & Business Etiquette

Robbi Forrester Atilgan

Survival Books • London • England

First published 2009

Survival Books Limited
26 York Street, London W1U 6PZ, United Kingdom
☎ +44 (0)20-7788 7644, 🖷 +44 (0)870-762 3212
✉ info@survivalbooks.net
🖥 www.survivalbooks.net

British Library Cataloguing in Publication Data.
A CIP record for this book is available
from the British Library.
ISBN: 978-1-905303-44-1

Printed and bound in India by Ajanta Offset

ACKNOWLEDGEMENTS

I would like to thank the many friends, family members and colleagues – unfortunately too many to mention – who provided information for this book. In particular, I would like to give huge thanks to my *dost*, Louise Robinson, for supporting the leap of faith which brought me to live in Turkey – and to *canım benim* Erden for giving me a reason to stay. Also, a special dedication to my late father Tom Forrester, who was charmed by the courtesy of the Turkish people and so looked forward to reading this book.

I would also like to thank Joe Laredo for editing, Peter Read for proof-reading, Di Tolland for DTP and photo selection, and Jim Watson for the cover design and maps. Finally a special thank you to all the photographers (listed on page 239) – the unsung heroes – whose beautiful images add colour and bring Turkey to life.

THE AUTHOR

Robbi Forrester Atilgan was born in the UK and has worked as a journalist for many years. She spent her early career in the music press, travelling around the world with rock acts such as Ozzy Osbourne and Bon Jovi, before settling for the more sedate world of freelance editing. Robbi first visited Turkey in the mid-'90s, and was soon tempted back to live there. She became a citizen through marriage in 2001 and now considers herself to be at least half Turkish. As well as writing for a living, Robbi has worked as a tour and airport representative, English teacher, estate agent and business owner. Robbi is married to Erden and divides her time between the UK and their Turkish home in Dalyan, a small riverside town near the Mediterranean coast. Robbi is the co-author of *Life in the UK: Test & Study Guide*, also published by Survival Books.

What readers & reviewers have said about Survival Books:

'If you need to find out how France works then this book is indispensable. Native French people probably have a less thorough understanding of how their country functions.'

Living France

'It's everything you always wanted to ask but didn't for fear of the contemptuous put down. The best English-language guide. Its pages are stuffed with practical information on everyday subjects and are designed to compliment the traditional guidebook.'

Swiss News

'Rarely has a 'survival guide' contained such useful advice – This book dispels doubts for first-time travellers, yet is also useful for seasoned globetrotters – In a word, if you're planning to move to the US or go there for a long-term stay, then buy this book both for general reading and as a ready-reference.'

American Citizens Abroad

'Let's say it at once. David Hampshire's Living and Working in France is the best handbook ever produced for visitors and foreign residents in this country; indeed, my discussion with locals showed that it has much to teach even those born and bred in l'Hexagone – It is Hampshire's meticulous detail which lifts his work way beyond the range of other books with similar titles. Often you think of a supplementary question and search for the answer in vain. With Hampshire this is rarely the case. – He writes with great clarity (and gives French equivalents of all key terms), a touch of humour and a ready eye for the odd (and often illuminating) fact. – This book is absolutely indispensable.'

The Riviera Reporter

'A must for all future expats. I invested in several books but this is the only one you need. Every issue and concern is covered, every daft question you have but are frightened to ask is answered honestly without pulling any punches. Highly recommended.'

Reader

'In answer to the desert island question about the one how-to book on France, this book would be it.'

The Recorder

'The ultimate reference book. Every subject imaginable is exhaustively explained in simple terms. An excellent introduction to fully enjoy all that this fine country has to offer and save time and money in the process.'

American Club of Zurich

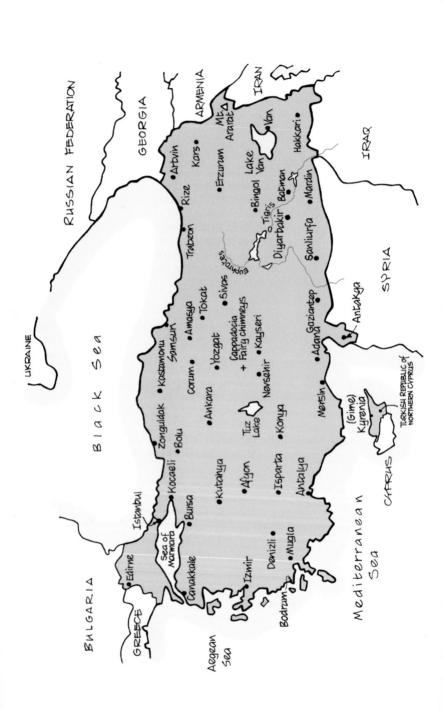

CONTENTS

Blue Mosque, Istanbul

INTRODUCTION

I
f you're planning a trip to Turkey or just want to learn more about the country, you'll find the information contained in *Culture Wise Turkey* invaluable. Whether you're travelling on business or pleasure, visiting for a few days or planning to stay for a lifetime, Culture Wise guides enable you to quickly find your feet by removing the anxiety factor when dealing with a foreign culture.

Adjusting to a different environment and culture in any foreign country can be a traumatic and stressful experience, and Turkey is no exception. You need to adapt to new customs and traditions, and discover the Turkish way of doing things; whether it's sharing a polite afternoon of *çay* and *pasta* with neighbours or toasting a colleague's success with copious glasses of *rakı* at a *meyhane*, learning the rules of *tavla* played at lightning speed or sweating out your stress at the *hamam*, watching a young boy's (painful) coming of age at his *sünnet* or wishing a couple '*Mutluluklar*' in their new married life. Whatever you do, it's sure to involve a little bit of *kader* and a large amount of *keyif*.

Turkey is a land where many things are done differently: where strangers are welcomed as guests (as long as they only stay for three days) and nobody needs an excuse to dance, where people eat olives and cucumber for breakfast and ladies' thighs and twisted turbans for lunch, where camels wrestle and Dervishes whirl and people live in fairy chimneys – and where the entire population stands silent to honour the memory of a leader who died before the Second World War.

Culture Wise Turkey is essential reading for anyone planning to visit Turkey, including tourists (particularly travellers planning to stay a number of weeks or months), business people, migrants, retirees, holiday homeowners and transferees. It's designed to help newcomers avoid cultural and social gaffes; make friends and influence people; improve communications (both verbal and non-verbal); and enhance your understanding of Turkey and the Turkish people. It explains what to expect, how to behave in most situations, and how to get along with the locals and feel at home – rather than feeling like a fish out of water. It isn't, however, simply a monologue of dry facts and figures, but a practical and entertaining look at life in Turkey – as it really is – and not necessarily as the tourist brochures would have you believe.

A period spent in Turkey is a wonderful way to enrich your life, broaden your horizons, and hopefully expand your circle of friends. We trust this book will help you avoid the pitfalls of visiting or living in Turkey and smooth your way to a happy and rewarding stay.

İyi şanslar! (good luck!)

Robbi Forrester Atilgan

February 2009

mosaic detail, Hagia Sophia, Istanbul

1.

A CHANGE OF CULTURE

With almost daily advances in technology, ever-cheaper flights and knowledge about almost anywhere in the world at our fingertips, travelling, living, working and retiring abroad have never been more accessible, and current migration patterns suggest that it has never been more popular. But, although globalisation means the world has 'shrunk', every country is still a world of its own with a unique culture.

Some people find it impossible to adapt to a new life in a different culture – for reasons which are many and varied. According to statistics, partner dissatisfaction is the most common cause, as non-working spouses frequently find themselves without a role in the new country and sometimes with little to do other than think about what they would be doing if they were at home. Family concerns – which may include the children's education and worries about loved ones at home – can also deeply affect those living abroad.

> 'There are no foreign lands. It is the traveller only who is foreign.'
>
> Robert Louis Stevenson
> (Scottish writer)

Many factors contribute to how well you adapt to a new culture – for example your personality, education, foreign language skills, mental health, maturity, socio-economic situation, travel experience, and family and social support systems. How you handle the stress of change and bring balance and meaning to your life is the principal indicator of how well you'll adjust to a different country, culture and business environment.

TURKEY IS DIFFERENT

Many people underestimate the cultural isolation that can be experienced in a foreign country, particularly one with a different language. Even in a country where you speak the language fluently you'll find that many aspects of the culture are surprisingly foreign (despite the cosy familiarity that can be engendered by cinema, television and books).

Turkey is a world away from Europe (although it's often considered to be a European country and is a member of many European institutions, most of the country is physically situated in Asia) or America. Not only is it a Muslim country, where religion is an integral part of daily life, but its development, while rapid, is still years behind that of North America and western Europe. The further you go from Istanbul and the tourist resorts, the more devout – and superstitious – the people are, and the more backward life appears to be.

Turkey is popularly perceived by many foreigners – particularly the British, Dutch and Germans – as a fairly easy expatriate option because of the well-established foreign communities on its Mediterranean and Aegean coasts, and the cosmopolitan atmosphere of Istanbul. They see it as a place where they can live the good life on a budget – with access to some, if not all, of the comforts of home.

However, despite the availability of foreign television, Dutch cheese and German newspapers, sooner or later they come up against the real Turkey, in the form of an obstinate bureaucrat, an untrustworthy property developer or a Turkish acquaintance who cannot afford medical care for his sick child. The blinkers drop away and they realise that they're no longer on holiday but living in a country where they will always be a *yabancı* (stranger or foreigner) and where life, for many people, is exceedingly tough. It's at this point that some book their plane ticket home.

> 'Burası Türkiye!' ('This is Turkey!') is an expression of despair, resignation and not a little pride, which you will hear many Turks exclaim when the bus breaks down, the *vezne* (cashier) closes his counter 15 minutes early or the electricity goes off for the fourth time that day.

Life isn't supposed to be comfortable in Turkey, when the unexpected is taken for granted. Westerners who are used to a life of order and predictability find this difficult to comprehend. The fatalistic attitude of many Turks when faced with discomfort or adversity is especially difficult to come to terms with. Some foreigners, particularly those who have juggled a family and business and developed a 'can do' attitude, cannot comprehend how the Turks simply accept (or appear even to enjoy) the inefficiency of their civil servants, the chaos of their road system or the ineptitude of their plumbers. The only way to cope is to 'let go'.

Before you try to get to grips with Turkish culture, however, you first need to adapt to a totally new environment and new challenges, which may include a new job, a new home and a new physical environment, which can be overwhelming.

Turkey experiences extremes of climate and weather, and you mustn't underestimate the effects that these can have on you. Intense heat and cold can lead to a lack of energy, poor sleep and dehydration. In the summer in many parts of the country, temperatures rise to a physically draining 50°C (122°F). In winter, Istanbul usually grinds to a halt for a while, under a blanket of snow, while even the Mediterranean coast can be damp and depressing, especially if you live in an open-plan villa with no central heating.

Those who move to a new job or attempt to start a business in Turkey may encounter a (very) steep learning curve – indeed, even finding a job can be a struggle, as the Turks put their own people first. The chances are that you've left a job in your home country where you held a senior position, were extremely competent and knew all your colleagues. In Turkey, you may be virtually a trainee (especially if your

Turkey attracts a great number of older people and retirees from western Europe, partly due to its low cost of living. However, many miscalculate the level of loneliness they will feel in a community of people who don't speak their language nor understand that people aged 60-plus can have a lot of life left in them. In Turkey, the average life expectancy for a man is 70, while a woman can expect to live to 75. To the Turks, many of whom expect to retire at 50, anyone who makes it into their seventh decade is decidedly elderly. This means that foreign 'snowbirds' may struggle to find Turks of their own age to socialise with and end up spending much of their time with each other – or with expatriates of their own age, which makes it more difficult to integrate with the community.

Turkish isn't fluent) and not know any of your colleagues. The sensation that you're starting from scratch can be demoralising.

Even if you move to a part of Turkey with a well-established expatriate community, such as the resort towns of Antalya, Fethiye or Marmaris, items that you're used to and took for granted in your home country may not be available, e.g. certain kinds of food (pork is forbidden by Islam), opportunities to engage in your favourite hobby or sport, and books and magazines in your language. The lack of 'home comforts' can wear you down. You'll also have to contend with the lack of a local support network. At home you had a circle of friends, acquaintances, colleagues and possibly relatives who you could rely on for help and support. In Turkey, there may be no such network, which can leave you feeling isolated and vulnerable.

The degree of isolation you feel usually depends on how long you plan to spend in Turkey and what you'll be doing there. If you're simply going on a short holiday you may not even be aware of many of the cultural differences, although if you are it will enhance your enjoyment and may save you a few embarrassing or confusing moments. However, if you're planning a business trip or intend to spend an extended period in Turkey, perhaps working, studying or even living there permanently, it's essential to understand the culture, customs and etiquette at the earliest opportunity.

CULTURE SHOCK

Culture shock is the term used to describe the psychological and physical state felt by people when arriving in a foreign country or even moving to a new environment in their home country

(where the culture and in some cases language may vary considerably by region or social class). Culture shock can be experienced when travelling, living, working or studying abroad, when in addition to adapting to new social rules and values, you may need to adjust to a different climate, food and dress code. It manifests itself in a lack of direction and the feeling of not knowing what to do or how to do things, not knowing what's appropriate or inappropriate. You literally feel like a fish out of water.

Culture shock is precipitated by the anxiety that results from losing all familiar rules of behaviour and cues to social intercourse – the thousand and one clues to accepted behaviour in everyday situations: when to shake hands and what to say when you meet people; how to buy goods and services; when and how much to tip; how to use a cash machine or the telephone; when to accept and refuse invitations; and when to take statements seriously and when not to. These cues, which may be words, gestures or facial expressions, are acquired in the course of our life and are as much a part of our culture and customs as the language we speak and our beliefs. Our peace of mind and social efficiency depends on these cues, most of which are unconsciously recognised.

The symptoms of culture shock are essentially psychological – although you can experience physical pain from culture shock – and are caused by the sense of alienation you feel when you're bombarded on a daily basis by cultural challenges in an environment where there are few, if any, familiar references. However, there are also physical symptoms including an increased incidence of minor illnesses (e.g. colds and headaches) and more serious psychosomatic illnesses brought on by depression. You shouldn't underestimate the consequences of culture shock, although the effects can be lessened if you accept the condition rather than deny it.

> **'When you travel, remember that a foreign country is not designed to make you comfortable. It is designed to make its own people comfortable.'**
>
> Clifton Fadiman (American writer)

Foreigners are often attracted to tourism-based businesses or end up in relationships with people who work in tourism, but many underestimate the pressure of working in this fickle industry, where many people work 18-hour days, dealing with high expectations and trying to earn enough money to survive through the off-season. Physical exhaustion and depression are common complaints. A doctor in a small Turkish Mediterranean tourist village revealed that roughly half the population took anti-depressants during the winter.

Stages of Culture Shock

Severe culture shock – often experienced when moving to a country with a different language – usually follows a number of stages. The names of these may vary, as may the symptoms and effects, but a typical progression is as follows:

1. The first stage is commonly known as the 'honeymoon' stage and usually lasts from a few days to a few weeks after arrival (although it can last longer, particularly if you're insulated from the pressures of 'normal' life). This stage is essentially a positive (even euphoric) one, when a newcomer finds everything an exciting and interesting novelty. The feeling is similar to being on holiday or a short trip abroad, when you generally experience only the positive effects of culture shock (although this depends very much on where you're from and the country you're visiting – see box).

2. The second (rejection or distress) stage is usually completely opposite to the first and is essentially a negative stage, a period of crisis, as the initial excitement and holiday feeling wears off and you start to cope with the realities of daily life – a life that is nothing like anything you've previously experienced. This can happen after only a few weeks. The distress stage is characterised by a general

feeling of disorientation, confusion and loneliness. Physical exhaustion brought on by a change of time zone, extremes of hot or cold, and the strain of having hundreds of settling-in tasks to accomplish is a recognised symptom. You may also experience regression, where you spend much of your time speaking your own language, watching television programmes and reading newspapers from your home country, eating food from home and socialising with expatriates who speak your language.

What are the most annoying aspects of living in Turkey? Comments from clients collected by a Mediterranean-based estate agent reveal these top ten gripes:

1. Bureaucracy
2. Death-wish driving
3. Complete disregard for time-keeping
4. Pushy salesmen & restaurant touts
5. Bungling workmen
6. Being charged 'tourist prices'
7. Unfinished buildings, roads & pavements
8. Attitude to street animals
9. Noise – car horns, wedding drums, the call to prayer at 5am
10. Insensitive, know-it-all foreigners

You may also spend a lot of time complaining about the host country and its culture. Your home environment suddenly assumes a tremendous importance and is irrationally glorified. All difficulties and problems are forgotten and only the good things back home are remembered. Some expats in Turkey exhibit a 'we and they' mentality, in which 'we' (the foreigners) are constantly trying to educate 'them' (the Turks) about the 'right' way to do things – an endeavour which is doomed to end in disappointment.

3. The third stage is often known as the 'flight' stage (because of the overwhelming desire to escape) and is usually the one that lasts the longest and is the most difficult to cope with.

   During this period you may feel depressed and angry, as well as resentful towards the new country and its people. You may experience difficulties, such as not being understood and feelings of discontent, impatience, frustration, sadness and incompetence. These feelings are inevitable when you're trying to adapt to a new culture that's very different from that of your home country, and they're exacerbated by the fact that you can see nothing positive or good about the new country and focus exclusively on the negative aspects. You may become hostile and develop an aggressive attitude towards the country. Other people will sense this and, in many cases, either respond in a confrontational manner or try to avoid you.

   There may be problems with the language, your house, job or children's school, transportation … even simple tasks like shopping may be fraught with problems, and the fact that the local people are largely indifferent to these only makes matter worse.

They may try to help but they just don't understand your concerns, and you conclude that they must be insensitive and unsympathetic to you and your problems.

Relinquishing your old customs and adopting those of your new country is difficult and takes time. During this process there can be strong feelings of dissatisfaction. The period of readjustment can last six months, although there are expatriates who adjust earlier and those (few) who never get over the 'flight' stage and are forced to return home.

Many expatriates who have stayed the course in Turkey have a love-hate relationship with the country. They love the people but accept that there are aspects of Turkish life which they strongly dislike and will never understand – such as the Turks' submission in the face of authority or the 'it'll do' attitude, whereby things are never quite finished. Accepting these uncomfortable differences is a key stage in overcoming culture shock.

4. The fourth (recovery or autonomy) stage is where you begin to integrate and adjust to the new culture and accept the customs

of the country as simply another way of living. **The environment doesn't change – what changes is your attitude towards it.** You become more competent with the language and you also feel more comfortable with the customs of the host country and can move around without feeling anxiety.

You still have problems with some of the social cues and you don't understand everything people say, particularly colloquialisms and idioms. Nevertheless, you've largely adjusted to the new culture and are starting to feel more familiar with the country and your place in it – more at home – and you begin to realise that it has its good as well as bad points.

The above-mentioned estate agent also revealed the top ten reasons why people fall in love with Turkey:

1. Generous, hospitable people
2. Laid-back attitude to life
3. Long summers & short winters
4. Low cost of living
5. Family values
6. Cheap, fresh fruit & vegetables
7. Politeness
8. Feeling safe & secure
9. Glorious countryside & ancient sites
10. Spontaneity

---

5. The fifth stage is termed 'reverse culture shock' and occurs when you return home. You may find that many things have changed (you'll also have changed) and that you feel like a foreigner in your own country. If you've been away for a long time and have become comfortable with the habits and customs of a new lifestyle, you may find that you no longer feel at ease in your homeland. Reverse culture shock can be difficult to deal with and some people find it impossible to re-adapt to their home country after living abroad for a number of years.

The above stages occur at different times depending on the individual and his circumstances, and everyone has his own way of reacting to them, with the result that some stages may last longer and are more difficult to cope with than others, while others are shorter and easier to overcome.

Reducing the Effects

Experts agree that almost everyone suffers from culture shock and there's no escaping the phenomenon; however, its negative effects can be reduced considerably by the following – some of which can be done even before you leave home:

● **Positive attitude** – The key to reducing the negative effects of culture shock is a positive attitude towards Turkey (whether you're visiting or planning to live there) – if you don't look forward to a holiday or relocation, you should question why you're doing it. There's no greater guarantee for unhappiness in a foreign environment than taking your negative prejudices with you. It's important when trying to adapt to a new culture to be sensitive to the locals' feelings and try to put yourself in their shoes wherever possible, which will help you understand why they behave as they do. Bear in mind that they have a strong, in-bred cultural code, just as you do, and react in certain ways because they're culturally 'trained' to do so. If you find yourself frustrated by an aspect of the local culture or behaviour, the chances are that they will be equally puzzled by yours.

> Turks often complain that foreigners are distant and aloof – they find many westerners difficult to get to know. For example, even those who have visited the UK many times, speak excellent English and have many foreign friends often describe the British as 'cold'. Try to see yourself as the Turks see you and avoid giving the wrong signals.

● **Research** – Discover as much as possible about Turkey before you go, so that your arrival and settling-in period doesn't spring as many surprises as it might otherwise. Reading about Turkey and its culture before you leave home will help familiarise yourself with the local customs and language, and make the country and its people seem less strange on arrival. You'll be aware of many of the differences between your home country and Turkey and be better prepared to deal with them. This will help you avoid being upset by real or imaginary cultural slights and also reduce the chance of your inadvertently offending the locals. Being prepared for a certain amount of disorientation and confusion (or worse) makes it easier to cope with it.

This book will go a long way towards enlightening you. For further details, there are literally hundreds of publications about Turkey as well as dozens of websites for expatriates (see **Appendices B** and **C**). Many sites provide access to expatriates already living in Turkey who can answer questions and provide useful advice. There are also 'notice boards' and 'forums' on many websites where you can post messages or questions.

● **Visit Turkey first** – If you're planning to live or work in Turkey for a number of years, or even permanently, it's important to visit the country to see whether you think you'd enjoy living there and be able to cope with the culture before making the leap.

Before you go, try to find people who have visited Turkey and talk to them about it. Some companies organise briefings for families before departure. Rent a property before buying a home and don't burn your bridges until you're certain that you've made the right decision. The Turkish property boom from 2003 onwards has attracted many would-be foreign investors, many of whom came on holiday, bought a home the same week and leapt into the Turkish lifestyle, without thinking about the consequences. Some even sold up in their home country. Many of those holiday homes ended up back on the market when their owners found they couldn't cope with life in Turkey. However, selling isn't as easy as buying, and they've found climbing back onto the property ladder in their own country an uphill struggle.

● **Learn Turkish** – Along with adopting a positive attitude,

overcoming the language barrier will probably be your most powerful weapon in combating culture shock and the key to enjoying your time in Turkey. The ability to speak Turkish isn't just a useful tool (allowing you to buy what you need, find your way around, etc.) but the passport to understanding Turkey and its culture. If you can speak the language, even at a low level, your scope for making friends is immediately widened beyond the limited expatriate circle. Obviously not everyone is a linguist and learning a language can take time and requires motivation. However, with sufficient perseverance virtually anyone can learn enough of another language to participate in the local way of life.

Certainly the effort will pay off, and expatriates who manage to overcome the language barrier find their experience in Turkey much richer and more rewarding than those who don't. The Turks realise that their language is difficult for westerners and are always honoured by a foreigner's attempts to use it. If you make an effort at communicating with the local people in their own language, you'll also find them far more receptive to you and your needs.

'Americans who travel abroad for the first time are often shocked to discover that, despite all the progress that has been made in the last 30 years, many foreign people still speak in foreign languages.'
Dave Barry (American writer & humorist)

● **Be proactive** – Make an effort to get involved in your new culture and go out of your way to make friends. Join

in the activities of the local people, which could be a religious holiday, local festival or social activity. The Turks will make an effort to invite you to events which are important to them but may be strange to you, such as circumcisions – take a deep breath and accept. There are often local clubs where you can play sport or keep fit, draw and paint, learn to cook regional dishes, make handicrafts, etc. Not only will this fill some of your spare time, giving you less time to miss home, but you'll also meet people and make new friends. If you feel you cannot join a local club, perhaps because the language barrier is too great, you can always participate in activities for expatriates, of which there are many in the most popular destinations. Look upon a period spent abroad as an opportunity to redefine your

life objectives and acquire new perspectives. Culture shock can help you develop a better understanding of yourself and stimulate your creativity.

● **Talk to other expatriates** – Although they may deny it, all expatriates have been through exactly what you're experiencing. Even if they cannot give you advice, it helps to know that you aren't alone and that the effects of culture shock lessen with time. However, don't make the mistake of mixing only with expatriates as this will alienate you from the local people and make it much harder to integrate. Don't rely on social contact with your compatriots to carry you through, because it won't.

● **Keep in touch with home** – Keeping in touch with your family and friends at home and around the world by telephone, email and letters will help reduce and overcome the effects of culture shock.

● **Be happy** – Don't rely others to make you happy; otherwise you won't find true and lasting happiness. There are certain things in life which only you can change. Every day we are surrounded by things over which we have little or no control but moaning about them only makes us unhappier. So be your own best friend and nurture your capacity for happiness.

Culture shock is an unavoidable part of travelling, living and working abroad, but if you're aware of it and take steps to lessen its effects before you go and while you're abroad, the period of adjustment will be shortened and its negative and depressing consequences reduced.

FAMILIES IN TURKEY

Family life may be completely different in Turkey from what you're used to, and although you may not adopt the ways of a Turkish family, you'll have to adapt to certain unfamiliar conditions. For example, your new home may scarcely resemble your previous one (it may be much more luxurious or significantly smaller) and the climate may be dramatically different from that of your home country. The stress of adapting to a new environment can strain family relationships – especially if they were under tension before you moved to Turkey. If possible, you should prepare yourself for as many aspects of the new situation as you can and explain to your children the differences they're likely to encounter, while at the same time dispelling their fears.

> **'Travellers never think that THEY are the foreigners.'**
>
> Mason Cooley (American aphorist)

In a situation where one spouse is working (usually the husband) and the other not, it's generally the latter (and any children) who is more affected by the change of culture. The husband has his work to occupy him and his activities may not differ much from what he had been accustomed to at home. On the other hand, the wife has to operate in a totally new environment, which differs considerably from what she's used to. She will find herself alone more often, as there will be no close relatives or friends on hand. However, if you're aware that this situation may arise, you can take action to reduce its effects. Working spouses should pay special attention to the needs and feelings of their non-working partners and children, as the success of a family relocation depends largely on the ability of the wife and children to adapt to the new culture.

Breadwinners can take refuge in the office but at-home spouses are in the front line of Turkey's cultural assault, when neighbours keep visiting, bringing unfamiliar food, intrusive questions and the full force of their curiosity. On the other hand, working women may find the Turkish 'men at work and women at home' mindset difficult to deal with.

Good communication between family members is vital and you should make time to discuss your experiences and feelings, both as a couple and as a family. Questions should always be raised and if possible answered, particularly when asked by children. However difficult your situation may appear at the beginning, it will help to bear in mind that it's by no means

unique and that most expatriate families experience exactly the same problems, and manage to triumph over them and thoroughly enjoy their stay abroad.

A NEW LIFE

Although you may find some of the information in this chapter a bit daunting, don't be discouraged by the foregoing catalogue of depression and despair; the negative aspects of travelling and living abroad have been highlighted only in order to help you prepare for and adjust to your new life. The vast majority of people who travel and live abroad naturally experience occasional feelings of discomfort and disorientation, **but most never suffer the debilitating effects of culture shock.**

As with settling in and making friends anywhere, even in your home country, the most important thing is to be considerate, kind, open, humble and genuine – qualities that are valued the world over. Selfishness, brashness and arrogance will get you nowhere in Turkey or any other country. Treat Turkey and its people with respect and they will reciprocate.

The majority of people living in Turkey would agree that, all things considered, they love living there – and are in no hurry to return home. A period spent in Turkey is a wonderful way to enrich your life, broaden your horizons, make new friends and maybe even please your bank manager. We trust that this book will help you avoid some of the pitfalls of Turkish life and smooth your way to a happy and rewarding future in your new home.

'Twenty years from now you will be more disappointed by the things you didn't do than by the ones you did do. So throw off the bowlines. Sail away from the safe harbour. Catch the trade winds in your sails. Explore. Dream. Discover.'

Mark Twain (American author)

2.
WHO ARE THE TURKS?

Like a veiled beauty in a sultan's harem, Turkey is mysterious, fascinating and exotic. A bridge between Asia and Europe, for centuries it has been the stage on which east meets west. Greek warriors and Roman centurions, Crusader knights and Arab invaders, Mongol hordes and Oriental traders – all have crossed, conquered and settled in Turkey. The result is a land steeped in history, with a diverse culture, a cuisine which is ranked among the best in the world, and a people renowned for their pride and hospitality.

> 'We Turks are a people who, throughout our history, have been the very embodiment of freedom and independence.'
>
> Mustafa Kemal Atatürk (the founder of modern Turkey)

Turkey is now a major tourist destination, attracting almost 20m visitors in 2006. It's often referred to as 'the new Spain', as it offers a Mediterranean lifestyle at a bargain price, and there's a growing foreign investment market, with Europeans buying holiday homes along the coast and overseas companies targeting its 70m-plus population.

More than anything, it's a country of contradiction and constant, often unpredictable, change. Despite its advances in pursuit of membership of the European Union (EU), Turkey isn't an easy option when it comes to choosing a place to settle or buy a second home, or even where to spend a holiday. The language is alien to most western ears. The economy is notoriously erratic. There is continuous conflict between secular and religious ideas and ideals. And Turkey's bureaucracy is one of the most antiquated and infuriating you'll ever encounter.

The upside is the spirit of relaxed optimism and unforced generosity which colours life in Turkey. The openness and kindness of the people is in stark contrast to the prevailing insularity of western life. The streets feel safe, and there's a refreshing lack of need for political correctness and no 'culture of blame'. Life is an adventure and most people agree that the future is something to look forward to.

To help you understand Turkey and the Turks, this chapter examines the country's turbulent history, the character of the Turkish people and the factors that influence it, and the icons and symbols which represent 'Turkishness' – at home and abroad.

Demographics

Full country name: The Republic of Turkey (*Türkiye Cumhuriyeti*).

Capital city: Ankara.

Population: 71,158,647 (July 2007 estimate – *CIA World Factbook*).

Population density: 93 inhabitants per km² (240 per mi²); Istanbul has a density of 6,521 inhabitants per km² (13,523 per mi²).

Largest cities: Istanbul (10.3m); Ankara (5m); Izmir (4m); Bursa (2.1m); Adana (1.3m).

Number of foreign residents: Just over 200,000, according to official figures in March 2007, just under half originating from EU member states. However, many foreigners stay in Turkey by continually renewing a visitor's visa, so the true figure has been estimated to be as high as 500,000.

Largest expatriate groups: Officially Bulgarian Turks (around 50,000), Azerbaijanis (11,000); Germans (10,000); Britons and Russians (8,000 each – though the movement of pension payments between the UK and Turkey suggests that the true number of British 'residents' may be closer to 40,000); Americans, Greeks, Iraqis and Iranians (6,000 each).

State religion: Turkey is officially a secular state.

Most followed religion: Islam – 99 per cent of the population is Muslim.

A POTTED HISTORY

Turkey's history is long and complex, and it's sometimes difficult to separate fact from fiction, but the remains of its many civilisations are among modern Turkey's greatest treasures. The most significant dates and events are listed below.

Invaders & Settlers

ca. 7500BC – People settle at Çatal Höyük in central Turkey.

1900-1600BC – The Hittites rule the Turkish peninsula (which became known as Anatolia, from the Greek word for 'of the sunrise' or simply 'east') from their power base at Hattusas, vying with the Egyptians for control of the near East.

1250BC – The Aegean principality of Troy (modern Truva in Çanakkale province in north-west Turkey) opens its doors to a great wooden horse and is destroyed by raiders from Greece.

1200-700BC – The independent kingdoms of Caria, Ionia, Lycia, Lydia, Pamphylia and Phrygia vie for power in western and central Anatolia, while the Urartians govern in the east.

546BC – Cyrus leads a Persian invasion, overwhelming the smaller states, and builds a road linking Iran to the Aegean coast.

334BC – The teenage Alexander the Great unifies much of Anatolia. His arrival heralds the Hellenistic age, combining Greek and Middle Eastern culture.

129BC – The Romans establish the province of Asia Minor; its capital is Ephesus, now one of the most-visited archaeological sites in Turkey.

47-57AD – St Paul journeys through Anatolia, spreading the Christian word.

330AD – A new city is completed on the site of Byzantium by the Roman Emperor Constantine. He calls it New Rome but the world will know it as Constantinople – and, much later, Istanbul.

Fortress of Europe, Istanbul

1453 – Sultan Mehmet II (the Conqueror) wins Constantinople for Islam and the Ottomans.

1520-66 – The reign of the greatest Ottoman sultan, Süleyman the Magnificent, who extends the boundaries of his empire to encompass the Middle East, North Africa and the Balkans.

> Despite their popular image as bloodthirsty warriors with harems full of captive western women, for the most part the Ottomans were civilised and pragmatic, and largely tolerant of ethnic differences and other faiths. They established a legal system, provided education and were patrons of the arts.

570 – Mohammed is born in Mecca; within 100 years the followers of the new religion of Islam are conquering Anatolia and threatening Constantinople.

1071-1243 – The first Turkic tribes arrive from Persia and establish the Seljuk Sultanate of Rum, with its capital in Konya. They build exquisite mosques and trading posts along the Silk Road, many of which remain today.

1000s-1200s – The Crusades; although intended to help Byzantium combat the Seljuks, the plan backfires in 1204 when poorly equipped Crusaders sack Constantinople for supplies.

The Ottoman Empire (1299-1922)

1288 – The foundation of the Osmanlı state near Bursa; this will grow into the Ottoman Empire, which will last for over 600 years.

1700-1900 – The Ottoman Empire slowly declines, losing land and influence.

The Birth of Modern Turkey

1881 – Mustafa Kemal (later Atatürk) is born in Macedonia (now part of Greece).

1876-1909 – The rule of Abdül-Hamid II, the last absolute sultan. He tries to enforce modernisation but alienates his subjects and is finally deposed. Power is now in the hands of the Ottoman government and the Young Turks' Committee of Union and Progress.

1914 -18 – The Young Turks' leaders side with Germany during the First World War. Despite success at Gallipoli, the Ottomans are on the losing side and the Allies carve up their territories under the Treaty of Sèvres.

1915-1917 – A dark and controversial period of Ottoman/Turkish history. Between 500,000 and 1.5m Armenians are massacred on Ottoman soil or die from starvation and exhaustion during deportation to Syria. To this day, and contrary to the views of many westerners, Turkey refuses to classify these events as 'genocide' (a term not legally defined until 1948).

1919-22 – Mustafa Kemal, a hero of Gallipoli, organises a resistance army and government.

1922 – The Turkish War of Independence. Greece invades Anatolia but is defeated at the Battle of Dumlupınar.

1923 – The Treaty of Lausanne is signed, confirming Turkish rule of Anatolia. Both Greeks and Turks are repatriated to their country of origin – many are uprooted against their will. The modern Republic of Turkey is founded on 29th October. Its capital is Ankara and Mustafa Kemal was its first president. He governs for the next 15 years and instigates sweeping reforms (see **Atatürk** under **Icons** below).

1938 – Atatürk dies on 10th November at the age of 57.

1939-45 – Turkey wisely stays neutral through most of the Second World War and only enters the fray in 1945 – on the Allies' side.

Democracy & Unrest

1950 – True democracy begins when the opposition Democratic Party is elected under its leader Adnan Menderes.

1960 – Economic problems lead to anarchy, violence – and the first of several military coups as the army steps in.

> There have been three military coups, plus some lesser interventions, since 1960. Many Turks accept or even support military interference, regarding it as a useful way of upholding secularism – and keeping politicians in line.

1965 – Süleyman Demirel begins the first of seven terms as Turkey's prime minister.

1974 – Turkish troops invade northern Cyprus in response to a Greek military coup. The island is divided and remains so into the third millennium.

1980-83 – Political infighting, soaring inflation and growing crime prompt another coup and the army remains in charge for three years under the leadership of Kenan Evren, until Turgut Özal's Motherland Party comes to power and begins a series of economic reforms.

NE MUTLU TÜRKÜM DİYENE

Atatürk's image is everywhere

1984 – The Kurdish Workers Party (PKK) launches its guerrilla war against Turkish troops in the south-east.

1987 – Turkey applies to become a full member of the European Union (EU).

1991 – The First Gulf War. The US launches air strikes from its Turkish bases; more than 3m Kurds flee from Iraq to eastern Turkey.

1995 – The right-wing religious Welfare Party forms a new government – two years later, the party is forced to disband in a 'post-modern' military coup.

1999 – PKK leader Abdullah Ocalan is captured and the PKK declares a ceasefire. In August an earthquake measuring more than 7 on the Richter scale devastates Izmit, east of Istanbul, leaving more than 17,000 people dead – poor building standards are blamed for many deaths.

2001 – The new Civil Code is enacted, giving women equal rights with men, more than 70 years after they received the right to vote.

2002 – The Justice and Development Party (AK Party) wins a landslide election victory. Abdullah Gül becomes prime minister.

2003 – Recep Tayyip Erdoğan takes over from Gül as PM. Turkey pushes ahead with pro-EU reforms, easing restrictions on freedom of speech and the Kurdish language. In November, a series of bombs in Istanbul, one outside the British Consulate, leaves 57 dead and more than 600 injured. Al-Qaida claims responsibility.

2004 – Turkey bans the death penalty.

2005 – Launch of the new Turkish lira (YTL) as the government strips away the six zeros which made every Turk a millionaire. The PKK is blamed for a series of violent incidents, including a bomb on a minibus in the resort of Kuşadası. Long-awaited European Union (EU) accession negotiations begin.

January 2007 – Turkey is shocked by the assassination of Armenian journalist Hrant Dink, and there are fears of a rise in nationalistic sentiment.

April-May 2007 – Mass rallies are held as supporters of secularism protest against the installation of an Islamist president – foreign minister Abdullah Gül. He fails to gain enough votes. As the stand-off between Islamists and secularists threatens to divide Turkey, the date of the next general election is brought forward.

July-August 2007 – The AK Party sweeps back into power with 46 per cent of the vote, although the nationalist and Kurdish parties also gain seats. Gül is elected president.

> **Istanbul lies in a precarious position on the North Anatolian Fault Line, along which there have been seven serious earthquakes since 1939, each occurring further west. Seismologists forecast the Izmit quake and predict that the next big one may well strike Istanbul.**

October 2007 – Relations with a long-time ally falter after a US congressional committee votes to recognise the killing of Armenians under Ottoman rule as genocide. Turks press for action after 13 soldiers are killed in PKK ambushes, and Turkey's parliament gives the green light to cross-border operations into northern Iraq in pursuit of PKK rebels.

November 2007 – Changes to the constitution are under discussion, in particular the controversial Article 301 of the Penal Code, which makes it illegal to 'insult Turkishness'.

December 2007 – Turkey sends troops into northern Iraq to strike at PKK separatists. Iraq protests but the US gives low-key support.

January 2008 – Police arrest a gang of high-profile nationalists, dubbed the 'Untouchables', for threatening the security of the state.

February 2008 – A seven-day ground offensive against the PKK in northern Iraq is announced as a success.

March 2008 – A top judge seeks an indictment against the governing AK Party for crimes against secularism. This is accepted by the Constitutional Court, and the country's president, prime minister and other members of its leading political party prepare to go on trial.

THE PEOPLE

It's usually a mistake to generalise about any people, and the Turks are no exception and especially difficult to categorise. On the one hand they appear generous, free-spirited and optimistic, on the other they can be withdrawn, sentimental and difficult to get to know. This contrary nature is due in no small part to Turkey's place in the world, balanced between east and west, religion and secularity, country and city, the past and the future.

Throughout history, the Turks have been misunderstood by much of the outside world, which has labelled them as cruel, indolent and unreliable. From Shakespeare to *The Simpsons*, there have been derogatory comments about them, and many European languages feature anti-Turkish sayings. Even today, a lot of foreigners' opinions are based on a few stereotypes – the smooth-talking carpet-dealer, the eager-to-please waiter – which have little to do with the average Turk.

In the same way, the picture of the 'typical' Turk is based on the short and swarthy Mediterranean physique, whereas the population encompasses features from across the globe – blue eyes in central Anatolia, red hair along the Black Sea coast, even the Negro features of the 'black Arabs' whose ancestors arrived as slaves from East Africa.

Just as their physical traits reflect their locality, so the Turks' attitudes vary from place to place, and these are further influenced in areas such as Istanbul and the tourist towns by the influx of foreigners from Europe and elsewhere.

But in spite of the many differences, there are some characteristics which are shared by most Turks. The main ones are as described below:

> '*Ne mutlu Türk diyene*' ('**How happy is he who can say "I am a Turk"!**'), which has become a national slogan.
>
> Mustafa Kemal Atatürk (Turkish leader, reformer & supreme icon)

National Pride

Turkey is one of the most patriotic nations in the world. From their first day at school, Turkish children are taught

to be proud of – and pledge allegiance to – their country. All young men must perform national service and, while some are reluctant, most would consider it shameful to try to duck this duty.

On national holidays, such as Republic Day (*Cumhuriyet Bayramı*), buildings are draped in flags and smaller versions are waved enthusiastically by onlookers at parades, while Atatürk's words are recited to rapt attention. Witnessing such an event can be overwhelming for someone from a country where national pride has lost its power or purpose – but this fervour is warmly and genuinely felt. Though most Turks welcome the outside world and its influences, at heart they still believe that 'Turkey is best'.

This is not to say that Turks cannot criticise their country – they frequently do – but it would be unwise for a foreigner to do so. Turkish law protects the flag, the people and the country itself, and there are penalties for denigrating these national pillars.

Honour & Respect

These two qualities are the glue which holds Turkish society together. It's a society in which everyone knows their place – at home, in the workplace and in social settings. Age and authority receive the greatest respect. Children defer to teachers, young people to their elders and employees to their boss, and no one resents (or even questions) this status quo. This is one aspect of the Turkish character which most delights foreigners – how pleasant to receive polite greetings from a gang of leather-clad teenagers!

Good manners really do matter in Turkey and there's no situation too urgent for them to be swept aside. Even in the midst of flood or earthquake, Turks still take the time to offer a welcome and exchange pleasantries with those offering assistance. And they expect you to do the same.

Honour, however, can be taken to extremes. Someone who brings dishonour on their family may be shunned or, in extreme cases, killed.

Turks forgive most social blunders by unwary foreigners but if they feel you've seriously damaged their honour, the breach will be difficult to mend.

Dignity & Saving Face

The Turks are a formal and dignified people, especially in business. They strive to avoid any situation which creates embarrassment or causes anyone to lose face, i.e. suffer humiliation or a loss of dignity. Most of all, they hate to say 'no', as a flat rejection implies a lack of respect. It's quite normal to ask favours through a third party to avoid the discomfort of giving or receiving a negative response, or to tell a white lie to preserve a client's dignity – 'the manager is out' rather than 'the manager doesn't want to see you'. Foreigners may find this evasive attitude frustrating, but it's an aspect of the culture which you need to adapt to – and employ. Western-style straight-talking won't get you very far in Turkey and could even be regarded as rude.

Gregariousness

Turks do everything together, in families or large groups. Meals are communal affairs (it's difficult to buy a meal-for-one in Turkey) and even the smallest house has several sofas to accommodate an extended family. Women gather in groups to cook and knit, men spend all day side by side at the tea house, and one of the most popular holiday options is a coach tour. Togetherness equals happiness, and the wishes of the group or family override personal desires.

The cult of the individual has yet to take hold in Turkey and people find it strange that westerners enjoy their own company. The pressure to 'join in' can be exhausting and you may find yourself making (polite) excuses or hiding behind your front door. But the group dynamic also means there's always someone to help in times of crisis.

Hospitality

Newcomers to Turkey are amazed by the unforced hospitality (*misafirperverlik*) which they receive from total strangers, but this shouldn't be confused with friendship. It's a matter of honour to look after guests, whether it's whipping up a last-minute meal or giving up the most comfortable bed in the house. In Anatolian villages, a stranger knocking on the door will automatically be invited to stay. However, guests also have responsibilities and shouldn't embarrass their host by offering money or assistance; nor should they overstay their welcome. Three days is generally considered long enough.

> **'A guest brings ten blessings, eats one and leaves nine behind.'**
> Turkish proverb

Keyif

This is the art of pure enjoyment, something which Turks are especially good at. They have the ability to switch off and live in the (pleasurable) moment – whether it's a boisterous wedding celebration or time spent sipping tea under a shady tree. Turks aren't great ones for planning, and *keyif* is often spontaneous – it can only take seconds for a quiet gathering to erupt into a frenzy of finger-clicking, hip-wiggling Turkish dancing.

Sentimentality & Melancholy

Songs about unrequited love and films with sad endings are much loved by the Turks. They tend to express nostalgia about people and places – in particular loyalty to a home town or village (*memleket*) and kinfolk (*hemşehri*) – and can be excessively sentimental. Mass migration to the cities in search of work means that many people live far from their birthplace, but they never forget their roots. Often they rebuild their 'village' around them – many cities have areas inhabited by communities who have arrived from the same place, and the names of their businesses reflect the owners' roots, e.g. *Kayserili Ali'nin Yeri* (Ali from Kayseri's Place).

Fatalism

One of the most frequently used words in Turkish is *inşallah* (as God wills it). Rooted in Islam, the concept of fate (*kader*) has a strong hold on the Turks – it's this which causes drivers to ignore speed limits, builders to teeter precariously on home-made scaffolding and electricians to test live circuits with a well aimed screwdriver. If your time is up, it's up. Those from countries where health and safety issues cannot be ignored find this attitude perplexing and even frightening; others find it refreshing.

Fatalism has its good points – Turks who believe in the power of fate suffer far less from guilt and recrimination; the downside is that some people use it as an excuse for not taking responsibility. Homes are uninsured, credit-card debts accumulate and medical help isn't sought until it's too late.

Fatalism has more power in poorer parts of the country – a 2001 survey of 400 women living in rural Konya (reported in the *Turkish Daily News*) revealed that nearly half believed they couldn't change anything by their will alone.

SENSE OF HUMOUR

The Turks have an irrepressible sense of fun. They're as willing to laugh at themselves as at others, and their humour ranges from quiet irony to slapstick – Jackie Chan is a huge hit in Turkey, as is the UK's bumbling Mr Bean. For such a conservative country,

some newspaper cartoons are surprisingly near the knuckle. And although television serves up the usual diet of bland sitcoms, Turks can also produce some sharp satire – of which politicians are a prime target. During the 2007 presidential campaign, a youth group called Young Civilians put up a fictitious candidate,

Aliye Öztürk, a headscarf-wearing Armenian–Kurd who pledged to serve Turkish pizza to diplomats. 'She' received requests for interviews until the media caught on to the joke.

The roots of Turkish humour are best illustrated by two very different characters – Nasreddin Hodja and Temel. Hodja, which means teacher (*hoca*) in Turkish, is a folk hero from the 13th century. Though often pictured sitting backwards on his donkey, he's a 'wise fool' and his humorous anecdotes always carry a profound and often satirical message. Variations on his stories have infiltrated cultures from Africa to China – so much so that UNESCO proclaimed 1996 as 'Nasreddin Hodja year'.

Turks laugh with Hodja, but they laugh at Temel. He's a buffoon from the Black Sea, whose limited intelligence makes him the butt of many jokes. Black Sea folk are a frequent target for Turkish humour, just as the Irish are for the British and the Poles for the Americans, but few can be as dumb as the hard-drinking, hen-pecked and hapless Temel.

A Nasreddin Hodja Story

'Hodja saw a group of ducks in the lake. He tried to catch one but couldn't. So he sat by the lake and took a loaf of bread from his saddlebag. He broke it into pieces and started dunking them in the water and eating them. A passer-by saw Hodja and asked him what he was eating. Hodja dunked another piece and said, "Duck soup".'

(Story taken from *Nasreddin Hodja*, a collection of anecdotes by Alpay Kabacalı, published by Net Books in Turkey.)

CHILDREN

Turkey is a country of young people, which makes it a positive and vibrant place to live. The average age is 28 and a quarter of the population is aged 15 or under. While the West struggles to cope with an aging population, Turkey faces the problem of how to educate and employ its large army of youths.

The Turks adore children – their own and those of other people. This is possibly the only country where you can go to a restaurant and offload your offspring on a waiter, who will entertain them while you eat. You'll find no shortage of babysitters, especially if your children are blond.

Many Turks come from large broods, although the modern nuclear family is shrinking, as parents choose to concentrate their resources on one or two children. As a result, children can be over-indulged, and in wealthier families they have access to all the gadgets required by European kids –

including a television and computer in the bedroom. Even in poor families, parents go out of their way to provide for their children. As a result, some children are demanding monsters – aptly described as 'Little Sultans' – although most are surprisingly well adjusted, studious and polite, and a pleasure to spend time with.

Like children in Latin countries, Turkish children are treated like small adults. They eat out with the family from an early age and don't appear to have a set bedtime. However, they're also expected to take on adult responsibilities, such as looking after their siblings; even teenage boys will happily fuss over a baby.

Most of Turkey is safe; children can play outside and there's usually an adult or teenager to keep a watchful eye. Thus many Turks have a relaxed view of child-rearing, although foreigners may find it too relaxed. Stair gates, baby monitors and child car seats are fairly new concepts in a country where children are often transported (without a helmet) on the back of their parents' bicycle.

THE CLASS SYSTEM

There's no class system – at least not in sense of the British social hierarchy. Ottoman society was strongly rooted in class but the pashas (equivalent to English lords) were swept away by the republic, and Turkey is increasingly a meritocracy, where money, education – and religion – are the main elements that divide the population.

Villages have a defined hierarchy, a few land-owning families sharing most of the power. In cities, people tend to be more equal, although there's a gulf between those living in modern apartments and those inhabiting the illegal settlements or shanty towns (*gecekondu*) on the outskirts of towns.

In Turkey, most money is 'new' money. Some of the wealthiest dynasties – including the Koç and Sabancı families, who head two of the country's largest corporations – come from humble backgrounds. What made them successful was a willingness to study and work and an entrepreneurial spirit. Even today, many Turks believe that 'money breeds money' and if they can just get a foot on the ladder they're on their way to unimaginable riches.

The Kemalists & the 'New' Islamists

The widest division in Turkey is between the middle-class secularists – called Kemalists after their adherence to Atatürk's principles – and the 'new' Islamists, who want their country to face more firmly in the direction of Mecca.

The Kemalists are deeply suspicious of any power connected to Islam and were loud in their protests against the election of the Islamist President Gül. They have the support of the Turkish Armed Forces, which musters the second-largest standing force in NATO after the US, and minority groups such as the Alevis. The 'new' Islamists are conservative but educated, strongly Muslim but pro-Western. They see no reason why economic progress, democracy and adherence to Islam cannot exist side by side.

Many Turkish observers believe that religion has regained its importance in the last decade or so because of the rootlessness felt by the huge number of people who have moved from a village culture to city life. On the other hand, they feel that the next generation will be more settled and less in need of a religious anchor – keener to adjust to a Western way of life.

> According to Article 66 of the Turkish Constitution, a 'Turk' is anyone who is 'bound to the Turkish state through the bond of citizenship' – so anyone acquiring citizenship is automatically Turkish.

ATTITUDES TO MINORITIES

Since the formation of the republic, Turkey has tried to assimilate its ethnic groups into the general population in an attempt to unify it and to avoid the kind of civil unrest seen in the former Yugoslavia. Censuses don't record ethnic or racial statistics, therefore it's difficult to gain an accurate picture of the extent of the different ethnic groups – the information below is based on popular wisdom.

Turks constitute the main ethnic group, but theirs is a bond based on language and culture rather than geography – there are Turks throughout Asia and the Balkans, as well as communities in Europe and the US. Important 'minorities' include Kurds, Azerbaijanis, Georgians, Arabs, Jews, Armenians and Greeks, though only the last three are recognised as minority groups – they had a great deal of power in the days of the Ottoman Empire, in diplomacy, commerce and trade, but numbers are declining fast as older people migrate abroad. There are now thought to be fewer than 10,000 Greeks and around 25,000 Jews. Of the 10m or so Armenians in the world, less than 7 per cent live in Turkey.

In addition, there are up to 1m people of Arab descent, mainly living in the south-east, and a similar number of Azerbaijanis in the east. Around 1.5m Georgians live in the eastern Black Sea area, while smaller minorities include the Laz and Hemşin, who live along the Black Sea. The Yörük are nomadic tribes who live mainly in the southern Taurus (*Toros*) Mountains, migrating between the coast and the high pastures (*yayla*), according to the season. They're herdsmen who live in distinctive black goats'-hair tents and have a long tradition of carpet-weaving. Don't confuse the Yörük with gypsies (*çingene*) – the latter are found throughout Turkey and suffer similar discrimination to that experienced by gypsies in the rest of Europe.

Kurds

Kurds account for up to 20 per cent of Turkey's population, according to the *CIA World Factbook*. Their long struggle for an autonomous state has led to violent clashes between the military and radical Kurdish groups such as the Kurdistan Workers Party (PKK) in the south-east of the country since 1984. This ongoing conflict has claimed the lives of more than 37,000 people and poses one of the main threats to Turkish unity – one reason why they're often referred to in Turkey as 'eastern' or 'mountain' Turks, rather than Kurds. In early 2008, it was also threatening stability in the Middle East when Turkey sent troops into northern Iraq to root out PKK terrorists.

The majority of Kurds in Turkey abhor the violence. You'll meet many who have built businesses in the cities and resort areas and are fully integrated into their Turkish neighbourhood. There is prejudice – some Turks talk disparagingly of Kurds – but the country is slowly facing up to the need to tackle its human and ethnic rights issues as part of its progression towards EU membership. Meanwhile, the Kurds' influence is growing – the 2007 general election saw 23 pro-Kurdish deputies voted into parliament on an independent ticket.

> The 'Kurdish problem' is a topic of conversation which is best avoided, as is the subject of the 'Armenian genocide'. Turkey doesn't see eye to eye with many other countries on these subjects, and Turkish people are acutely sensitive to any hint of foreign interference in ethnic issues.

ATTITUDES TO FOREIGNERS

Turks are especially welcoming to foreigners. They're tolerant of and courteous to holidaymakers and go out of their way to make new residents feel at home. By and large, they appreciate the investment made by foreign companies and the money spent by foreign tourists, and even the surge in property prices on the coasts – fuelled by villa-buyers from Europe and responsible for pricing some Turks out of the market – hasn't (as yet) dented that goodwill.

In resort towns, the welcome becomes slightly jaded towards the end of the season, and some foreign residents find that the locals' friendliness cools a little once they put down roots (and have less disposable income than a two-week tourist). However, there appears to be less tension between westerners and Turks than there is between Turks and some of the indigenous minorities.

> **Over 200,000 residence permits were issued in the year to March 2007, the majority of them to ethnic Turks born in other countries.**

Statistics also show a large number of German and British residents (around 10,000 and 8,000 respectively), followed by Russians, Dutch, Americans, Greeks, Australians and Scandinavians. It's impossible to give exact figures for these 'settled foreigners' as many people stay in the country by continually renewing their visitor's visa without officially registering as residents.

Where the Expats Live

There are expatriates in most corners of Turkey, except for the eastern and south-eastern provinces, with different nationalities favouring different areas:

- Germans mainly live along the Mediterranean coast around Antalya, although they now have to share their beaches with Russians – there's even a hotel called the Kremlin Palace in Antalya, complete with onion-shaped domes. This coast is also popular with the Dutch and Scandinavians.

- British expats prefer the Aegean, in particular Altınkum, Marmaris and Fethiye (known as 'Little Britain'), while the Irish favour Kuşadası.

- A mixed bag of foreigners – French, Italians, Americans, Aussies and Japanese – is drawn to the lunar landscape of Cappadocia in central Anatolia.

- The Russians use the Black Sea coast as a trading base, and Trabzon is notorious for its large number of 'Natashas' (prostitutes from the former Soviet Bloc countries).

- The most cosmopolitan city is Istanbul, attracting expats from throughout the world, mostly for work rather than pleasure.

NATIONAL ICONS

Every country has its icons – people, places, symbols, flora and fauna, food and drink – which are unique to that country and have special significance to its inhabitants. Turkey is no exception, and the following is a list of some of the icons that you can expect to see, experience or hear reference to.

Icons – Atatürk

Mustafa Kemal Atatürk (1881-1938) – The ultimate Turkish icon, Atatürk enjoys god-like status. He was born into a comparatively humble family but succeeded through intelligence, military genius and sheer bloody-mindedness to transform his country into a modern state. A workaholic and inveterate drinker, he died in his 50s. The whole of Turkey still stops to remember him at the time of his death – 9.05am on 10th November.

Founder of the modern republic, Atatürk is everywhere in Turkey. His statue is in every town or village. Streets, stadiums and airports are named after him. His portrait has pride of place in shops and businesses across the country and pops up in the corner of television screens on national holidays. His life and philosophy are part of the school curriculum, and there's even a law against insulting his memory.

Atatürk's single-minded determination to unite, modernise and Westernise his country after the First World War was achieved with a series of sweeping reforms designed to delete the last vestiges of the Ottoman Empire and drag Turkey firmly into the 20th century. These included:

- **Erasing religion from government** – Atatürk established a secular government. He replaced Islamic law with civil codes based on European law, abolished the Caliphate (the Sultan had been nominal leader of the world's Muslims) and put the state in control of education and religious affairs.

- **Outlawing polygamy** – Men were no longer allowed to have more than one wife and women could file for divorce.

- **Giving women the vote** – They also received the right to education and to own and inherit property.

- **Introducing the Latin alphabet** – see **Atatürk's 'New' Turkish** in **Chapter 5**.

- **Banning the fez** – Atatürk regarded this brimless headgear as backward and insisted on European-style hats. He also encouraged women to abandon the veil.

- **Establishing the use of surnames** – A law was passed which required all Turks to adopt a surname. Mustafa Kemal became known by the surname Atatürk (meaning 'Father of the Turks'), which was awarded to him by his devoted followers.

This period of reform was a tough time for many Turks. Atatürk believed in the stick as much as the carrot and allowed no disagreements. The last of the Ottoman tribe were banished from Turkey and many men were arrested – some were even executed – for continuing to wear the fez. But the fact that he led a single-party democracy with the full support of the military gave him all the power he needed to impose his new vision of Turkey.

Today, Atatürk is seen by many Turks as the great reformer, without whom their country could now be another Iraq. Others think that such devotion to a long-dead icon is holding Turkey back and that the secularism which Atatürk imposed is at odds with progress in a modern Muslim society. However, few

would deny his success in transforming Turkey into the country it is today.

Icons – People

Sezen Aksu (b. 1954) – The 'Queen of Turkish pop', Aksu has sold over 40m albums in her 30-year career and is often voted Turkey's most popular artist. She's best-known outside Turkey for her song-writing collaborations with pop idol Tarkan (see below) and 2003 Eurovision winner Sertab Erener.

Cüneyt Arkın (b. 1937) – Prolific actor-director-producer with more than 300 movies under his belt. Many are historical action pictures which give him an opportunity to display his martial arts' skills.

> **Arkin's best-known film outside Turkey is** *The Man Who Saves the World*, **a spoof sci-fi film often referred to as** *Turkish Star Wars* **as it 'borrows' footage from the George Lucas original.**

Yunus Emre (1238-1320) – Poet and Sufi mystic whose humanist works were among the first to be composed in the Turkish language.

Bülent Ersoy (b. 1952) – Larger-than-life celebrity, best known for her sex change in 1981, when she defied the military regime of Kenan Evren in championing transsexuals' rights.

Ahmet Ertegün (1923-2006) – Turkish-American founder of Atlantic Records, who signed such artists as Ray Charles, Aretha Franklin and Led Zeppelin.

Sabiha Gökçen (1913-2001) – Turkey's first female aviator, Gökçen was also the world's first female fighter pilot, completing 32 hours of active combat with the Turkish Air Force. Istanbul's second airport is named after her.

Nazım Hikmet (1901-63) – The foremost Turkish poet, Hikmet was frequently imprisoned for his communist sympathies but is revered by most Turks for the romantic lyricism of his poems.

Yaşar Kemal (b. 1923) – One of Turkey's most influential novelists, Kemal came from a poor Kurdish family and his stories record the tribulations of working people in south-eastern Turkey. Many have been translated into English – the best known is the acclaimed *Ince Memed* (*Memed, My Hawk*).

Barış Manço (1943-99) – This unconventional folk-rock singer was one of Turkey's best-loved entertainers. Hugely popular with children, his outlandish appearance (long hair and knuckleduster rings) belied his thoughtful lyrics. His sudden death, of a heart attack, prompted national mourning.

Hüsnü Özyeğin (b 1944) – Turkey's richest person according to figures released by *Ekonomist* magazine in 2006, and the owner of FIBA Holding, a major finance group. He went to the US at the age of 20 with the equivalent of $1,000 and built up a career in banking. His net worth in 2006 was estimated at $3.5bn.

Orhan Pamuk (b. 1952) – Winner of the 2006 Nobel Prize for literature, Pamuk is Turkey's most acclaimed writer. He's a strong secularist and his outspokenness has got him into trouble with the authorities – when he voiced his opinion on the Armenian 'genocide' issue, he was charged with 'insulting

Naim Süleymanoğlu (b. 1967) – Turkey's most successful athlete, this pint-sized weightlifter – just 1.5m (4ft 11in) tall and known as the 'Pocket Hercules' – has won ten gold medals in Olympic and World championships and set several word records.

> Süleymanoğlu was born a Bulgarian but defected to Turkey in 1986. Two years later, Bulgaria demanded a million-dollar 'ransom' to allow him to represent his new country in the 1988 Seoul Olympics. Turkey paid up.

Turkishness'. The charges were later dropped.

Güler Sabancı (b. 1955) – Probably the most powerful woman in Turkey, Güler heads up Sabancı Holding, the second-largest financial and industrial conglomerate in the country. Her uncle Sakıp chose her over male relatives to be his successor – a rare occurrence in the masculine world of Turkish finance and a tribute to her skills.

Mimar Sinan (1489-1588) – The most important Ottoman architect, Sinan built many of the signature buildings which make up the Istanbul skyline, including the awesome Süleymaniye Mosque, which towers over the Golden Horn.

Kenan Sofuoğlu (b. 1983) – Ace motorcyclist Sofuoğlu broke the record for the most wins in a season to become 2007's World Supersport Champion. His nickname is Superglue.

Kemal Sunal (1944-2000) – Turkey's answer to Norman Wisdom, this lovable comedy actor starred in more than 80 films. His naïve but optimistic characters struck a powerful chord with his audience.

Türkan Şoray (b. 1945) – 'Sultan' to her fans, the sultry Şoray is a grand dame of Turkish cinema, with over 150 acting credits and a wealth of awards. She's also a true diva – her 'rules' include not working on Sundays and not kissing her leading men. The latter rule has rarely been broken.

Hakan Şükür (b. 1971) – The Galatasaray striker is Turkey's greatest footballer (although fans of rival Istanbul team Fenerbache may disagree). He has been capped over 100 times for the national team and is the highest scorer in Turkish football league history – 242 goals by September 2007, including the fastest goal ever scored in a World Cup match in the 2002 third-place play-off against South Korea – 11 seconds after the kick-off.

Tarkan (b. 1972) – The green-eyed 'bad' boy of Turkish pop, Tarkan has sold more than 15m albums. His fan base stretches from Russia to the Americas and his biggest hit, *Şımarık*, has been re-recorded by other artists in 17 languages including English – a version entitled *Kiss Kiss*.

İbrahim Tatlıses (b. 1952) – 'Ibo' is the undisputed king of arabesque (see below). Turkey's answer to Frank Sinatra, he's as well known for his slightly shady gangland connections and tumultuous love life as he is for his 20-plus best-selling albums. The Tatlıses 'brand' doesn't stop at music. It also includes a holiday club, a private airline and a chain of kebab shops.

Icons – Places & Structures

Blue Mosque – Though not the grandest mosque in Turkey, the Blue Mosque, with its huge domes and six minarets, is a classic symbol of Istanbul. Completed in 1616 for Sultan Ahmed I, it's properly called the Sultan Ahmed Mosque – the 'blue' comes from the tiles which adorn its vast interior.

Bosporus Bridge – The longest suspension bridge outside the US – at 1,510m (4,954ft) – links Europe to Asia. Opened in 1973, it was designed by a British civil engineer, Sir Gilbert Roberts, and one of the first people to cross it was US comedian Danny Kaye. Around 180,000 vehicles pass through its toll booths every day.

Ephesus – One of the best-preserved ancient cities in the world, Ephesus (*Efes*) is also one of the most visited: each year around 1.5m people explore its temples and theatre. Past inhabitants include the Apostle John, the Virgin Mary and St Paul.

Fairy Chimneys of Cappadocia – These bizarre rock formations form one of the landscapes unique to Turkey. Located in central Turkey, Cappadocia (*Kapadokya*) is equally fascinating underground, where early Christians carved out churches, and even subterranean cities, from the soft volcanic rock.

Pamukkale – Deservedly declared a UNESCO World Heritage Site in 1988, Pamukkale translates as 'Cotton Castle' and describes the chalk and limestone platforms, carved out by thermal waters, which hang from the hillside beneath the ancient city of Hieropolis like a frozen waterfall.

Icons – Symbols

Arabesque – Folk music with a Middle Eastern twist, this was the soundtrack to most working class life throughout the '50s and '60s, and while its appeal has declined, arabesque refuses to die – many pop, rock and dance artists have fused it with more modern sounds. To hear the original version, just take a taxi ride or tune in to any vintage Turkish film.

Arçelik – This consumer durables manufacturer is the top-selling brand name in Turkey – its fridges and washing machines are found in 17m households across the country – and is now making serious inroads into Europe, although British consumers buy its Beko brand; the word Arçelık has unfortunate connotations for those unfamiliar with the Turkish alphabet.

Fez – Memorably worn by British TV comedian Tommy Cooper, this icon is unique in that it's rarely seen in Turkey. A maroon felt hat in the shape of a flower pot, it was introduced in the 19th century as a replacement for the turban – its lack of a brim meant it could be worn during Muslim prayer. But Atatürk banned it, so you'll see the fez only in tourist resorts – usually on tourists' heads.

Hookah – A single or multi-stemmed (often glass-based) water-pipe for smoking, a hookah (*nargile*) operates by water filtration and indirect heat. Fashionable during Ottoman times, they can be found in special water-pipe cafés (*nargile kahvehanesı*).

Kurtlar Vadisi (Valley of the Wolves) – A hugely popular television series following the adventures of a special agent who goes undercover with the Turkish mafia. Violent and controversial, it had a number of spin-offs, including a feature film set in northern Iraq called *Kurtlar Vadisi Irak* (Valley of the Wolves Iraq), the most expensive Turkish movie ever made.

Migros – Swiss supermarket chain Migros has been credited with bringing Western-style shopping to Turkey. By early 2008, it had more than 950 stores across the country and a deal was struck to sell the majority of its shares to UK-based private investment consortium BC Partners.

Nazar beads – Also known as *mavi boncuk*, these blue glass beads resemble eyes and are a talisman to ward off the *nazar* or 'evil eye'. Hung from rear-

view mirrors, cemented into the walls of houses and pinned into cloth pockets on children's clothes, they're believed to reflect jealous looks and negative energy and keep the bearer safe from harm.

Oil Wrestling – Turkish oil or grease wrestling (*yağlı güreş*) is the Turkish national sport, in which wrestlers cover themselves in olive oil. Wrestlers, known as *pehlivan* (meaning hero) wear a kind of hand-stitched lederhosen called *kisbet* (or *kispet*), traditionally made of water buffalo hide but nowadays also made from calf leather.

Tavla & Okey – Two of the most popular games in Turkey. *Tavla* is a version of backgammon, played at lightning speed, while *okey* is played with numbered tiles and is similar to rummy.

Topkapi Palace – Constructed in the 15th century, Topkapı Palace in Istanbul was the official and primary residence of the Ottoman sultans from 1465 to

1853. At its height it was home to some 4,000 people and was a setting for state occasions and royal entertainments. Today it's a major tourist attraction.

Turkish Bath – The Middle East variant of a steam bath, the Turkish bath (*hamam*) is best categorised as a wet relative of the sauna. It plays an important role in Turkish culture, serving as a place of social gathering and ritual cleansing. They were introduced to the west from contacts with the Ottomans, hence the 'Turkish' part of the name.

Whirling Dervishes – The Mevlevi, a Sufi order, are known as Whirling Dervishes because of the trance-like whirling dance, or *sema*, which they perform to gain spiritual closeness to God. They do this in Konya every December to commemorate the death of their 13th-century founder, Mevlana – a truly uplifting experience.

'Come, come, whoever you are,
Wanderer, idolater, worshipper of fire,
Come even though you have broken
your vows a thousand times,
Come, and come yet again,
Ours is not a caravan of despair.'

Mevlana (founder of the Mevlevi)

Zurna & Davul – There are many musical instruments peculiar to Turkey but these are the ones you hear the most: the clarinet (*zurna*) and drum (*davul*). Once the core of the Ottoman Janissary bands (part of the sultan's guard), they now provide the soundtrack to every wedding and circumcision, and are also used to wake people in time to eat before sunrise during the fasting month of Ramadan.

Icons – Flora & Fauna

Denizli rooster – This long-necked cockerel is the symbol of its city in western Turkey, where the breed has been preserved since Ottoman times. Denizli *horozlar* (roosters) are characterised by their colour – and by the tone and depth of their crowing. Denizli is not a place to enjoy a quiet lie-in.

Kangal dog – Tough, brave and independent, this shepherd dog from the central province of Sivas is Turkey's national dog. Similar to a mastiff, it was bred to protect Anatolian livestock from attacks by bears and wolves, and some still wear an intimidating spiked collar.

Tulip – Associated with the Netherlands, this elegant flower originated in central Asia and is known in Turkish as *lale*. Its cultivation was an obsession for the Ottomans, reaching its peak in the 16th century under Ahmet III, a time of peace and prosperity which became known as the 'Tulip Era'. The name is derived from the Ottoman word for turban. Tulips appear throughout Anatolian art and there are magnificent displays every spring across Turkey.

Van cat – Originating in the south-eastern province of Van, these rare and beautiful cats are almost all white, with fur like cashmere and startling blue and amber eyes – some, like David Bowie, have one of each colour. Sociable and inquisitive, they are also love water. Van cats are protected under Turkish law and you aren't allowed to sterilise or intentionally kill them.

Icons – Food & Drink

Baklava – Many countries around the eastern Mediterranean have laid claim to this rich concoction of pastry, nuts and syrup, but the version most popular in

Turkey, made with honey and pistachio nuts, was developed in the kitchens of the Ottoman sultans. The best Turkish baklava is made in the south-eastern city of Gaziantep.

Çay – Despite the fame of Turkish coffee, most Turks drink tea (*çay*). It accompanies breakfast, follows every meal and forms a liquid punctuation to the events of daily life. Like the Japanese, Turks attach much importance to the ritual of making, serving and drinking tea (see **Tea & Coffee** in **Chapter 4**).

Döner kebab – A freshly-made *döner kebab* (and other Turkish *kebabs*) is quite different from the greasy post-club snack on offer in the UK and other countries. Consisting of thin slices of grilled lamb or chicken, rolled with salad in warm thin bread, the *döner* kebab was invented in Bursa but now has imitations across the globe. The name *döner*, meaning 'it spins', comes from the rotating spit on which the meat is cooked.

Efes beer – Despite being Muslim, the Turks are fond of their beer – and their favourite is Efes, a light, malty German-style brew. It accounts for 80 per cent of the market and is usually the first Turkish brand name foreigners get to know.

Lokum/Turkish Delight – A sticky sweet confection, Turkish delight is usually flavoured with lemon, rosewater and nuts, which unfailingly finds your teeth fillings. It was invented by an Ottoman confectioner to satisfy the cravings of an 18th-century sultan and is now served to guests at weddings and other important celebrations. It's an acceptable gift for any occasion.

Pide/Lavaş – Delicious Turkish flatbread made with yeast is the national food, *pide* and *lavaş* (a long, puffed up flatbread) are sold in every store and baked on every street corner. A staple of Turkish cuisine, *pide* is also the name of a Turkish pizza-like food, when it's topped with lamb, onions, cheese, tomato or any variety of combinations.

Raki – The unofficial Turkish 'national drink', *raki* is a non-sweet usually anise-flavoured aperitif (similar to *pastis* and *ouzo*) produced by twice distilling suma (a pomace wine obtained by fermenting must) or suma that has been mixed with ethyl alcohol. It's traditionally drunk mixed with water in Turkey, which causes it to turn a milky-white colour, popularly referred to as *aslan sütü* (lion's milk).

Simit – Turkey's version of the bagel, this crunchy, chewy ring of dough sprinkled with sesame seeds is a ubiquitous snack food.

Turkish Coffee

Coffee prepared by boiling finely powdered roast coffee beans in a pot (*cezve*), possibly with sugar, and served in a cup where the dregs settle. Very strong and an acquired taste.

REPUBLIC OF
TURKEY
TÜRKİYE CUMHURİYETİ
REPUBLIC OF TURKEY
PASAPORT
PASSPORT

3.
GETTING STARTED

One of the most difficult stages of adjustment to a new country is those first few days, when you have a million and one things to do. This is stressful enough without the addition of cultural differences. This chapter will help you overcome the challenges of arriving and settling in Turkey, including those posed by obtaining a residence permit, finding accommodation, hiring or buying a car, opening a bank account, registering for taxes, obtaining healthcare, council services and utilities, finding schools for your children, getting online, staying informed and coping with Turkish bureaucracy.

> The petition still exists in the form of a *dilekçe*, a form which asks the recipient (very politely) to do what is required. The *dilekçe* is a necessary part of almost every Turkish transaction.

IMMIGRATION

Turkish immigration officials are formal but polite. Some may appear abrupt to foreigners, but this is usually due to communication difficulties rather than rudeness. Turks can be submissive in the face of authority and some officials expect everyone to act this way – just remain calm and polite, you shouldn't have any problems.

To enter Turkey, you need six months' validity on your passport. Many nationalities can buy a visitor's visa on arrival, which you must do before queuing at passport control, but some may need to obtain a visa before arrival (check with a Turkish embassy or consulate). Visas are valid for 30 to 90 days' and cost €10 or €20 – the length and fee depend on how openly your home country welcomes Turkish visitors. Citizens of the UK, US and most European Union (EU) countries receive a 90-day, multiple-entry stamp.

Visa Run

A visitor's visa can be renewed by crossing the border to Bulgaria, Greece or one of the Greek islands, and getting a new stamp on the way back, which is known as a 'visa run'. An 'official' extension can be obtained in Turkey but involves a lot of bureaucracy, and the visa can be extended only once. The 'visa run' has become an institution among expatriates, many of whom have been doing it for years. There's a (slim) possibility you'll meet an obstructive official, who could hold you up at the border or (at worst) insist that you return to your country of origin and travel back to Turkey from there. If you overstay your visa, you'll incur a fine as you leave the country.

> **It's compulsory to carry photo identity at all times. Suitable documents include your passport, national identity card or residence permit.**

Residence Permits

You need a residence permit (*ikamet oturma izin*) if:

- you want to reside in Turkey for more than three months, without the hassle or uncertainty of making 'visa runs' (see above);

- you're married to a Turkish national;

- you're applying for a work permit or plan to start a business;

- you want to import personal goods or bring a car into Turkey for more than six months.

Residence permits are issued for between one and five years. You can apply at the Turkish consulate in your country of origin or go directly to a police headquarters (*emniyet müdürlüğü*) in Turkey – many have a foreigners' office (*yabancılar bürosu*).

It's a complicated process, which can take up to three months in areas with a large expatriate population. The fee varies according to your nationality – British and American citizens must pay around €275 per year, while some western European nationals pay a good deal less. There are discounts for children.

You aren't permitted to work unless you also have a work permit, therefore you must show that you have an adequate income from your home country to support yourself – €500 per month is normally enough. You don't need a residence permit in order to purchase property or a vehicle.

Citizenship

In theory, you can apply for citizenship after five years' residence – or three years if you're married to a Turk. Turkey allows dual citizenship, as does the UK and the US. Other countries, such as Germany and Japan, don't – and it may be unwise to give up your original nationality to obtain Turkish citizenship.

The main benefit of citizenship is being able to reside and work in Turkey without permits. It also opens a lot of doors, as people will be honoured that you've chosen to become a 'Turk'. However, there are drawbacks. You risk having a tax liability in two countries; your home country's embassy may not offer you diplomatic help and men aged 40 or under are theoretically eligible for military service.

BUREAUCRACY

Bureaucracy is a way of life in Turkey. Most Turks despair of the amount of form-filling and counter-hopping required for something as simple as obtaining a telephone line – and the many photocopies and 'official stamps' needed to supplement most applications. However, they're very patient when dealing with a system which drives the majority of foreigners crazy. The system dates back to Ottoman times, when all requests were passed through an endless chain of officials before arriving at the Sultan, and each stage required a 'humble petition' for the request to be passed further up the line. The petition still exists in the form of a dilekçe, a form which asks the recipient (very politely) to do what is required. The dilekçe is a necessary part of almost every Turkish transaction.

Increasing pressure from a streamlined and effective private sector is forcing Turkey's public sector to improve its efficiency. Most government departments have websites giving reasonably clear information – sometimes in languages other than Turkish. Officials are more courteous, and public offices are more welcoming. Turkish bureaucracy is now probably no worse than bureaucracy in many western European countries, such as Italy or Spain.

It's just as well, since you'll encounter officialdom repeatedly, particularly during your first few months in Turkey. There's no way around the system, but there are ways to make you feel more in control:

- When planning to visit an office, check the opening times and don't go on a public holiday.

- Check and double-check everything you need. Start by consulting the relevant the website (if there is one) and talk to other expatriates who have been through the same process recently. It's difficult to obtain any information over the phone.

- Always arrive early – if you turn up after lunch (and offices always close for lunch), you'll probably have to return the next day. Friday afternoon is the worst time to approach civil servants.

- Carry spare copies of everything. If you don't have a residence permit, you'll need a notarised translation of your passport, and it's advisable to have several copies prepared. Always take plenty of passport photographs.

- Accept that rules may have changed without warning, and that it's sometimes necessary to return with extra paperwork and repeat the whole process.

Proof of Address

Officials sometimes require proof of identity and/or address (*ikametgâh ilmühaberi*). You can obtain this from your *muhtar* (the equivalent of a local councillor), who keeps a record of everyone living in his neighbourhood. You'll need some photographs and may have to pay a small fee.

Civil Servants

A job in Turkey's civil service has always been highly desirable. Civil servants (who include police, health workers and teachers, as well as the great army of bureaucrats) work shorter days and take longer holidays than private-sector workers. Job security and a good pension makes up for low wages. The Turkish public approach civil servants with a mixture of envy, trepidation and scorn. But, despite their formidable reputation, officials are as susceptible to charm as anyone else and the more courteous you are, the better they will treat you (see **Dealing with Officials** in **Chapter 4**).

It's advisable to try to build a relationship with officials that you see on a regular basis, such as staff at the local municipality (*belediye*) and the police officer in charge of the *yabancılar bürosu*. They meet a lot of impatient and angry foreigners and will always remember a polite one, especially one who is well prepared and makes an effort to speak Turkish.

Donations

Corruption frequently makes headlines in the press, but Turks may be offended if you suggest that their system is corrupt. (Even if it is, that's their business, not yours.) Never offer a bribe to get something done. You may, on the other hand, be asked for a 'donation' (*bağış*), especially when applying for certain permits. This usually goes towards a fund for the local school or other worthy cause, and you can ask for a receipt (*makbuz*). A donation should not, of course, be confused with a bribe.

Getting Around Bureaucracy

In Spain, a *gestor* can be hired to run through the bureaucratic minefield on your behalf. Turkey's version is called a *takipci* (quite literally 'one who pursues'); *trafik takipci* are hired to deal with the endless red tape involved in buying and registering a vehicle, but it's also possible to find a *takipci* willing (if not always totally able) to guide you through the property maze.

Reputable estate agents (*emlakçı*) will assist you with getting utilities connected and arranging insurance, and may do this at no charge if you buy or rent through them. Lawyers (*avukat*) can make all applications on your behalf – and have the advantage of being impartial. Accountants (*muhasebeci*) will help you establish a business and deal with the tax authorities. A certified translator (*tercüman*) ensures you understand documents – all documents must, by law, be translated into your language – and strictly contracts are worthless without the stamp of a notary public (*noter*), although few foreigners pay for this safeguard.

19th century Ducats

You may need to give professionals power of attorney (*vekâletname*) to act on your behalf, but you should only do so if you're sure of their credentials; always ensure that the document is specific to your requirements and has a deadline (i.e. is a for a limited period only). You can revoke a power of attorney without giving a reason.

Networking

Who you know is every bit as important as what you know. Turks 'collect' useful people and trade in favours as well as in commodities. This is especially important in business but is equally useful in daily life. Getting to know the officer who handles your taxes or the assistants at the notary's office can oil the wheels of many transactions. If you meet these people on a social basis, always take the time to exchange pleasantries.

ACCOMMODATION

Finding somewhere to live is one of your most urgent tasks on arriving in Turkey. The type of accommodation you choose depends largely on where you want to live. In cities, most people live in apartments, while houses are easier to find in the suburbs or rural areas. There's a surplus of new villas in coastal resorts – many are holiday lets and you can rent one over the winter while looking for something more permanent.

Be cautious when looking at older properties, especially apartment blocks in Istanbul whose rent is unusually low. Many are not 'earthquake-proof' and some were destabilised by the 1999 quake and are, in theory, awaiting demolition.

Buildings constructed since 2000 are generally safer.

> **Almost 70 per cent of Turks are owner-occupiers, while a quarter live in rented accommodation, according to research by the Turkish Statistics Institute (Türkstat).**

Rented Property

Renting makes sense if your stay in Turkey is temporary or you aren't sure exactly where you want to live. Always rent for a while before you commit to buying. Local newspapers carry advertisements for rental properties, and there are websites and forums offering rentals and flat-shares. Most estate agents market rentals but charge commission of a month's rent. Some of the best deals are discovered by word of mouth or by accident – walk around the area and look for signs saying *Kiralık* (to let).

Turks assume that foreign tenants will look after a property and pay their rent on time. However, some also think they can charge a foreigner a higher rent, so it can help to have a Turkish friend negotiate the agreement for you.

Furnished or Unfurnished

'Furnished' is an arbitrary term in Turkey. Unfurnished (*mobilyasız*) can mean a totally empty shell, while furnished (*mobilyalı*) property may have a (basic) kitchen and bathroom but no furnishings. Décor is unlikely to be to your taste. If urgent work needs doing, e.g. fitting a kitchen, ask the landlord if you can offset the expense against rental payments.

Safety is a fairly new concept in the Turkish construction business, and some properties have dangerous equipment, such as ageing boilers and dodgy wiring. Get an independent builder to check a property before you agree to rent it.

Contracts & Payment

Turkish law favours the tenant (*kiracı*), but you should still insist on a rental contract (*kira sözleşmesi*). Some landlords (*ev sahibi*) are reluctant to sign one but be persistent, and include a clause allowing you to give two months' notice in case you want to move before the lease is up. The contract will be in Turkish. Never sign anything you don't understand.

Rents are increased annually in line with inflation, which was just under 9 per cent in early 2008. Don't hand over cash without obtaining a receipt. It's best to pay it directly into the landlord's bank account, which was under consideration as a legal requirement in 2008, so that you have a record of payment.

Deposits & Advances

All landlords ask for a deposit against damages and, by law, can demand up to three months' rent. In theory, it's lodged in a holding account, although in practice most landlords spend it, and some invent 'damage' to justify not repaying it. Because of this, some tenants withhold their rent before vacating a property. A few landlords demand several months' or even a year's rent in advance, which makes it costly to move out early.

Landlords

Private landlords can be accommodating or downright devious. Some are both, and will bring you bags of lemons while calculating how much more rent they can squeeze out of you. Many landlords object to pets and fear foreigners' strange ways; some have a habit of popping in unexpectedly (with a bag of lemons) in order to check that you aren't keeping 15 cats and haven't painted the living room orange! You encounter more interference – and more generosity – if you both live in the same block.

Both landlords and tenants have liabilities and responsibilities, as follows:

- **Landlords** – Pay property taxes, building insurance and the cost of maintenance and repairs. They should ensure that the property is clean and tidy, with everything in working order, before you move in.

- **Tenants** – Pay for all utilities – you should take meter readings on moving day so that you don't pay the previous tenant's bills. In a block, you may be liable for a share of the communal heating costs and the services of the *kapıcı* (doorman). Tenants should leave the property as they found it. This includes filling any nail holes and applying a coat of paint if necessary.

Both landlords and management companies can be slow to sort out problems or make repairs. But provided you're a good tenant, you get along

nationals owned 13,402 and Greeks 10,059. The most popular province with foreign investors was Antalya.

Purchasing property in Turkey isn't particularly complicated, although it can be time-consuming, and you should be aware of some unusual and, if you don't take the proper precautions, risky aspects of the purchase procedure:

● It's necessary to set up a public limited company in order to own village land.

● Checks are required to ensure that the property isn't in a military or security zone (e.g. near an army base), as these areas are also off-limits to foreigners.

● Completion can take up to six months.

● The title deed is called a *tapu*. All property transactions take place at the deeds office (*tapu müdürlüğü*), which holds all titles, along with a record of any charges or encumbrances.

> Never buy a property without a *tapu* (title deed) It's also risky to buy in a Turkish friend's name (e.g. to speed up the process or obtain land in a restricted area), because if your name isn't on the *tapu* you have no legal right of ownership.

with your neighbours and abide by any community regulations, you have every right to insist, calmly and politely, that things are done.

Buying a Home

Ownership by foreigners is based on reciprocity – if a Turk can own property in your country, you can own Turkish property on the same terms. However, the amount of land you can own is limited to 2.5ha (6.2 acres) and it must be residential or commercial property within an area administered by a *belediye*.

Figures released by the General Directorate of Land Registry and Cadastre (Tapu ve Kadastro Genel Müdürlüğü) revealed that as of 13th January 2008, 70,366 foreign nationals owned a total of 3,700ha (9,143 acres) of Turkish land. Germans came top, owning 15,911 properties, British

● Estate agents act for the vendor and the purchaser and take 3 per cent commission from both parties. This, plus another 6 per cent to cover surveyor's and local authority fees and government taxes, can add up to fees of 9 per cent of the purchase price for the buyer.

● When a sale is agreed, the buyer pays a deposit (usually 10 per cent) and a binding contract is signed – if either side backs out, there are financial penalties. Gazumping is rare.

● A large number of properties are built illegally and it has been estimated that more than half the country's housing stock is unregistered for habitation. If you buy an unregistered house, it may not be possible to connect utilities and if it's built illegally (e.g. on government-owned land) it could be demolished.

> **Though it isn't mandatory, it's highly advisable to contract a lawyer to assist with all property transactions, contracts and inheritance issues. Lawyers who speak your language can be found by recommendation or through your embassy.**

Furnishings

Furnishings, kitchen appliances and building materials cost roughly the same as they do in many western European countries, while labour charges are considerably lower. Many people have items such as furniture and kitchen units built to order. Good second-hand goods are scarce as Turks hate to throw things away, but you can search the expatriate forums to find goods on sale by other foreigners, some of whom sell off their entire house contents when moving abroad. To import your possessions you need a residence permit, which involves a lot of bureaucracy. Note that it isn't worth importing some items, such as old electrical goods, which are heavily taxed.

BUYING OR HIRING A CAR

Before you buy a car, think about whether you really need one. In a rural area, it's essential, but a car is more of a liability than an asset in the middle of traffic-choked Istanbul. In resorts with long summers, many people prefer to use a scooter or quad-bike.

Below are some tips on hiring (renting) or buying a vehicle:

Car Hire

Car hire (rental) is expensive – from €30 per day – making it extravagant as a long-term option. But you may want to hire a car on arrival while you look for one to buy. Try to negotiate a long-term discount with the agency and make sure the price includes adequate insurance, e.g. collision damage waiver and cover against damage to tyres and glass. The minimum age is 21 and you need a credit card as security. Don't choose the cheapest car if you're planning on driving long distances or out of town, as you need something tough and agile to cope with bad roads and unpredictable drivers. If you're hiring in the summer, make sure you have a car with air-conditioning.

Buying a Car

To buy a vehicle in Turkey, you need your passport and a tax number (see below). Be prepared to pay cash, as it's unlikely that a bank or dealership will offer a foreigner a loan or a hire purchase (time payment) arrangement.

Inevitably, buying and registering a car involves a lot of red tape.

New Cars

If you buy new, the dealer should handle the registration and insurance process for you. List prices are high, so be prepared to haggle hard and insist that all the paperwork is done for you. Most major makes are available, but those which are manufactured in Turkey, such as Renault and Fiat, are easier and cheaper to repair.

Used Cars

Few Turks can afford a new car, therefore used cars (*ikinci el arabası*) hold their value well. Inventive mechanics, rudimentary car tests and lower taxes on older cars have all helped keep a vast number of old bangers on the road. The reputation of used-car dealers (*oto emlak*) is no better in Turkey than anywhere else, and you may prefer to buy privately by searching one of the used-car websites or looking for cars with 'For Sale' ('*Satılık*') signs in the window. However, you should get a mechanic (*motor tamircisi*) to check a car before agreeing to buy it.

Private sales must be notarised; the buyer pays for this, while the seller pays any outstanding taxes. The car must be insured, and then registered, which involves visits to the tax office, the drivers' association (*şoförler odası*) and the traffic police. All this takes at least a day, but you can pay a *trafik takipci* (see **Getting Around Bureaucracy** above) to do it for you. They can also handle the necessary safety and emissions tests.

> Every province has its own vehicle registration number, so you can tell immediately where a car is from. Ankara plates starts with 06 while Istanbul plates start with 34 – which is a warning to provincial Turks who consider Istanbul drivers the worst in Turkey.

Blue-plate Cars

Blue-plate cars are so called because they used to have a blue number plate. Turks call them *yabancıdan / yabancıya arabası* (literally 'from foreigner to foreigner cars') because they're imported under strict conditions (see below) and can be sold on only to foreigners who meet the same criteria. They're often advertised at temptingly cheap prices, because the owner is in a hurry to leave Turkey. However, the bureaucracy – which is double that of the normal registration process – rarely justifies the savings.

Importing a Vehicle

It's difficult to import a car or motorbike and Turks make it much easier for you to support their automotive industry by buying a new one. You can bring your

car in on a visitor's visa, but only for six months. If you want it for longer, you need a work permit, a student visa or a retired resident's permit.

The import process requires a dozen documents plus a security deposit in the form of a bank guarantee, which reflects the import duty and can be as much as the actual value of the car. You have to re-export the vehicle when you leave Turkey or when your visa expires – or sell it to another foreigner. Most people who have imported a car say they'd never do it again. For more information on this subject, go to the Turkish Touring and Automobile Club website (🖳 www.turing.org.tr/eng/mavikarne.asp).

Your visibility is limited when driving a right-hand-drive car in Turkey, where traffic drives on the right – overtaking is especially dangerous – and this makes the experience of driving even more stressful and hazardous.

Driving Licences

You can drive on your home country's licence for up to six months. After this you must obtain a Turkish licence. Many foreigners, and even some Turks, have been driving on a foreign licence for years. Police often turn a blind eye, but your insurer is unlikely to do the same if you have an accident. You can take a driving test, but it's easier to have your licence translated and reissued as a Turkish licence.

EMERGENCY SERVICES

In an emergency (*acil durum*), you can phone for assistance, and you'll need to do this in Turkish. Be prepared to explain where you are and also the type of emergency – some useful numbers and phrases are shown in the box below.

Emergency Numbers	
110	Fire service (*yangın servisi*)
112	Ambulance service (*ambülans*)
155	Police – towns and cities (*polis*)
156	Military police – villages and rural areas (*jandarma*)
158	Coastguard (*sahil güvenlik*)
177	Forest fire service (*orman yangını*)

There's a shortage of ambulances, therefore Turks often call a taxi instead. Most private hospitals have their own ambulances – such as Istanbul's International Hospital (☎ 0212-663 3000) and Bayindir Hospital in Ankara (☎ 0321-287 9000). Find out which is the nearest private hospital to you with a properly equipped ambulance (i.e. one with life-saving apparatus on board) and keep the phone number at hand.

Police

Turkey has several types of police. State police (*polis*) enforce the law in cities, towns and airports, and wear a dark uniform and cap, emblazoned with the word '*polis*'. Village areas (and some resorts) are served by military police (*jandarma*), who dress in camouflage combat gear, whether they're helping tourists or hunting down terrorists. Both *polis* and *jandarma* are armed and sometimes carry machine guns. Council 'police' (*zabita*) enforce the municipality's bylaws; they dress like state police but have far fewer powers – although some would like to think otherwise.

HEALTH SERVICES

Turks are obsessed by their health (*sağlık*) and many have an irrational fear of draughts, ice-cold drinks and pet hair, and quite a few are hypochondriacs – few Turks catch a cold (*nezle*) when they could have flu (*grip*). Many complain about their healthcare system, which they regard as lagging well behind those of western Europe. However, the World Health Organization's 2000 report on worldwide health, ranked the Turks 33rd out of 191 countries for their health, while its healthcare system came 70th. This is a far better performance than those of Bulgaria or Romania, who have already joined the EU. Turks are healthier

---

Emergency Phrases

accident (car accident) – *kaza (araba kazası)*
allergic reaction – *alerjik reaksiyonu*
attack (armed attack) – *hücum (silahlı hücum)*
bleeding (a lot) – *(çok) kanama*
broken arm – *kırık kol*
broken leg – *kırık bacak*
burglary – *hırsızlık*
fire – *yangın*
heart attack – *kalp krizi*
I need an ambulance – *ambülansa ihtiyacım var*
I need a doctor – *doktora ihtiyacım var*
intruder – *davetsiz misafir*
mugging – *soygun*
not breathing – *nefes almıyor*
(I am) on the road to X – *(Ben) X yolunda(yım)*
overdose – *aşırı doz*
unconscious – *baygın*
wounded – *yaralı*

---

than they think and their healthcare system isn't as disabled as they believe it to be.

Because Turkey isn't in the EU, there's no reciprocal healthcare agreement between western European countries and Turkey. Foreigners must pay for treatment if they aren't covered by one of the social insurance schemes or a private plan.

State Healthcare

Most Turks qualify for state healthcare through their social insurance (*sosyal sigorta*), which covers their dependants and also provides unemployment, maternity and retirement benefits. In early 2008, social insurance consisted of three separate plans – SSK (Social Security Authority) for employees, Bağ-Kur (Social Insurance for the Self-Employed) and Emekli Sandık (Pension Fund) for civil servants –

although the government was in the process of merging them into a single social security scheme. There's also a provision for those on low or no income.

Health benefits include free care in state clinics and hospitals, as well as discounted care in some private hospitals. It also discounts the cost of prescription medicines, which as a result is among the lowest in Europe.

Foreigners employed in Turkey qualify for SKK and employers are obliged to contribute towards this, while the self-employed and business owners pay into the Bağ-Kur scheme – your accountant will arrange this. Both systems use a prescription book (due to be replaced by a card), which you must present when attending a clinic or hospital or obtaining prescription medicine.

Private Healthcare

Distrust of the state system causes many Turks to go private; some pay cash while others have insurance. Some doctors who work in state or university hospitals have private practices to boost their income, and people refer themselves for treatment, with a consultation costing from €25 to €100. Dentists (*diş hekimi*) and opticians (*gözlükçü*) are also often consulted on a private basis – fees are low compared with those in Europe and the US. This has led to a growing trend in medical tourism and people travel to Turkey specifically to have their teeth fixed or to undergo laser eye surgery.

Choosing a Doctor

Turks don't register with a family doctor (*doktor*) and there's currently no system of GP referral, so when a Turk

is ill he selects a private doctor based according to his speciality (see below). If he cannot or doesn't want to pay, he attends a local health clinic (*sağlık ocağı*) or hospital outpatients department. One of the reasons why state hospitals are overcrowded and chaotic is because Turks treat them like doctors' surgeries.

As a foreigner, you may be asked to pay a small fee at a health clinic or hospital, unless you're registered to one of the Turkish social security schemes and can prove it. You can, of course, see a private specialist.

> **Turks like to self-diagnose and they consult whoever they think most appropriate, e.g. a cardiologist (*kardiyolog*) for chest pain or a gynaecologist (*kadın hastalıkları uzmanı*) for women's problems, the latter being among the busiest doctors in Turkey!**

The best way to choose a doctor is by recommendation. You may prefer one who speaks your language and those in resorts often speak English or German, while those who don't are happy for patients to take along a translator. Finding a female doctor isn't a problem, as more than a third of Turkish doctors are women.

The American Embassy in Ankara's website (🖳 http://turkey.usembassy.gov/list_of_doctors_ankara.html) maintains a comprehensive list of doctors and medical facilities in Istanbul, Ankara, Izmir and Antalya.

Visiting the Doctor

An appointment (*rendevu*) is necessary only if you wish to see a private doctor or have treatment at a private clinic or hospital. If you're eligible for public healthcare, you just turn up and wait your turn, but it will be crowded, so expect a long wait. The public service is overloaded and consultations are brief (even brusque), although you may find that medics take more time and attention over you, as a foreigner brave enough to enter a state facility! You certainly get more time and attention in a private consultation.

Women's Health

The state runs mother-and-baby clinics, which also offer family planning, as do clinics run by the Turkish Family Planning Association (Türkiye Aile Planlaması

Derneği) in major cities. The birth-control pill is available over the counter in pharmacies, along with hormone replacement therapy. Sanitary towels are sold in supermarkets but tampons can be difficult to find and are of poor quality.

Emergency Treatment

All hospitals have an emergency (*acil servis*) department, although these are often overwhelmed by non-emergency cases. They do, however, give priority to genuinely urgent cases, and you won't be turned away, however busy they are. If the situation is serious, call a private ambulance.

Pharmacies

Turkish chemists' or pharmacies (*eczane*) stock many medicines (drugs) for sale over the counter, without a prescription – including antibiotics,

antidepressants and even Viagra. The chemist can undertake minor procedures, such as checking blood pressure or dressing a wound, and is well qualified to give advice on suitable treatments. For this reason, many Turks go to the *eczane* for medical help, rather than queue at a clinic or pay to see a doctor. There's always one open 24 hours, especially near a hospital.

Doctors often obtain medicines and equipment from the nearest *eczane* to administer treatments in the surgery, e.g. intravenous antibiotics; injections are given frequently, as they're deemed faster and more effective than pills. Doctors also set up intravenous drips – sometimes in the patient's home with a family member supervising!

If you have social insurance, you pay only 10-20 per cent of the cost of prescribed medicines. However, medicines (especially generics) are cheap by western standards.

> Over-prescribing is common in Turkey. Antibiotics, especially, are handed out like sweets, and most prescriptions feature several items, including the inevitable vitamins. Doctors are pressured by patients, who don't feel they have been treated properly unless they go home with a bag full of pills and potions.

Hospitals

There are two kinds of hospital in Turkey – state and private. State hospitals (*devlet hastanesi*) have a reputation for being overcrowded, understaffed and dirty, while private hospitals (*özel hastane*) are seen as clean and caring, with the latest equipment. However, the distinction is beginning to blur as Turkey undertakes a radical transformation of its health service. The government has greatly increased the number of state medical facilities, beds, examination rooms and full-time physicians, and is now buying in services from the private sector. Changes to the social security system should allow patients to obtain subsidised treatment at some private hospitals.

State hospitals have wards with up to six beds, as well as private rooms with en-suite facilities and TV, while private hospitals have individual hotel-style rooms. There's a lack of privacy in state hospitals and Turkish patients have many visitors, so it's a noisy (though friendly) environment.

Food is provided, although the quality varies considerably – but there are always shops and food stalls nearby.

Nursing Care

There's a shortage of nurses (*hemşire*) in the state sector and they provide little more than urgent medical care. Turkish patients invariably have a family member on hand to tend to their non-medical needs, such as feeding, cleaning and morale-building. These are designated as patient carers (*hasta bakacı*) by the medics, who will be concerned if you go into hospital with no one to look after you.

Medical Procedures

Turks accept what a doctor says without question and procedures such as blood tests and scans are prescribed with minimal explanation. A few doctors, especially those in state hospitals, lack what westerners might describe as a 'bedside manner'; one or two seem to suffer delusions of omnipotence, which are reinforced by the obsequiousness of their patients. However, the concept of patients' rights is taking hold and people can now contact the Ministry of Health (Sağlık Bakanlığı) via a call centre (☎ 184 SABIM), which claims to resolve 90 per cent of problems within 24 hours.

Childbirth

Most women give birth in hospital and almost half are by Caesarean section, which is preferred by mothers, fathers and doctors, and is rarely questioned. If you insist on a natural birth, you'll find that epidurals are available but 'birth plans' and 'alternative' delivery

methods such as water births aren't. Home births are strictly for poor women in remote villages.

Turkey has a high infant mortality rate, mainly due to the limited facilities east of Ankara and the high proportion of home births in rural areas. The 2007 figure, according to the *CIA World Factbook*, was 38.88 deaths for every 1,000 live births, compared with the EU average of 4.8. It therefore makes sense to have your baby at the best hospital you can afford with the most up-to-date ante- and post-natal care facilities. (Even if you're on *SKK*, it's unlikely you'd want to give birth in a state hospital.)

You may spend a little longer in hospital than you would in your home country, but once you're discharged, the onus is on you to arrange and attend check-ups. Convalescent care is almost non-existent, and it's expected that your family will provide this.

INSURANCE

Two kinds of insurance (*sigorta*) are obligatory in Turkey: earthquake insurance for property owners and third-party insurance for vehicle owners. In addition, there are optional policies to protect your health, car and home. Smaller insurers offer the best deals, although the major international names, such as Koç Allianz and Axa Oyak, may be more reliable at settling claims.

Health Insurance

As a foreigner, you may have no option but private healthcare, therefore it's essential to have insurance. There are policies which cover the cost of healthcare in Turkey and expatriate policies which also include repatriation, both of which are expensive, especially if you need to insure a family. Turkish policies allow you to opt for in-patient (*yatarak*) cover, which pays for operations and emergency treatment, or *ayakta ve yatarak* cover which includes out-patient consultations.

Read the policy carefully. Check which hospitals you can be treated at, whether any treatments or existing conditions are excluded, and whether there's an excess (deductible), which makes you liable for a proportion of the cost.

Don't leave it too late to take out health insurance, especially if you're approaching retirement age. Turkish insurers have a cut-off point between the ages of 55 and 65 – if you apply too late they may turn you down or refuse to extend your cover in future years.

Car Insurance

Basic policies cover third-party liability only. To cover your car against fire, theft and accidental damage, you need comprehensive cover, known as *kasko*, which also allows you to use the insurer's roadside rescue service (similar to the UK's AA or RAC services). The policy insures the vehicle rather than the driver, therefore in theory anyone can drive the car – but check before you lend it to someone.

> Insurance policies, vehicle registration documents, and tax and car test certificates must be carried in a car at all times – they're usually tucked into the sun visor. If you leave them at home, the police can fine you.

Household Insurance

Since the Izmit earthquake of 1999, the government has insisted that all homes be insured against natural disasters, which is known as 'earthquake insurance' (*deprem sigortası*) or DASK. Additional household insurance (*ev sigortası*) is optional, and many Turks don't take it out, but building insurance covers most risks, such as fire, flood and storm damage; contents cover only is available for those in rented properties.

There may be special terms if you want to insure valuables, such as jewellery or antiques – e.g. installing a safe or security bars – and your cover may be increased if you let your property. Power cuts and surges are common in Turkey, therefore you should insure against electrical items being damaged or destroyed.

Claims

If your policy is sold by an agent, and many are, your contact with the insurer will be through that agent, including the submission of claims. In the case of theft, fire or any incident that may need to be investigated, you must obtain a police report (*polis raporu*) within 24 hours, without which your insurer may not consider your claim. The same applies if you have a car accident, therefore you shouldn't move your car until the police arrive.

EDUCATION

Education (*eğitim*) is of prime importance to Turkish parents, most of whom take a hands-on interest in their children's schooling, and teachers are respected and good grades demanded. Children give up free time to take extra lessons, and would-be university students attend a *dershane* (a specialist private school) to cram for important examinations. Most children accept the high expectations of their families, who will take on extra jobs or loans and sell assets to ensure that their child gets the best possible education.

In the 2006/07 academic year, 90 per cent of potential students were enrolled in education. Non-attendance is often the result of a child needing to work to support the family or, in rural eastern Turkey, the reluctance of parents to send girls to school.

Finding the right school is one of the biggest challenges faced by families relocating to Turkey, and you need to thoroughly investigate all available options. If your move is permanent, you will also need to consider your children's choices in higher education and the impact this will have on their career.

Turkish or International School?

This is your first, and most important, decision – and it may have a bearing on where you settle, as the choice of schools is far greater in major cities than rural areas or resorts. Money is another factor. Unless you're working for an overseas company or embassy which pays for your children's schooling, the fees for international schools will take a huge slice out of your budget.

International Schools

The best international schools are in Istanbul and Ankara, where many are long established and have an excellent reputation. There are also schools in Izmir and Antalya and some other cities, but to date few in resort areas. Many teach in English, although there are schools where the language of instruction is German, French or Japanese. Don't confuse international schools with the many private (*özel*) schools, which teach the Turkish curriculum in Turkish to Turks, but in a better equipped and less crowded environment than a state school.

If there's a chance that your children will wish to go to university outside Turkey, they must attend a school with a universally recognised accreditation, such as the European Council of International Schools or ECIS (💻 www. ecis.org).

An international school is the best choice if your stay is temporary, or your child is at a critical stage in his or her education. Standards are usually high – many teach the International Baccalaureate programme – but so are the fees. One year's primary education at a top international school in Istanbul costs around €8,000. Another drawback is that international schools expose your children to many different nationalities, but may insulate them from the country they're living in – therefore you should ensure that Turkey's language, history and culture are included in the curriculum.

State Schools

Attending a state school (*devlet okulu*) is much harder to begin with, but it gives your child a better chance of learning the language and fitting into the community. It's the best option if you're planning a permanent move, and younger children adapt surprisingly well, although children over ten may find it more difficult and need extra language coaching and a lot more support. In a resort, where there are other foreign children, look for a school which already has some expatriate students of a similar age.

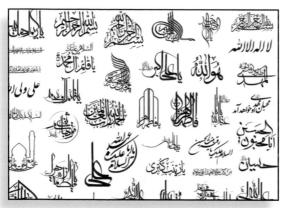

A Turkish school is more of a challenge for parents, too, as you must communicate with teachers, other parents and your children's friends in their language. Your first test will be navigating the Ministry of Education's website in order to enrol your child in a school.

Education System

Compulsory education consists of eight years at primary school (*ilköğretim*), commencing at the age of six.

Secondary school (*lise*) lasts four years, from 14 to 18, and students choose from a range of options: academic, vocational or specialist. Education is free, although parents pay for uniforms and stationery, and those who can afford to contribute towards equipment and activities.

Some aspects of the Turkish education system which may come as a surprise are listed below:

● Methods are old-fashioned, with teaching by rote (memorisation by repetition), rather than by research and innovation, although the curriculum is changing to include more team work and group projects.

● All subjects are taught in Turkish and foreign students have to get to grips with the language as soon as possible, or they risk being put back a year.

● Subjects taught include Turkish, mathematics, history and the sciences. All years have lessons in art, music and physical education, and foreign language tuition (usually English) starts in year three. Optional subjects include drama, computer studies, philosophy – and chess!

● Patriotism and hard work are instilled from an early age. Children start and finish the week singing the national anthem (*İstiklâl Marşı*), as they watch the Turkish flag being raised.

'I am Turkish, I am honest, I am hard working' (*Türkum, doğruyum, calışkanım*). **These are the words which every child chants at the start of the school day.**

● Atatürk (see **Chapter 2**) is part of the curriculum and children are taught him and his reforms from their first year in school.

● Text books are treated with reverence and, literally, followed to the letter.

● Uniforms are compulsory and all children have homework (*ev ödevi*) – up to a couple of hours a night in secondary school.

● The school day lasts from 8.50am until 3.20pm, with up to an hour for lunch. Food isn't provided so most children bring their lunch or go home to eat.

● The school year is from September to June, with a three-month summer break and a shorter break in winter.

There is also days off for religious and public holidays.

- Classes are large – up to 60 pupils in some primary schools. A few schools are so oversubscribed that they have to teach in two shifts.

- Children are disciplined and stand up to speak to a teacher – the disrespect seen in some western schools doesn't exist in Turkey.

- Exams (*sınav*) begin in the first year. Children are graded twice a year on a combination of exam results, course work and assessments, and receive a diploma (*ilköğretim diploması*) at the end of primary school.

Just over half of all students go on to secondary education, and they have to make a decision about their career path while still in their early teens. Choices include general high schools; vocational schools, which teach trades and professional subjects such as nursing; technical schools; and schools that teach in a foreign language.

Whether or not they obtain a place in their chosen school depends on how well they do in the examination (*Ortaöğretim Kurumlari Sınavı* or *OKS*) at the end of their last primary school year. It's much easier to get a place at a standard vocational school (*meslek okulu*) than at a popular Anatolian high school (*Anadolu lisesi*), where the curriculum is focused towards a university education.

Dershane are specialist private schools offering extra lessons during evenings and weekends so that students can brush up on their weaker subjects. They also provide courses tailored to the Student Selection Exam (*Öğrenci Seçme Sınavı* or *ÖSS*), which all students must pass if they wish to go to university. Many students forfeit their social lives during high school in order to cram for this life-changing test, and parents spend up to €3,500 on lessons. Students planning a career abroad or wishing to work in tourism may attend private language courses (*dil kursu*) in addition to their regular education.

University

Turkey has more than 90 universities (*üniversite*), both state and private, but the best ones are hugely oversubscribed. A degree is seen as a ticket to employment and many employers will only consider graduates, therefore the pressure to gain higher qualifications is immense. Selection takes place via the dreaded *ÖSS* exam (see above). The higher the score, the greater a students' chance of getting a place in a good university. Degree courses last four years, and even state universities charge tuition fees; grants and loans aren't easily available.

> **Foreign students can attend Turkish universities but must first pass an exam and then, if necessary, spend a year learning Turkish before enrolling in a course.**

COUNCIL SERVICES

The local municipality (*belediye*) is the organisation that lights your streets, fills the potholes outside your house and takes away your rubbish. As a property owner, you're required to register with it.

Refuse Collection

Collections are frequent – every day in summer – and paid for by a small environment tax (*çevre temizlik vergisi*), which is added to water bills. Rubbish is dumped in communal street bins – if you live in a block, the *kapıcı* (caretaker) may do this for you. Refuse includes household and garden rubbish and even the contents of wood-burning stoves – there are no restrictions on what you can put in or near a council bin. You aren't supposed to dump rubble in the countryside, although many people do.

Recycling

The Turks have been recycling for years, using old cola bottles to store olive oil, planting flowers in cheese tins and even appropriating Roman pillars to prop up their houses. But organised recycling is a relatively new concept. Some areas have recycling bins, usually for paper and glass, but there's no requirement to sort your rubbish in the home, as there is in many western European countries. Occasionally, councils provide bins for recyclable material, but these are often 'borrowed' in rural areas.

Some Turks make a living from selling other people's unwanted goods. Scrap metal merchants (*hurdacı*) tour the streets for custom, as do people collecting aluminium cans and paper. Unused food has a willing army of disposal experts in the stray dogs and cats which roam Turkey's streets.

UTILITIES

As with most things in Turkey, connecting to utility services involves some bureaucratic gymnastics. New customers must take out a subscription (*abonelik*) and may have to pay a deposit (in case they default on a bill), which requires a visit to the utility company's office. If you take over an existing supply, you're responsible for the previous occupier's unpaid bills, therefore you must check that they are paid up to date.

Electricity

All of Turkey is wired for electricity (*elektrik*), which is supplied by the state monopoly TEDAŞ (🖳 www.tedas.gov. tr/25,Bilgi_Edinme_Index.html). The voltage is 220v (as in western Europe) and sockets take two round pins – you can buy adapters for foreign plugs. If the power keeps cutting off when you switch on a high-power appliance, such as a kettle, you may need to upgrade your power rating – circuits in older homes aren't designed for all the appliances we use today.

Users are billed every two months, either by TEDAŞ or one of its local subsidiaries. Bills can be paid at a TEDAŞ office, post office (*postane* or *PTT*) or bank. Electricity is expensive in Turkey and using electric fires all winter – or air-conditioning unit all summer – will result in hefty bills.

Power Cuts

Power cuts (*elektrik kesintisi*) are a constant problem in winter, especially in rural areas – and also in resorts when demand is high. They rarely last long, but it's a good idea to have some back-up power, such as a gas heater, as well as candles and a torch. Connect your computer to a UPS (uninterruptible power supply) and fit surge protectors to expensive electric appliances such as televisions. There's little point in buying items with timers unless they have an integral memory.

Solar Panels

Ugly but economic, solar panels (*güneş enerjisi*) are ideal in areas where summers are long and hot, and can be fitted for around €850. Many people fit the whole system, including the heated-water tanks, on the roof. However, tanks are heavy and can sometimes leak, so it's better to site your system on a garage roof or in the garden, with the solar panels in an elevated position facing the path of the sun. If solar panels are your only source of hot water, you need to have an immersion element so that you can heat water during 'bad' weather.

Stoves

Wood-burning stoves (*soba*) are still the most popular form of heating in country

areas, where there's an ample supply of wood. The main advantage is their economy – around €50 buys enough wood (*odun*) to run a stove for a month. The disadvantages are the dirt, the hassle of loading and emptying them, and the potentially deadly fumes. A *soba* is sufficient to heat a small flat or bungalow, but not a two-storey villa.

Gas

Natural gas (*doğalgaz*) is only available in large cities – in Istanbul it's supplied by İGDAŞ (🖥 www. igdas.com.tr) – but having it fitted can be expensive and is worthwhile only if you own your property or are planning to rent long term. Elsewhere people use bottled liquid propane gas (LPG, *tüp gaz*) – small bottles to run cookers and large canisters to power hot water and central heating systems. These are delivered and fitted by companies such as Aygaz – flag down a van or order a bottle by phone (only 'camping' size bottles can be purchased in shops). Bottled gas is safe provided it's correctly fitted.

Central Heating

Many city apartments have central heating (*kalorifer tesisatı*), which usually runs on natural gas but may also use coal, diesel, electricity or bottled gas. Coal is the cheapest and electricity the most expensive. In some apartment blocks, central heating is controlled from a central point by the *kapıcı* or doorman, who will carry out the wishes of the majority of residents, therefore you may have little or no say about when it's turned on (or off). Turks like the heating up high, therefore you may have to pay extra to keep your neighbours warm.

Water

Water and waste services are supplied by the local authority, who generally read meters and send out bills every few months. Not all areas are connected to mains sewerage (*kanalizasyon*) and many rural homes have a septic tank (*fosseptik*), which needs to be emptied from time to time. Water is cheap, and Turks can be wasteful – 2007's unusually hot summer drained reservoirs, and water cuts were threatened. Pressure can drop (sometimes to virtually nothing) in resorts in high season, when tourists add to the demand, and brief water cuts may accompany power cuts; if you live in an area where this is common you should keep some bottles in reserve.

Quality

City water should be safe to drink but sometimes tastes of chlorine, while rural water supplies are more risky and include 'free' water from springs and wells, which should be boiled well before use (or you should stick to bottled water). Large water bottles (the type used in coolers) are delivered by shops and gas-bottle suppliers, which, when fitted with a pump, can save you money as well as effort.

Telephone

Telephone services are reliable and virtually the entire country is served by both fixed and mobile phone networks.

> If you're dialling Turkey from abroad, you need to dial the international code, which is 90. You then omit the first 0 in the local code, therefore to reach 0252 234 5678 from the UK you dial 0090 252 234 5678.

Installation

Türk Telekom is the sole telephone (*telefon*) service provider in Turkey, although since its privatisation in 2005 it's become more user-friendly; however, many people still complain about the time it takes to get a problem fixed.

To apply for a line, go to a Türk Telekom office with your residence permit and bank account details – there are offices in most towns. Note that you cannot have a landline installed (officially) without a residence permit, although some offices will quietly overlook this while others will insist you take out the contract in a Turk's name (the same applies if you want an internet connection). Many foreigners find it easier to use a mobile phone.

It can take up to a week (or longer) to get a line installed. Installation and line rental charges are low, and call costs were slashed in 2007, with local calls now costing the same as national calls, and a ten-minute call to most EU countries less than €1. Bills are sent out monthly and can be paid at a Türk Telekom office, post office or bank.

For more information, see Türk Telekom's website (🖳 www.turktelekom.com.tr/eng_default.asp) or call ☎ 444 1444.

Mobile Phones

Mobile phones (*cep telefonu*) are ubiquitous in Turkey, despite a 40 per cent government tax on calls. Contracts are restricted to residents, but anyone can buy a pay-as-you-go SIM card and top up the units (*köntor*) in local shops. The service providers are Avea (🖳 www.avea.com.tr), Türkcell (🖳 www.turkcell.com.tr) and Vodafone (🖳 www.vodafone.com.tr) – both Avea's and Türkcell's websites have English options.

You can bring your own mobile phone and slot in a Turkish SIM card, but this only works if your phone isn't locked to a network in your home country. Also, you must register the phone with one of the mobile phone service providers' shops or risk it being blocked. It's simpler to buy a cheap handset in Turkey.

Internet

Turks have welcomed the internet like a long-lost relative, and with the introduction of ADSL/broadband connections in 2003, online communication has become (almost) as easy as it is in the West. Just over 20 per cent of Turks are regular internet users and virtually every company or organisation has a website, so finding things out no longer relies on phone calls or hearsay.

Türk Telekom's internet subsidiary is TTNet (🖳 www.ttnet.net.tr), which sells ADSL packages for as little as €15 per month, with connection costing roughly the same. Apply at one of the sales points (*satış noktaları*) listed on the website or at a Türk Telekom office – once online you can cut the cost of phone calls by subscribing to an internet call service, such as Skype.

If you don't have a home connection, you can get your internet fix at one of the many internet cafes. These are to Turkish youth what the tea house was to their fathers and are usually full of teenagers chatting on MSN or playing online games – the noise can be deafening. But they're cheap – around €1 per hour – and usually stay open late.

Paying the Bills

The easiest way to pay bills (*fatura*) is to set up automatic payments (*otomatik ödeme*) through your bank by direct debit. These prevent you from getting cut off when paper bills turn up late (as they often do) or when you're away, and having to pay a reconnection fee.

Most villages and smaller towns have a loudspeaker system run by the *belediye* through which important events, such as weddings, are announced. It's also used to remind people when it's time to pay taxes and bills. Each broadcast is prefaced by feedback and the word '*ilan*' (announcement) and is usually repeated.

Dealing with Utility Companies

Customer services are improving in Turkey, especially in private companies. However, if you have a complaint or problem, it's best to get your point across in person, at one of the company's shops or sales points. Although companies have a contact number (usually a 444 number, which can be dialled from anywhere in Turkey without a local prefix) – some even allow you to 'press 9 for English' – it's frustrating trying to explain your predicament over the phone, especially if you can't explain it in English. In any case, Turks always prefer to do things face to face. A few companies have online customer service sections which can be contacted by email – they will then either email you back or (more likely) phone you.

Useful Numbers	
Water problems	185
Electricity problems	186
Gas problems	187
Telephone problems	121
International operator	115
Directory enquiries	118

STAYING INFORMED

You need some knowledge of the Turkish language to follow the country's media – although not as much as you'd think, and watching television is a great learning aid. If it all gets too much, there's a choice of foreign-language newspapers, radio and television channels, the majority of which are in English.

Television

In Turkey, the television (*televizyon*) is part of the family and doesn't appear to have an 'off' switch – many Turks turn it up when visitors arrive. Much of the programming is low-brow entertainment, although the state channels (TRT 1 to TRT 4) broadcast a range of cultural entertainment and documentaries.

The most popular commercial channels are ATV, Kanal D and Show TV, which air the staple soaps, sitcoms and game shows. Some of these will be familiar to foreign viewers, as there are Turkish versions of many Western shows, including *Big Brother* and *Pop Idol*. There are also some expensive and well-made drama series, such as *Avrupa Yakası* and *Kürtler Vadisi*. Advertising breaks are frequent (and loud) and films are usually dubbed into Turkish (seemingly by the same three people). News content can be graphic, with repeated shots of people falling from buildings and close-ups of the aftermath of car accidents. Simple subtitles in Turkish help you follow the reporting.

Children's programmes consist mainly of cartoons. Some channels screen warnings before violent or otherwise unsuitable programmes (although not the news!), but there's no 'watershed' and most Turkish children stay up until midnight watching grown-up TV. You may therefore wish to monitor your children's viewing or keep

news, documentaries (National Geographic), sport (Eurosport, Fox Sports), films (Moviemax) and US dramas (CNBC-e and Dizimax). A big bonus is that on some channels, foreign programmes are broadcast in their original language (usually English) with Turkish subtitles, while on others you can switch the audio output between English and Turkish. To watch Digiturk, you need a dish, a 'digibox' (decoder) and a smart card – a basic package costs from €11 a month.

the remote control to hand. Digiturk allows you to block channels.

Satellite TV

Satellite dishes, large and small, disfigure every rooftop and balcony in Turkey. Analogue transmission is sparse. Turks need a dish and set-top receiver to watch even free national television channels via the Türksat satellite, which also transmits some free foreign channels such as BBC World. People in larger cities have access to Türk Telekom's cable TV, but it isn't available in resort areas.

It's possible to pick up a huge number of channels from the Astra satellite, provided you have a large enough dish, and you'll see some 4-metre whoppers in expat areas. These can also receive Sky TV provided you have a decoder box and a smart card, and a way to keep your card updated (see 🖥 www. storesatellite.com/index.php).

The best-known subscription service is Digiturk (☎ 212-473 7373 🖥 www.digiturk.tv) which transmits via the Eutelsat satellite and dominates the subscription TV market. It airs dozens of channels, including English, French, German and Russian TV, as well as

Radio

Turks are fond of the radio (*radyo*) and there are thousands of radio stations, national and local, broadcasting a non-stop barrage of news, chat and music. Among the most popular are Alem FM, Powerturk and Kral FM. There are also channels dedicated to sport and debate, which are difficult to follow unless your Turkish is excellent. Digiturk transmits over 30 stations in digital format.

The national broadcaster, TRT, has some foreign-language programming – its Voice of Turkey channel transmits programmes in several languages, while TRT Tourism Radio is available in resort areas and broadcasts in English, French and German (among others). You can access both BBC World Service and Voice of America through satellite radio, but the easiest way to tune into most foreign radio stations is via the internet.

The Press

There are over 30 national and more than 500 local newspapers in Turkey, although sales of national dailies barely top 5m copies as Turks prefer to obtain their news from the TV. Newspapers cost from around €0.50 and are more expensive at weekends when they're stuffed with supplements covering culture, travel, entertainment – and sport.

There are three English-language dailies:

- *Today's Zaman* – A successful spin-off from *Zaman*, which became the best-selling English-language daily less than a year after its launch in 2007.

- *Turkish Daily News* – Founded in the '60s and the oldest of the three, *TDN* has good international coverage but a slightly stodgy image.

- *The New Anatolian* – owned by the founders of *TDN* and similar to that paper.

Many resorts have an English newspaper, usually distributed free, and most are available online, although some read like a parish magazine. Virtually all are in English and the best include *Land of Lights* (Fethiye), *The Post* (Marmaris), *Voices* (Altinkum) and *Dalyan Times* (Dalyan).

It's possible to buy popular magazines, such as *Hello!*, and several foreign newspapers are available, e.g. *The Times*, *Le Monde* and *Bild*, but they're usually a day late. Some titles, such the UK's *Daily Mail* and *Guardian*, are published in issues focussing on the eastern Mediterranean. All imported publications are relatively expensive.

Turkish magazines are an enjoyable way to brush up your language skills. Try *Atlas* (Turkey's answer to *National Geographic*) and *Cornucopia*, a collectable glossy dedicated to Turkish culture.

The box below shows Turkey's most popular publications, all of which

are daily newspapers. Two of them, *Hürriyet* and *Sabah*, have English versions of their websites.

Turkey's Top-selling Publications

Zaman – pro-Islamic (circulation 766,472)

Posta – undemanding daily with popular puzzle pull-out (628,897)

Hürriyet – independent (518,871)

Sabah – independent (439,325)

Milliyet – liberal (244,242)

Fotomaç – top-selling sports (as in football) daily (241,593)

Vatan – centre-right and popular with men (232,768)

Fanatik – aptly named sports daily (228,243)

Takvim – daily (217,558)

Akşam – evening newspaper (197,195)

Cumhuriyet – the broadsheet founded by Atatürk, comes in at a lowly 17th.

Post

The Turkish postal system isn't noted for its reliability and letters often turn up late, especially post sent to or from overseas. Inbound parcels are checked by customs and you may be asked to pay duty. If you send a parcel within Turkey, it's better to use one of the cargo companies.

Post offices (*PTT*) are open from 8.30am to 5pm and sometimes close for lunch from 12pm to 1.30pm. Many people pay their bills at the *PTT* and the queues at the end of the month can be horrendous.

BANKING

Turkey is still a cash-based society, although a large proportion of television advertising is now devoted to credit cards, financial services and banks, and the western 'buy now pay later' philosophy is catching on fast The economic crisis of 2001 saw several banks fail and those that remain are modern, efficient and similar to western European banks. They often have staff who can speak English and other foreign languages (usually German), especially in resort areas. With over 40 banks, including some foreign banks such as HSBC, it's difficult to decide who to bank with; the three largest banks are Akbank, Turkiye İş Bankası and Yapı ve Kredi Bankası.

Whichever you choose, there are some quirks of Turkish banking which you should be aware of:

● **Accessing your account** – Most banks have internet access, usually with an English-language version. The main banks have secure websites, but you should take sensible precautions, such as not giving out confidential information by email or replying to emails claiming to be from your bank.

● **Bank charges** – Banking isn't free in Turkey and account charges (*hesap ücreti*) are

applied every few months. Turks rarely use cheques and there may be charges for transferring money between banks (*havale*), as well as for using your debit card in another bank's cash machine (ATM).

● **Cash withdrawals** – There are ATMs everywhere, with instructions in various languages. For extra security, you should use one at a bank.

● **Changing money** – Banks, post offices and foreign exchange bureaux (*döviz*) can all change foreign currency (euros, dollars and sterling notes – coins and less familiar currencies are more difficult or impossible to change). Check the rate and ask if there's a commission charge.

● **Cheques** – These are rarely used and take several weeks to clear. Payments are usually made by credit card, bank transfer or in cash.

● **Credit & debit cards** – Most businesses use the chip and pin system with credit and debit cards, and commission is sometimes charged on credit card transactions – you'll almost certainly be charged when using a foreign credit card.

Foreign debit cards are useful for withdrawing money from ATMs, for which your bank will usually charge a fee (unless the card is issued by the British post office or Nationwide building society). Credit cards issued by Turkish banks are available only to Turkish citizens – interest rates are high and national credit card debt is growing at an alarming rate. Card companies campaign vigorously for custom, offering deals whereby people who cannot obtain any other credit can use their card to buy goods in stages (*taksit*), sometimes at no extra charge.

● **Opening an account** – To open a current account (*vadesiz hesap*), all you usually need is your passport, especially if it's a foreign-currency account, although some bank managers demand a residence permit if you want a new Turkish lira (YTL) account. You need a tax number to open a deposit account (*vadeli hesap*) and can obtain this from the tax department at your local Finance Ministry (Maliye) office. Take your passport and residence permit (if you have one), plus photocopies of both – tax numbers are usually issued the same day. Tax on interest earned is always deducted at source.

● **Opening hours** – Banks are open from 9am to 5pm and often close for lunch (12 or 12.30 until 1.30pm). The busiest times are just before and after lunch.

● **Overdrafts & loans** – There are no unauthorised overdrafts and loans are difficult to obtain for non-Turks unless you use your property as security.

● **Savings** – The Turkish lira (YTL) investment rate was 17 per cent in summer 2007, compared with around 9 per cent inflation. You can therefore earn good interest (*faiz*) on Turkish lira investments, and a few enterprising expats claim they can live on their investments. How much you earn depends, of course, on how much you invest and how long you're brave enough to leave it there.

> If you invest a lot of money in Turkish currency, you could be a huge loser if the lira suddenly plummets against foreign currencies, as it did in 2001. There's a limit on the amount of funds the government guarantees if a bank fails, which was just YTL 50,000 (around €27,000) in 2007.

● **Transferring money** – It's easier to transfer money into Turkey than out, and charges vary with the bank. You should always transfer into a foreign currency account, e.g. euros into a euro account. Some banks charge if you withdraw transferred funds in the same currency within a certain period, but will allow you to withdraw them in YTL without charge.

● Anti-money-laundering regulations mean that any transaction over YTL8,000 (around €4,325) must be made through a bank or the post office, although this can work in your favour (see **Tax Fraud** below). Always keep a copy of the receipt.

TAXES

It's a national joke that most Turks will do anything to avoid paying tax, including tax officials, and one of the country's biggest economic problems is its failure to collect all taxes due. The government struggles to prise revenue out of the public, many of whom are self-employed and experts in concealing their income. Most of those who cannot escape the tax man are in low-paid public-sector jobs, and their contributions aren't enough to balance the budget.

The tax system isn't especially complex, but residence can have an effect on your tax liabilities. Turkey has a double-taxation agreement with the UK (and most western European countries) and the US, which means that you won't pay tax in two countries. However, you must take expert advice on tax planning before taking up residence or buying property in Turkey. Once there, you may need to use an accountant (*muhasebeci*) owing to the lack of bilingual tax officers.

The Turkish tax year runs from January to December, with income tax levied on a sliding scale from 15 to 35 per cent. Tax is withheld from employees' salaries, but the self-employed and business owners are expected to declare their income and make payments several times a year.

Other taxes you may have to pay include:

- **Motor vehicle tax** – This can be frighteningly high on new and petrol-hungry cars, and is paid in two instalments in January and July.

- **Property tax** – This is satisfyingly low and is between 0.1 and 0.3 per cent of a property's value paid annually.

- **Property sale & acquisition tax** – This is paid by both buyer and seller on the transfer of property and is levied at 1.5 per cent of a property's declared selling price.

- **Capital gains tax** – There's nothing to pay on property, provided that you've owned it for five years (four years if it was purchased before 1st January 2007). If you sell sooner, tax is charged at the same rate as income tax.

- **Tax on rental income** – This must be declared and paid in Turkey, even if you're a non-resident. The rates are those applied to income.

Tax Fraud

Tax evasion is rife, especially among small (and not so small) businesses and the self-employed, and many foreigners fail to declare any income, either in Turkey or in their country of origin. The tax authorities are aware of this – a recent campaign targeted non-resident foreigners who rent out holiday homes – and the penalties for tax fraud are high.

It's especially tempting to deal 'under the table' with property transactions and cash deals are common, as is under-declaring a property's value is routine in order to reduce the amount of property sale and acquisition tax due. The risk for the buyer is not just a large fine, but also having a low value recorded on the title deed, which will have further tax implications when you come to sell.

If you pay tax in Turkey, you must retain all personal tax-related paperwork for five years – the period during which the tax authorities can claim unpaid back taxes.

COST OF LIVING

Turkey is popularly perceived to be a cheap country, where a foreign pension goes a long way towards providing a comfortable lifestyle. However, many expatriates, once settled, are shocked at the speed with which prices are rising. Basic foodstuffs, clothing and public transport are reasonable, but if you smoke, drink, run a car or buy imported food or wine, you'll soon count the cost.

Inflation is (officially) around 9 per cent (based on 2007 figures), but the cost of fuel is increasing inexorably and this is having a knock-on effect on the price of many goods and services. Petrol prices are frightening and in mid-2008 a litre of unleaded petrol cost more in Turkey than in the UK and other western European countries. Electricity bills have also risen sharply in recent years, as has anything deemed to be a 'luxury'.

High levels of 'special consumption' tax are levied on petrol, cars, alcohol, cigarettes and even cola! The governing AK Party makes no secret of its aversion to the 'demon drink' and has repeatedly raised tax on alcohol. VAT (known in Turkey as *KDV*) and private consumer taxes make up 65 per cent of the price of a bottle of *rakı*, Turkey's 'national' spirit, which costs almost €13 for a 75cl bottle. The price of a packet of locally produced cigarettes has increased threefold since 2000 to €1.50.

Rental payments account for 30 to 50 per cent of a worker's income. Landlords are permitted to increase rents annually by the rate of inflation, but many push them higher. Rents are especially crippling in Istanbul and tourist resorts. A two-bedroom apartment in Marmaris can easily cost €250 per month, which is twice as much as a similar property in a provincial town, but only half the price of one in a smarter suburb of Istanbul.

In the 2008 Mercer *Cost of Living Survey* (www.mercer. com), Istanbul was in 23rd place – up from 38th place in 2007 – and just one place below New York city.

4.
BREAKING THE ICE

One of the best ways of getting over culture shock and feeling part of life in Turkey is to get acquainted with the Turks. Making new friends anywhere takes effort, and the language and cultural barriers in Turkey add to the pressure. You'll need to make adjustments to fit into the social order, which is highly structured and family-orientated, formal (though gregarious), and built on a foundation of religion and tradition. But the warm and welcoming Turks will go more than halfway to meet you.

This chapter provides information about important aspects of Turkish society and family. It advises how to make acquaintances and behave in social situations, as well as topics to steer clear of in conversation. It also deals with the question of mixing with the expatriate community and gives guidance on handling confrontation – especially with Turkish officials.

> 'The most important trip you may take in life is meeting people halfway.'
> Henry Boye (writer & publisher)

COMMUNITY LIFE

Turks don't live behind closed doors. Neighbours and family interact on a daily basis, visiting each other's houses and meeting in the street, as well as chatting endlessly on the phone. The downside is that everybody knows – or thinks they know – everybody else's business. The upside is that there's a great sense of community and always someone ready to help.

Neighbours (*komşu*) are important and are regarded as a second family. Make the effort to talk to your neighbours. A friendly *merhaba* (hello) as you pass on the stairs goes a long way, and shopping at the local grocer's helps you to feel a part of the community. It also encourages you to speak their language.

Community life differs according to where you live, but whether it's in rural Anatolia or modern Istanbul, there are many similarities.

Country Life

Village doors are always open. During summer, life is lived outdoors – most houses have a large terrace and an outside 'kitchen', and the occupants go inside only to sleep or when bad weather forces a retreat. Even then, there's a constant ebb and flow of visitors.

A foreign resident is an object of much interest and speculation, especially a foreign woman who lives alone! Being the centre of a village's attention can be exhausting. Your guests will be monitored and even your laundry inspected. Most of this is down to curiosity – many villagers' experience of foreigners is limited to what they've seen on television – but it's also to do with honour. In a small community, everything you do reflects on your neighbours.

You'll have to accept them interfering in your life, at least until you've learned enough Turkish to tell them, gently, that you sometimes need privacy. Their nosiness is rarely malicious and most just want to offer support.

> A friend of the author once spent three weeks in a remote farming village in the centre of Turkey. Her Turkish language skills were basic and the villagers were suspicious at first – until she put her experiences as a Girl Guide and dairy farmer's wife to good use by administering first aid to an injured villager and tending to a sick cow. The villagers immediately accepted her.

City Life

City living is less conservative, although you'll still have regular contact with the people around you. Most Turks live in apartment blocks with be 20 or more apartments – and walls can be thin. Noise is a constant problem, especially in summer when windows are open, televisions blaring and children playing in the street until midnight and calling up to their mothers to open the front door. But living on top of each other has advantages; potential thieves are easily spotted, and

there's always someone to keep an eye on your home when you're away.

Neighbours welcome newcomers, usually with food – they assume you're too busy with the move to cook – and will be keen to tell you about your other neighbours and even more keen to learn about you. Be careful how you handle these initial advances. Reject them and you may be considered strange or stuck up; welcome them unequivocally and your new neighbours may think your home is an 'open house'.

If someone brings food, you should never refuse it, even if it's something you don't eat. It's also bad manners to return the plate or container empty; some of your home cooking will be appreciated. Be prepared for the dish to return to you once more, with a new Turkish delicacy, and for the process to continue for some time.

Community Regulations

These are the rules which apply to the residents of an apartment block or other 'community' development – check if any apply to your block. Generally, only upmarket gated complexes have a list of

rules and regulations, which are usually decided by a committee, who also set the annual management fee. Regulations may include where you can park, how you should dispose of rubbish, who may use the pool and communal areas, and how much you can alter the outward appearance of your property.

Single blocks are often managed by a *yönetici* (administrator) – details are usually posted on a notice board – and residents may take turns to fulfil the role or appoint a professional. Duties may include collecting the rent, handling accounts and ensuring the *kapıcı* (see below) is doing his job correctly.

There's also an unwritten code of conduct. This usually means turning a blind eye to your neighbour's child leaving his bike in the stairwell, and not watering plants too vigorously after your neighbour below has cleaned her balcony or objecting when she fries fish beneath yours!

Apartment life is held together by the *kapıcı* or caretaker, who's the equivalent of a janitor in the US; his job is to clean and secure the block, fix things, regulate the central heating and deliver post. He may also run errands and keep a set of keys in case you lock yourself out. The *kapıcı* often lives in the basement, with his wife, who is invariably a cleaner, and all residents contribute to his wages.

FAMILY

By Western standards, most Turkish families are large. A family (*aile*) usually consists of a husband, wife and children, but can expand to include grown-up children and their spouses (and offspring), elderly relatives, unmarried sisters and distant relatives on long-term visits. The more rural the area, the larger the family unit will be.

It's considered shameful to bundle off old folks into a home, so many are looked after by their children – in turn, they help to look after their grandchildren. It's considered unseemly for single women to live alone, so female relatives will stay with the family and assist with cooking and other chores.

The average house cannot cope with this extended brood, therefore some families inhabit entire apartment blocks or build several houses on one plot.

Family Names

Members of Turkish families rarely refer to their elders by their first names. Instead, they use an appropriate 'title'. Even non-family members can use these titles, which saves you having to remember a lot of unfamiliar names. Typical family titles are show below:

● *anne* – mother;

● *baba* – father;

- *abla* – older sister;

- *ağabey/abi* – older brother;

- *yenge* – older brother's wife (or uncle's wife). The term is also used for a foreign woman who has married into a Turkish family.

- *enişte* – sister's husband;

- *babaanne* – paternal grandmother;

- *anneanne* – maternal grandmother;

- *büyükbaba* – paternal grandfather;

- *dede* – maternal grandfather;

- *amca* **&** *hala* – paternal uncle & aunt;

- *dayı* **&** *teyze* – maternal uncle & aunt;

- *kaynana* – mother-in-law;

- *kayınpeder* – father-in-law.

SEXUAL ATTITUDES

At first glance, Turkey appears to be as sexually liberated as any western European country. Newspapers carry pictures of topless girls and advertisements for 'chat' lines, condoms and birth-control pills are sold openly, there are state-run brothels and homosexuality isn't a crime (but see below). But this progressive picture obscures the reality of Turkish sexual values, which are similar to those of Catholic countries and are rarely challenged, even in the anything-goes atmosphere of a resort town. You may see mixed groups of teenagers holding hands, but you're less likely to see a couple kissing passionately in public. If you do, it's odds on that the boy is a Turk and the girl is foreign.

Your encounters with Turks, whether liberated or conservative, will be easier if you understand why the different sexes behave as they do.

Men

In Turkey, men appear to 'have it all'. The foreign stereotype (which most Turkish women would recognise) is the macho male, who spends his free time smoking and socialising with his friends, knowing his house is spotless and his faithful wife is patiently awaiting his return.

Turkish culture doesn't repress male sexuality and a man who has affairs appears to have the admiration of his peers – although, deep down, most Turks disapprove of adultery, which was illegal until recently. But he's not as free as he appears to be and with his role as breadwinner and patriarch mapped out for him, he faces unavoidable responsibilities. He may spend his youth chasing foreign tourists but his family expects him to settle down with a 'nice Turkish girl' and provide (and provide for) as many grandchildren as possible.

There are 'new men' in Turkey and as more women work, their husbands take on a share of household duties. These unions of equality are seen more in areas with a high percentage of foreigners, where Western ideas – and mixed marriages – have penetrated the culture. But in rural Anatolia, where couples marry young – often in arranged marriages – and wives stay at home, they're rare.

> Marriage is almost universal for women. The Turkish Democratic Health Survey in 2003, which questioned over 8,000 women from all regions of the country, revealed that 95 per cent were married, 3 per cent were divorced or separated and 2 per cent were widowed. None were single.

Women

In Turkey, women appear to be the lesser sex, but in truth they have a great deal of power. A girl's most important possession is her virginity and most wouldn't dream of sleeping around – to do so could damage her and her family's honour and ruin her for marriage prospects. In a survey of university students, only 18 per cent of females questioned admitted to having had sex.

Marriage is still the goal for both sexes, and most Turkish men want to marry a virgin – or, at least, a girl who his family thinks is a virgin. Courtship is often a game of 'catch me if you can', in which the man does all the running with no guarantee of a prize.

Housewives & Breadwinners

A Turkish man's home is not his castle – it's his wife's castle. The man holds the power outside the home, but inside the woman's word is law. Turkish women keep control of the household, even if they go out to work. They don't trust their husbands with important tasks such as cleaning, cooking and childcare, and some wives even control the household budget. In return they expect their men to supply all the appliances necessary for their high standards to be maintained – even at the risk of running up huge debts. In wealthier households this may include a (live-in) cleaner and a nanny.

Turk-foreigner Marriages

An increasing number of Turkish men are marrying women from Europe, the US and the former Soviet states. Sadly, many such marriages fail, not just through a clash of cultures but also due to differences in wealth, education, language and age. Tales of twenty-something waiters taking fifty-something foreign brides to gain a visa to a new life abroad are part of modern Turkish folklore.

Even when a couple are of a similar age and social standing, they may have very different views on child-rearing and the woman's role. Turkish men can be jealous and some expect their liberated girlfriend to turn into a conservative wife – staying at home, covering up and not drinking. Foreign wives often complain about interference from their mothers-in-law, who may resent their son's choice of bride (*gelin*) – in rural households, the *gelin* is expected to live in the family home and undertake menial chores until she has children.

Unions between foreign men and Turkish women tend to be more successful, but men who embark on a relationship with a Turk should be aware that she probably expects it to end in marriage.

> In 2006, 15,905 Turks married a foreign spouse, according to statistics from the Turkish Interior Ministry – of these, 11,678 were male.

Harassment & Abuse

By law, Turkish women have equality in the home as well as the workplace, and in theory they're protected against sexual harassment and domestic violence, but many women suffer both – and worse. There are no official figures, as much abuse goes unreported, but Amnesty International estimates that up to half of women in Turkey are subjected to violence by family members. Especially in the east, there have been incidences of girls being killed by a relative for having pre-marital or extra-marital sex, or even for being the victim of rape. These so-called 'honour killings' are one of the country's most pressing human rights issues.

Foreign women often complain about sexual harassment, such as cat calls, over-friendly men and offers of sex. Unfortunately, disrespectful behaviour by a few tourists has led some men to think all foreign women are 'available', but if you dress modestly and act with decorum, you'll deflect all but the most persistent 'admirers'. If you're assaulted or feel threatened, you should always call the police.

Homosexuality

Homosexuality was an acknowledged ingredient of the Ottoman court and it isn't illegal in modern Turkey, but it isn't acceptable either. There are provisions in Turkish law prohibiting 'indecency and offences against public morality', therefore overtly gay behaviour is asking for trouble, although what you do in your own home is your own affair. You'll see men holding hands with men (and women with women) but this is a social custom and doesn't infer that they're gay.

There's a gay scene in Istanbul and Bodrum, and many gay couples have bought property in Turkey, but it's a long way from Mykonos or San Francisco, and there's no official gay movement. The law doesn't recognise same-sex marriages or partnerships, and the majority of homosexuals keep their sexuality hidden from family and colleagues. The best-known (unofficial) gay organisation in Turkey is Lambda (🖥 www.lambdaistanbul.org).

MEETING PEOPLE

It's easy to meet Turks as they're overwhelmingly sociable and keen to discover what makes foreigners tick. They regard it as an honour to make strangers feel welcome, so chance meetings on public transport or in a shop often lead to social invitations. But as with many things Turkish, there are rules to friendship, and you must learn the difference between an acquaintance and a friend. Most Turks have a huge number of acquaintances (*arkadaş*) but only a few friends (*dost*), which conveys responsibility. A Turk has fun with his *arkadaş* but it's his *dost* he turns to in times of trouble, and if you become a friend, you'll be expected to prioritise his needs.

It's less effort to make 'friends' with expatriates – you understand each other's culture – but you need to try to make friends with Turks as well, in order to reduce the effects of culture shock. Fortunately, there are many ways to meet people in Turkey:

- **At work** – You can quickly build acquaintanceships, if not friendships, with work colleagues, who will want to help you fit in. Workers socialise on their own level, while meetings with the boss are usually about business. After-work drinks and office parties are rare, unless organised by expat staff, but Turks bring food to work and arrange outings, and will invite you along. Using specialist skills, such as knowledge of your language, to help co-workers will help you to integrate.

- **Family & neighbours** – If you marry into a Turkish family, you have an immediate network of friends – maybe more than you want! Neighbours, too, will invite you to weddings and family events, which you should accept and return the gesture.

- **Local clubs & groups** – Check local newspapers and notice boards for details of clubs and societies (*dernek*) and contact any which interest you, whether it's an amateur football team or a walking group. Sport, art and other activities can cross cultural and language barriers and are a great way to make friends.

- **Language classes** – Not just a way to meet other foreigners who are learning Turkish, but also to meet Turks learning your language. You could offer to help as a language assistant or arrange a language exchange with local students.

- **Expatriate groups** – There are expat groups and networks throughout Turkey, but especially in resort towns – local newspapers and expat websites are a good place to start. In larger cities, embassies and consulates may maintain a list of local expatriate groups.

- **School & childcare** – Turks take an active interest in their children's education, and most schools have an *aile birliği* (family association), which organises social and fund-raising events. There are also mothers' support groups (*anneler destek grubu*) in many areas – check out nurseries and crèches. Your children will be an object of fascination to their Turkish school friends and this provides a handy link to their parents.

It's difficult, though not impossible, for a man and woman to be friends in Turkey. If both are in a relationship, they may socialise when in their respective couples but will rarely meet alone. Same-sex friendships are easier in Istanbul or a coastal resort, but much more difficult in villages, where tongues will wag. If you do become friends with a Turk of the opposite sex, be aware of the boundaries (especially if you're a man) and don't give people an excuse to misinterpret your actions.

Where & When to Meet

Most socialising goes on at home, especially between women, and usually takes place during the afternoon, when cleaning has been done and there's a respite before the demands of cooking and children. In cities, women may arrange to meet on the neutral territory of a coffee shop – Starbucks is a favourite in Istanbul. Men often meet in the evening, in bars or restaurants or at each other's place of business. Couples socialise at weekends or in the evening, depending on whether they have children, and arrange group outings such as picnics and barbeques, and also meet for dinner at restaurants and at each other's houses.

Paying the Bill

In Turkey, the host provides, therefore if you arrange an outing you pick up the bill. Younger Turks may share the cost of a meal, but it's not a good idea to suggest 'going Dutch' – known in Turkey as '*Alman usulü*' or 'going German' – as your friends may think you're tight-fisted.

> Some friendships come with strings attached, especially in resorts. Your 'friend' may be hoping you'll buy a villa or a carpet, or eat at a certain restaurant – all of which will gain him commission. Some expats are guilty of this, too. Use your judgement, and if someone tries to monopolise your attention, ask yourself if he has a hidden agenda.

INVITATIONS
Receiving Invitations

Visiting is the number one social activity in Turkey, which is sometimes completely spontaneous although usually it's meticulously planned. It's as much a chance for the hostess to show off her culinary skills as it is for her guests to enjoy them.

Visiting usually takes place in the afternoon or evening and may involve a meal or just tea, which needs to be established at the outset. Lunch is usually served between 12 and 2pm, while dinner is eaten around 8pm. If you're invited for dinner, don't arrive too early as Turkish women don't like guests hanging around in the kitchen.

Invitations include your partner, unless it's clearly a single-sex gathering such as a ladies' afternoon tea party – if you aren't sure, ask. If your hosts have children, you can ask if it's OK to bring yours along. In the countryside, people turn up with their neighbours, house guests and other hangers on, and no one minds, but this wouldn't be appreciated in Istanbul.

If you're a vegetarian, you should let your hosts know in advance – vegetarians aren't regarded as odd in Turkey, as they might be in, say, France.

A lot of Turkish cuisine revolves around rice, pulses and imaginatively cooked vegetables, so your hostess won't have to cook separately for you, although she's unlikely to understand the difference between a vegetarian and a vegan.

Dress Code

This depends on who you're visiting and where. Country folk dress for comfort and practicality, and will only expect you to look decent and clean. Loose clothing is advisable as you may be sitting on the floor. City dwellers dress smartly, especially when they're going out.

Gifts

Unless you know that your hosts are drinkers, it's best not to bring alcohol. Flowers are a nice gift for your hostess (always an odd number – even numbers, like red roses, are reserved for your beau), as is a box of chocolates or *baklava*. It's customary to leave your gift on a side table rather than thrusting it at your hostess. The gift reflects her 'value', so quietly leaving it to one side intimates that it's probably not

worthy of her, and it also saves mutual embarrassment if she doesn't like it.

Greetings

Turks aren't great at making introductions, therefore it's important that you circle the room and greet everyone there, even if you don't know them (see **Greetings** in **Chapter 5**). It's polite to greet older people first and children last.

The Meal

In many families, meals are much like those in the West. You sit at the table and are served several courses in order – usually soup and/or *meze* (a selection of starters), followed by a main course with side dishes and, later, dessert. Each diner has a place setting, and wine or soft drinks may be served with the meal. Your hostess will insist on serving you, although you help yourself to bread. The meal will end with strong, black Turkish coffee, although Nescafe is sometimes offered as an alternative for foreigners.

A village meal is much more traditional, where everyone sits on the floor with a *sofra* (communal tablecloth) tucked over their laps. Food includes soup, salad, a main course (often vegetarian but sometimes with a little chicken or other meat), rice, yogurt and lots of bread. It's all served at once, and you eat from the serving dishes – spoons and forks are provided, plates and knives are not. Water is passed around during the meal – sometimes just one glass which is handed from one diner to the next. The meal concludes with plenty of tea.

Villagers may compromise for foreign guests by setting up a table with individual plates and a large bottle of cola. Alcohol, if it makes an appearance, is usually *rakı*, an aniseed-flavoured spirit, and served to the men. Your hostess may press you to eat as much as possible – it's ill-mannered to say no but also impolite to appear greedy, therefore you should make a show of declining before you give in and graciously accept.

> Turks expect guests to do absolutely nothing – therefore you shouldn't offer to help serve or clear up. Instead, say '*Zahmet etmeyin*' (Don't go to any trouble). You can also say '*elinize saglik*' ('Health to your hand'), which is the equivalent of 'compliments to the chef' as you're tucking into or finishing a meal. This is the set response to '*afiyet olsun*' ('Enjoy your meal') which Turks say repeatedly when serving anything from food to a glass of water.

Tea & Coffee

Turkish tea is made in a double kettle (*çaydanlık*) and served in small tulip-shaped glasses. Water is boiled in the bottom of the *çaydanlık* and tea is brewed in the top, then the two are poured together to achieve the desired mix. You should ask each guest how he likes his tea – *demli* is strong, *açık* is weak. Sugar is handed round separately – Turkish tea is never served with milk. Refills are frequent and it's usual to drink at least two glasses, preferably three – place your spoon across the top of the glass to indicate when you've had enough.

Turkish coffee is 'black as hell, strong as death and as sweet as love'. It's brewed in a small pot (*cezve*) and sugar is added at the beginning – Turks drink it plain (*sade*) or, more usually, slightly sweet or very sweet (*az şekerli* or *çok şekerli*). Once it boils, it's poured frothing into delicate cups and sipped; if you swig it back and you'll get a mouthful of the bitter grounds!

Turkish coffee is reserved for special occasions – to mark the end of a good meal, an afternoon work break or a guest's visit. It's also a good excuse for some fortune telling. Some people like to invert the empty cup on the saucer, wait a while and then read their future in the grounds ...

Leaving

You should start hinting that you need to leave at least an hour before you intend to go. Your hosts will do their best to persuade you to stay and may offer you a bed (usually their bed) for the night – the longer you stay, the better this reflects on their hospitality. That said, afternoon guests usually leave by 6pm, while dinner guests should depart by midnight – although your hostess will release you only after extracting a promise that you'll visit again.

You may be offered a memento, such as a scarf or embroidered guest towel. She will say, '*Yine buyurun gelin*' ('Come again soon'). If you don't want to commit, or even if you do, the polite response is, '*inşallah*' ('As God wills it').

Making Invitations

It's expected that you'll reciprocate invitations, but don't feel you have to produce a gourmet meal. Your guests will be more interested in how you live than in your culinary skills, and will be most impressed if you get the etiquette right (see below). Do, however, ensure that your house is clean, and any pets are out of the way; most Turkish homes are spotless and animals usually stay outside.

If you're serving lunch or dinner, state the time – don't arrange dinner any later than 8pm. You can also invite guests to tea at any time – mid-afternoon or after dinner.

The Welcome

First impressions are all-important. Greet all guests by saying '*Hoş geldiniz*' ('Welcome'), ask after their health and provide slippers. It's traditional to seat the eldest guest in the best seat – usually the one furthest from the door. Splash a little lemon cologne (*kolonya*) into their cupped hands – this charming ritual can be repeated just before they leave – and then sit and chat for a while. If you produce food too soon, your guests may think you're trying to get rid of them!

> Never openly admire something in a Turkish person's home or you may end up taking it home. It's extremely difficult to say 'no' without causing offence.

What to Serve

Drinks and 'nibbles' are unnecessary if you're serving dinner; it's more important that there's enough food, which doesn't have to be Turkish. The Turks have a saying, '*Misafir umduğunu yemez, bulduğun yer*' ('A guest can't eat what he hopes for, only what is served') and will eat whatever you give

them. Don't serve any pork products or anything too unfamiliar or spicy (save your Thai green curry for expat friends), and ensure you provide salt, lemon (if there's soup), toothpicks – and lots of bread! No one will object if you drink alcohol in your own home, but you must have soft drinks and water available.

If you don't know your guests very well or there's a language barrier – or you aren't a great cook – invite them for tea. They will be delighted if you know how to make Turkish tea or coffee (see below). Turks often serve just tea, accompanied by snacks such as biscuits, fruit (always served peeled and sliced), nuts and sunflower seeds, which should arrive from the kitchen in a steady procession.

RESPECTING PRIVACY

Turks aren't especially private people but they do like to be prepared. They have a room reserved for socialising, which contains the best furniture and most valuable possessions, and enough food in the fridge to feed all-comers. They will drop everything else to attend to guests, but unless you know them well – or they live in a village where

One area that is off limits is family problems, which are rarely discussed outside the clan. Don't bring up such sensitive subjects unless your Turkish friend does – the fact that he trusts you enough to talk about them is a sign of trust and respect and means that you're his *dost*.

every house is an open house – never drop in unannounced. If you catch your hostess in her house clothes, elbow deep in flour, she will welcome you, but she won't be pleased.

TABOOS

Turks accept that foreigners make mistakes, but there are a few unforgivable gaffes and taboo subjects of conversation which you should be aware of. This section is a brief guide to potentially embarrassing actions and words.

Conversation

Turks like to talk about family, local events, football, politics and the economy – and they'll be fascinated to learn about your own country. Turks talk openly, and few areas of conversation are deemed to be intrusive – this includes your marital status, children, job and salary. Turks will also tell you, in a matter-of-fact way, that you're looking tired or have gained weight since they last saw you – women, especially, describe in detail their health problems. All this can be challenging if you're used to keeping such matters to yourself. Taboo subjects are listed below:

The Kurds and the PKK

Turkey's ongoing battle against Kurdish separatist group the PKK has resulted in the deaths of many young men on compulsory military service. A few Turks are in favour of Kurdish independence (usually those with some Kurdish blood), whereas a larger proportion believe the Kurds to be troublemakers who should accept (or be grateful for) being Turkish. Most Turks' views sit somewhere in between, but you won't know their feelings, therefore it's a subject best avoided.

The 'Armenian Genocide' Issue

The claim that more than a million Armenians were massacred or died during deportation in the last years of the Ottoman Empire in an attempt to exterminate them, is disputed by Turkey. The country's formal stance is that deaths did occur but that they didn't constitute genocide. Many nations have officially denounced the events as 'genocide', including France, Germany and the USA. This subject is hazardous for a Turk to discuss, never mind a foreigner.

Human Rights

Turkey's human rights record is frequently under the spotlight, especially with its accession to the European Union (EU) high on the agenda. Turks are well aware that issues such as women's rights and the treatment of prisoners are in need of attention, but they won't welcome your input on the subject.

Headscarves

The subject of whether women should, or shouldn't, be allowed to wear the headscarf in certain places is highly contentious (see **Religion** in **Chapter 10**). This issue combines two sensitive subjects in Turkey (or in any society) – religion and politics – both may be loudly debated in your presence but you shouldn't contribute unless you know your company (and the issues involved) very well indeed.

Article 301

Article 301 of the Penal Code makes it an offence to 'insult Turkishness', which has caused a lot of controversy – at the end of 2007, the government was debating cancelling or toning it down. However, voicing your opinion on any contentious subject could, in theory,

result in a visit from the police or even arrest – as a number of Turkish writers and journalists have discovered to their cost.

Turkish Customs

Turks are proud. When you're with Turkish people, avoid any negative comments about Turkey and its customs – if you must sound off, do it among expats whom you trust.

> Disrespecting Islam can have dire consequences, as teacher Gillian Gibbons discovered in Sudan in 2007 when she gave a teddy bear the name of the Prophet Mohammed. Even if Turks don't appear to be strongly religious, they do take offence to insults against their religion. Always show respect towards Islam. Never give pets religious or 'human' names – an acquaintance may be highly insulted to find your poodle shares his first name.

Dress

Turks don't display much flesh – and they don't like seeing it displayed by other people, unless they're celebrities. This creates problems in resorts, many of which retain a 'village' mentality. It's considered insulting for a woman to wear a bikini anywhere other than by the pool or on the beach – and you should never sunbathe topless unless you're certain nobody can see you. Shops and restaurants may refuse entry to people in swimsuits or bare-chested men, and even exposing your arms and legs can be offensive in more conservative towns and villages. Shorts and vests are the mark of the tourist and you'll gain far more respect if you stick to trousers and sleeves.

Behaviour

There are some things which Turks just don't do, and neither should you. These include:

- **Wearing shoes in the house** – Streets are often dusty or muddy so this is a practical matter as well as a cultural gaffe. When visiting, you'll be provided with house slippers, but ensure you have clean socks on.

- **Sitting next to a stranger of the opposite sex** – This applies in public places and people's homes and is especially important in a village house, where unrelated men and women always sit apart.

- **Pointing the soles of your feet at someone** – Throughout the Middle East, this part of the anatomy is considered unclean.

- **Turning down someone's offer of food** – Taste a little, even if you don't like the look of it, as to refuse is an insult to your host.

- **Displaying your smalls** – Peg out laundry so that underwear isn't visible to neighbours or passers by.

EXPATRIATE COMMUNITY

Officially, less than 1 per cent of the Turkish population are foreigners. Statistics from the General Directorate of Security (Eminyet Genel Müdürlüğü or EGM) revealed that on 1st March 2007, a total of 202,085 foreigners had residence permits in Turkey. But these figures are only part of the story. Many

'settled foreigners' don't apply for residence, which can be an expensive and time-consuming undertaking – instead, they keep renewing their visitor's visa – see **Chapter 3**. Thus the total number of expatriates may be as high as half a million.

> EGM statistics also reveal where foreigners live. In 2007, Istanbul had the highest number of foreign residents with 106,156, followed by Bursa with 16,772 and Antalya with 13,832; while the capital Ankara had 12,157. (See Where the Expats Live in Chapter 2.)

If you choose to live in an area popular with people of your nationality, you'll find it easier to fit in – at least to begin with. But there are dangers in relying on expatriate society. People come and go, so friendships may be temporary, and there's often an undercurrent of gossip. Resorts are unsettling places to live – crowded with tourists in summer, and inhabited by cliques of expats in winter. Many are still villages at heart and some locals resent their economic dependence on outsiders.

On the plus side, expats provide an instant support system of people who speak your language and know how to get things done. You understand their culture and they understand your culture shock, and it's good to have people you can talk to when you're frustrated, confused or just plain homesick.

A lot of expats are fascinating people – writers, artists, genuine adventurers – but some spend all their time complaining about Turkey and the Turks, and too many negative vibes are unsettling. Even worse, some are possessive or even predatory, and there are many stories of new arrivals being ripped off by their own countrymen.

Don't fall into the trap of mixing with people simply because they're from the same country as you; you could end up socialising with people who you'd avoid in your home country. Resist the temptation to immerse yourself in 'safe' expatriate culture and make an extra effort to meet Turkish people. You may well find that you prefer their company. In the end, the more time you spend with expats, the less time you spend with Turks and the less reason there is for you to be – and to remain – in Turkey.

CONFRONTATION

Turks have a long fuse and do their best to avoid confrontation. A quarrel can escalate into a feud – or even a blood feud in the east – and create tension for a long time to come. When a Turk is angry, he often says nothing at all, which is a signal not to pursue the subject – what a westerner may consider lively debate, a Turk may regard as a prelude to a fight. Stay quiet and the situation may resolve itself, as most people are quick to forgive and are patient with foreigners' mistakes.

It's especially rude to confront someone in front of other people, even worse in front of his peers or superiors.

This will cause him to lose face and he may never forgive you. Insulting a Turk's family is also unforgivable.

Losing your temper won't get you very far in Turkey. If you have a grievance, discuss it quietly and calmly, away from other people. Turks are good at negotiating and you'll gain far more through diplomacy than through conflict.

DEALING WITH OFFICIALS

Public-sector officials, who include police, civil servants and municipality workers, aren't well paid, but they have power over the general public, who need their assistance to get things done. Because of this, civil servants sometimes have an inflated sense of their own importance, which is reinforced by the way in which many people defer to them. Officials may look upon a foreigner, especially one with poor language skills, as a little light relief in a boring day. They will be either extremely helpful – foreigners are often treated better than Turks – or frustratingly obstructive.

You may find your patience being tested severely at times, but resist the

temptation to lose your temper as this will only result in your file going to the bottom of the pile. The best way to deal with officials is to treat them with quiet courtesy. You should also apply the following rules:

● Wear your smartest clothes.

● Always use the polite form of address (see **Chapter 5**).

● Be prepared to speak Turkish or use an interpreter. If officials make the effort to communicate in your language, speak slowly and clearly, and thank them for their efforts.

● Turn up the charm – excessive courtesy is a much stronger weapon than rudeness.

● Thank them profusely – you never know when you'll need them again.

The Police

Turkish police have a reputation for being heavy-handed and corrupt, and many Turks regard them with great suspicion. However, they're usually extremely courteous and helpful towards foreigners, unless you're on the wrong side of the law. Traffic police operate speed traps and impose spot fines – and have the power to stop vehicles and check licences, while city police and village *jandarma* keep records of foreigners, and assist with residence and other permits.

Always be polite to police and use formal grammar. If you think you've been stopped and fined illegally, don't make a fuss – it may be misinterpreted, but make a complaint at a police station. All police and *jandarma* stations provide an interpreter.

> **'One of the greatest victories you can gain over someone is to beat him at politeness.'**
>
> Josh Billings (American humorist)

Civil Servants

Turkish civil servants dispense numerous permits and licences, and you will deal with them on a regular basis. Most requests require encounters with several people in different offices, and this can be exasperating – even more so if you don't understand what's going on. Just stay calm and remember the above points.

Some municipalities in areas with high foreign populations make an extra effort for foreigners and have liaison staff who can speak (a little) English or German. But very few officials speak any language other than Turkish, therefore you may need an interpreter.

Teachers

Teaching is accorded a great deal of respect in Turkey. Atatürk credited teachers with 'saving nations' and there's a Teachers' Day (24th November) when children take gifts to school. State schoolteachers are civil servants and they work civil servants' hours. There are no parents' evenings, therefore if you want to discuss your child's schoolwork you must make an appointment during school time or attend meetings of the family association. Many teachers know some English, but they may not be willing or able to discuss schoolwork in English – ask first and, if necessary, take someone along to translate.

5.

THE LANGUAGE BARRIER

The ability to communicate with the Turks and know what to do and say when you meet them is a priority when you move to Turkey, especially when you arrive. Learning to speak a foreign language is never easy and is full of potential pitfalls – all expats have stories to tell of when they said the 'wrong' thing, often with embarrassing consequences. To help keep your collection of anecdotes as small as possible, this chapter offers tips on learning Turkish, some useful expressions, and explanations of body and sign language (and their importance in communication), false friends, forms of address and greetings, and telephone and letter etiquette.

> 'A different language is a different vision of life.'
> Federico Fellini (Italian film maker)

Turks are great communicators and will go out of their way to understand – and be understood – by foreigners. Many university-educated Turks have been taught in English and some also speak German or French. In resort areas the local traders' survival depends on their knowledge of the majority foreign (*yabancı*) language, be it English, German or, increasingly, Russian – and in popular holiday destinations, such as the British enclaves of Marmaris and Fethiye, it sometimes feels as if Turkish has been relegated to second place. Even in villages people will make an effort, producing a tattered dictionary or even a schoolchild to act as a translator.

The result is that many foreigners live in Turkey for years and learn little, if any, of the language – indeed, it's a country where you really can 'get by' with just a few phrases. But if you want to truly understand the culture, or to work or conduct any business, learning Turkish is a priority. Not only will it make your life easier and richer and win you a great deal of respect, but it will also save you from relying on other people to get things done. Turks are renowned for their helpfulness but there are some untrustworthy characters – and quite a few are expats – who earn a good living by relieving new arrivals of their cash.

LEARNING TURKISH

Experts on relocation and culture shock agree that learning the local language is an essential step when settling into a foreign country. Without this knowledge you can feel helpless, drowning in a sea of alien vowel sounds as you try to communicate with nods and (sometimes incorrect) gestures. But mastering the basics will boost your confidence and help you feel more in control.

Turkish is a fascinating language which bears little relation to English or other European languages. Some of its older vocabulary comes from Arabic and Farsi (Persian), but the reform of the language in the '20s saw an increase in loanwords from German and French – and more and more English is creeping in.

The following peculiarities set Turkish aside from most western European languages:

● Turkish features letters not found in other languages, such as ğ and ı.

● Word order appears strange – the verb usually comes at the end of the sentence.

● The same word can mean many different things, depending on the context.

● Rather than using separate words, Turkish often adds endings (suffixes) to words, which can make them very long and difficult to pronounce.

● Turkish has tenses not found in other languages.

● Turkish uses 'vowel harmony' – a way of matching.

But on the positive side, Turkish is a phonetic language – you speak it as you see it – with very few exceptions to grammar 'rules', and no genders to grapple with. Moreover, Turks aren't obsessive about their language, in the way the French are. They will welcome your attempts to speak it – warts and all.

One of Atatürk's most controversial reforms was his introduction of the Latin alphabet in 1928. The old Ottoman script was consigned to history as new letters were introduced, designed to imitate the sounds in Turkish speech. Atatürk's intention was to purify the Turkish language and rid it of Ottoman, Arabic and Persian influences, and he insisted that the reform take place within a few months. He even travelled around the country with blackboard and chalk, giving impromptu lessons in village squares. The 'new' Turkish was designed to be clear, precise and easy to learn, and literacy received an immediate boost. Today's literacy rate is 87 per cent – a point worth remembering as you struggle with the language.

The Alphabet

Turkish has 29 letters – 21 consonants and eight vowels. Three English letters are absent (q, w and x) while three are pronounced differently (c as the j in John, j as in the French Jean and v halfway between v and w in English). The three extra consonants are ç (pronounced like the 'ch' in chat), ş (like the 'sh' in ship) and ğ, which is silent and lengthens the preceding vowel. The three extra vowels are the undotted ı, which sounds like 'er' in butter, ö and ü, both of which are pronounced as in German.

There are many dialects, but Istanbul Turkish (*Türkçe*) is the official language and the standard used by the media and education system. All Turkish words in this book are Istanbul Turkish. It's spoken as a first or second language by the entire population, including those who speak regional languages such as Kurdish.

Why Turkish is Essential

- In an accident or emergency, your ability to communicate with the police, fire or medical services makes the situation less stressful – and could even save lives.

- Dealing with Turkey's infamous bureaucracy is always frustrating, but less so if you understand some of what's going on. All documents are in Turkish and few bureaucrats speak another language.

- It greatly enhances your job prospects. Non-Turkish speakers are often limited to badly paid or even illegal work in the tourism and property sectors. You pay the local price – as opposed to 'tourist' prices – at markets and shops.

- You can give instructions to tradesmen, builders and cleaners

– and they feel more comfortable, knowing that you understand them. And you won't have to rely on translators, estate agents and other 'experts'.

- Knowledge is power – you can obtain information from Turkish newspapers and television instead of receiving it second-hand.

- It helps you to appreciate Turkish culture – and the more you learn, the less you'll feel like a stranger in a strange land.

- Language classes are a great way to meet like-minded people in a similar situation.

- Neighbours, colleagues and in-laws will respect your efforts and include you in their lives. You'll quickly widen your circle of acquaintances and won't have to rely on other expats for company.

- If you're in a relationship with a Turk, sharing their language brings you closer together; if you aren't in a relationship with a Turk, it's highly unlikely unless you learn Turkish.

Know Before You Go

Aim to start learning Turkish at least three, and preferably six months before your move to Turkey. Don't imagine that learning the language will be easier once you're there – 'immersion learning' only works if you can give it your undivided attention and that's impossible when you're juggling all the demands of relocation. It's far better to get a grounding in the language in advance so you can at least exchange greetings, count to ten and ask for things you need, all of which make your first days easier.

Many schools, colleges and universities offer language courses, which vary from classes targeted at holidaymakers to intensive courses for business people. Areas with a Turkish community are likely to offer more choice as some expatriate Turks send their children to classes.

> **If you're pushed for time you could hire a private tutor – you can find these through online community websites such as Gumtree (💻 www.gumtree.com) or through one of the organisations which match tutors and students.**

Whichever you choose, remember to allow extra time for practise and homework. Other options include 'teach yourself' books and CDs; and online courses where tutors monitor your work via the internet – such as those offered by TÖMER, Ankara University's Turkish & Foreign Languages Research and Application Centre (💻 www.turkish-center.com). With either of these options you need to find someone to practise with.

Some useful language learning websites are listed in Appendix C, while a list of words and phrases you might need during your first few weeks in Turkey can be found in **Appendix D**.

When in Turkey

When you arrive, you'll be busy arranging accommodation, transportation and so forth, and may be tempted to let your studies slip – but it's vital you commit to continuing your language study as soon as possible.

If you delay, you may never improve on a few pleasantries and the ability to order a beer. There's a wide choice of language schools in the larger cities, offering courses in various degrees of intensity, although prices and quality vary – you'll find some recommendations in the appendices.

In resort towns there are fewer organised Turkish classes, maybe because so many locals speak European languages – check out expatriate groups and local newspapers. If you're living off the beaten track, an online course may be your only option.

When starting a course, ensure that your knowledge of Turkish is assessed and that you're put in a class to suit your level. There's nothing more dispiriting than struggling to follow a group of intermediate speakers while you're still a beginner. Ask for a free trial lesson and try not to pay for a full course until you're sure that you're comfortable with the teacher and method.

Pir Sultan, Turkish Poet

Teaching is a prestigious profession in Turkey and you'll find many private tutors available, which allow you to have lessons at your convenience and tailored to your ability. The downside is the cost – expect to pay at least €15 per hour, more in Istanbul. You can reduce your expenses by sharing a tutor with another learner, which will make your classes more sociable and give you someone to practise with.

> **'Learn a new language and get a new soul.'**
> Czech proverb

However you choose to learn, lessons are only part of it. Practise is essential and the more you use your Turkish, the easier it will become. Most locals will be delighted that you're trying to learn their language and will be happy to chat with you, and there's no shortage of people keen to brush up their foreign language skills. It's easy to set up a language exchange, where you meet and spend half the time talking Turkish and the other half English (or your native tongue). You can place adverts in local newspapers, on notice boards in bars and clubs, and on website bulletin boards – or ask your or your partner's employer for contacts.

Tips for Learning Turkish

- **Learn the alphabet** – Once you master the more unusual vowels and consonants, you'll be able to pronounce most words and make yourself understood.

- **Use the language** – Speak Turkish whenever you can, to shopkeepers, waiters, your neighbours, as the more you use a language the more it comes alive.

- **Ask for help** – If someone speaks too quickly and you don't understand, ask them to say it again: *Anlımıyorum; lütfen onu tekrarlar mısınız?* ('I don't understand; please could you repeat that?'). Turks are patient teachers.

- **Set sensible targets** – It's better to learn three new words a day and remember them than to try (and fail) to absorb a whole chapter of grammar points in a week.

- **Don't be obsessed by the grammar** – Some of the rules, such as vowel harmony, are difficult concepts but will come naturally as you use the language.

- **Make use of the media** – Having a talk radio station on in the background will get you used to the rhythm of the language, while watching television puts it into context – trashy soaps are a good place to start and there's no shortage of these on Turkish TV. The digital TV provider Digiturk transmits films in Turkish and English and subtitles foreign series in Turkish – a useful and entertaining learning aid.

- **Don't lose heart** – There will come a time when you've mastered the basics and feel you're making little or no progress, but this intermediate 'plateau' will pass if you persevere.

- **Keep your sense of humour** – You're sure to make verbal blunders (see **Some Tricky Words** below). Laugh at your mistakes and be proud of your achievements – remember what your Turkish was like when you arrived.

Children

If your move to Turkey involves the whole family, your children will need to learn Turkish as well. The younger they are, the easier it will be – children aged ten or under can often pick up a new language in a few months, while older children and teenagers may struggle. If they've already learnt a second language at school, it will be less of an ordeal; if they have siblings in the same situation, the challenge can be shared. But an only child, especially one who has no experience of other languages, may find the process daunting.

Like you, your children will need language classes before they leave home. Being able to say their name and communicate basics with local children will boost their confidence, and for safety reasons it's vital that they known

how to say their address and phone number in Turkish.

All state and much private schooling is in Turkish and little allowance is made for children who don't speak it. Teachers will do their best and Turkish children are brought up to be welcoming and caring towards strangers, but Turkish schools aren't used to coping with foreign students (though this will probably change in the future) and the onus is on you to get your kids' language skills up to a level where they can learn alongside their peers. This will mean taking extra language classes and practising as much as possible.

> If your children are at a crucial stage in their education or cannot cope with the transition to a Turkish school – on top of the stresses of a new lifestyle – they may be better off at an international school. These schools are situated in the larger cities, therefore this may have a bearing on where you settle.

OTHER LANGUAGES

The only official language is Turkish and it's used in commerce and bureaucracy throughout the republic. Even speakers of second languages must use Turkish in these situations. However, the republic has never quite managed to break the linguistic connections with its Ottoman past and it's still possible to hear Greek, Armenian and Arabic spoken in certain parts of the country, alongside the new languages of the settled foreigners – English, German, Russian and French.

Kurdish

The largest minority language is Kurdish. Figures for the number of Kurdish speakers in Turkey are difficult to come by, as the language has been restricted in the past, but there are thought to be around 15m people who speak a Kurdish dialect. Before 2003 it was forbidden to teach or broadcast in Kurdish, although more recently private television channels have been allowed to air programmes in Kurdish, albeit with Turkish subtitles.

Black Sea coastline

There are several dialects, Kurmanji being the most widely spoken – it can be heard throughout the eastern and south-eastern provinces. Unless you plan to live and work in these areas, or your partner is Kurdish, it's unlikely you'll need to learn the language but if you're interested in the subject, the appendices include some useful contacts for information.

Turkey is also home to the following minority languages:

- **Hemşince** – spoken by the Hemşin, an ethnic people of Armenian origin who live along the Black Sea coasts of Turkey, Russia and Georgia;

- **Ladino** – spoken by around 8,000 people, members of the Sephardic Jewish communities in Istanbul and Izmir;

- **Laz** – the language of the Laz people in the eastern Black Sea area, which has several dialects and may be spoken by as many as 500,000 people;

- **Syriac** – an Aramaic language spoken by the Syriac Christians in various parts of the Middle East, a small number of whom live in the area around Mardin in south-eastern Anatolia.

Dialects & Accents

Turkey is a large country with a corresponding variety of regional accents and dialects. Someone from Istanbul may struggle to follow a conversation in the south-eastern provinces, where consonants and vowels are swapped, added and subtracted so much that the local dialect can sound like a completely different language. Similarly, visitors to the Black Sea coast are bamboozled by the sheer speed of the natives' machine-gun patter.

Some parts of Turkey even have their own vocabulary – in the Antalya area, for example, the words *iyi* (good) and *kötü* (bad) may be replaced by *eş* and *uş*, while people in the western province of Denizli eat *kumpir* rather than *patates* (potatoes) and wear *potur* instead of *pantalon* (trousers).

If you've started learning Istanbul Turkish but end up in an area with a distinctive local accent or dialect, it will take time, but you'll 'tune in' eventually. In the meantime persevere with your Turkish studies so that you can at least make yourself understood.

Turklish

In areas with a strong expatriate presence, there's a strange hybrid of Turkish and English vocabulary and grammar which can best be described as 'Turklish'. Some Turks speak it, too. You may hear a scorching August day described as '*çok* hot' or be asked 'Happy *misin*?' ('Are you happy?').

Turklish is creeping stealthily into the national vocabulary, encouraged in part by the media, who have adopted many English phrases to market goods. A surprising number of new products have English names, e.g. a chocolate bar called 'Wanted' and a cleaning product called 'Mr Proper'. Meanwhile, old words are being dropped in favour of new, so *gözde* loses out to *favori* (favourite) and *seçenek* to *alternatif* (alternative).

There are also words borrowed from German, Arabic and, especially, French, as Atatürk was a Francophile.

SLANG & SWEARING

If you go by the subtitles to foreign films on Turkish television, the only swearword is *lanet olsun* – a fairly mild oath which roughly translates as 'damn you' and is widely used to replace the 'F' word and other strong swear words. But the Turkish language features a lot of colourful and insulting oaths, many of which refer to animals, some of which refer to your mother (and various parts of her anatomy), and all of which should be avoided!

Turkish people put great emphasis on respect and good manners and consider it demeaning to swear, and you're unlikely to hear any but the mildest oaths from women or older people. Young lads may call each other *salak* (idiot) but rarely resort to crude insults. If you hear a Turk let rip with blue language you know that he's really angry.

Turkish also includes a rich feast of slang (*argo*), which is widely used by younger people; as in other languages, street talk is constantly changing and it's hard to keep up if you're over 25. You're sure to pick up a few phrases, but you shouldn't use them unless you know your company well, as it's easy to cause offence.

> Those who are interested in slang and swearwords may find the following webpage entertaining:
> 🖥 www.practicalturkish.com/off-color-turkish-slang-dictionary.html
> – it's certainly comprehensive.

Everyday Expressions

Turkish has a number of stock phrases which are always used in certain situations; they're great for breaking the ice and save you from being tongue-tied – and they indicate that you've made an effort to understand the language and culture. Some useful ones to learn are given below (many of these expressions don't translate very well into English):

- *geçmiş olsun* (may it soon pass) – said to someone who has suffered a setback, illness or other problem;

- *kolay gelsin* (may it come easy) – said to someone who is busy or preoccupied;

- *çok yaşa* (live long) – said to someone who sneezes; *gözünüz aydın* (your eyes are sparkling) – said to someone who has received good news;

- *sıhhatlar olsun* (may it be healthy) – said to someone who has just had a shave, haircut or Turkish bath;

- *başınız sağolsun* (may your head be alive) – said to someone who has just been bereaved.

Invoking Allah

The use of the name of Allah in certain phrases is perfectly acceptable and carries no taint of blasphemy; you'll hear them all the time, especially from older people, and there's no reason why you shouldn't use them yourself, even if you're a non-Muslim. The best known are:

- *inşallah* (as God wills it) – said when you hope or intend to do something, and also useful as a polite way of avoiding a commitment;

- *maşallah* (wonderful) – said in response to someone's good fortune and, especially, when admiring a baby or child as its alternative meaning is 'may God protect';

- *estağfurullah* (please don't mention it) – said in response to a compliment.

BODY & SIGN LANGUAGE

The Turks don't gesticulate in the same way as the Italians, for example, but their body language is a no less important part of their communication. They're more tactile than many western Europeans and will move in close and even touch you during conversation. Some Turkish body language is subtle but small gestures can mean a great deal and interpreting them is a key to understanding the people.

Gestures

Try to recognise these gestures, which may at first confuse you. Once you fully understand them, you can use them yourself, but beware of making mistakes and causing offence.

- A sharp nod of the head – Yes.

- A single tilt of the head backwards with eyebrows raised – No. This may be accompanied by a 'tsk' sound for emphasis.

- Shaking the head from side to side – I'm not sure. If you shake your head to mean no, a Turk will think you've

misunderstood him and will repeat what he has just said.

- A shrug of the shoulders – I don't know.

- Palm of the hand placed flat on the chest – No thank you. This is a polite way of refusing something, such as a third helping of *baklava*.

- Rubbing your two index fingers together side by side – This asks a couple if they're in a relationship.

- Scooping the hand with fingers pointing down – Come along, follow me. This is something you see the police do as they direct traffic. Never beckon with your forefinger, as this is considered rude.

> There are some other hand gestures which are considered rude, such as the American sign for OK. Making a fist with your thumb protruding between your index and middle fingers is extremely offensive.

Personal Space

In Turkey, as in much of the Middle East, people aren't protective of their personal space and Turks will crowd in on you in markets, at weddings and anywhere where large groups congregate. Before numbered queuing systems were introduced, it was normal to conduct your business at a bank or post office with the next customer leaning over your shoulder.

Turks are quite happy living cheek by jowl in apartment blocks and will all sit together on an otherwise unoccupied beach and take the seat nearest to you in a half-empty cinema. Much of this is down to their gregarious nature – they enjoy doing things in groups and cannot understand westerners' need for their own space.

If you find it uncomfortable being 'leaned into' during a conversation, just take a step back and a deep breath. Whatever you do, try not to take offence as you can be sure that none is intended.

FALSE FRIENDS

Some words in Turkish are similar in appearance to, or sound like, English words but have a different meaning, which can lead to misunderstandings and, on occasion, embarrassment. These words are known as 'false friends'. Because Turkish is unlike European languages there are fewer 'false friends' to trip you up than in, say, French, but you should be aware of the following (the correct Turkish words are given below):

- *baş* (sounds like 'bash'): head, chief, e.g. *baş ağrısı* (headache), *başbakan* (prime minister)

- to bash or hit: *vurmak* (all Turkish verb infinitives end in *-mek* or *-mak*)

- *boy*: height, size, length, e.g. *boy aynası* (full-length mirror)

- boy: *erkek çocuk*

- *bir* : one, a, e.g. *bir numara* (number one)

- beer: *bira*

- *çok* (sounds like choc): a lot, very, many, e.g. *Temmuz'da hava çok sıcak* (the weather is very hot in July)

- chocolate: *çikolata*

- *fabrika*: factory

- fabric: *kumaş*

- *fiş* (sounds like fish): receipt

- fish: *balık* – this always amuses tourists as it sounds like the English slang word for testicles

- *fon*: fund (as in savings fund)

- phone: *telefon*

- *grip*: flu

- to grip or hold firmly: *sıkı tutmak*, e.g. *elimi sıkı tut* (hold my hand tight)

- *hat*: route or line, e.g. *telefon hattı* (telephone line)

- hat: *şapka*

- *iç* (sounds like itch): inside, interior, drink, e.g. *içeriye gelin* (come inside), *su iç* (drink water)

- to itch: *kaşınmak*, e.g. *burnum kaşınıyor* (my nose itches)

Some Western names translate rather uncomfortably into Turkish. Anne means mother, Sue means water, and Don translates as underpants!

- *kan*: blood

- can (or tin): *teneke*

- *kar*: snow

- car: *otomobil* or *araba*

- *kaş* (sounds like cash): eyebrow

- cash: *nakit para*

- *kat*: floor, storey, level, e.g. *ikinci katı* (second floor)

- *mağaza*: large shop or store (the ğ is silent)

- magazine: *dergi*

- *pasta*: dry cake or biscuit

- pasta: *makarna* (from the Italian macaroni)

- *piç* (sounds like peach): bastard

- peach: *şeftali* – this is one fruit you must learn the name of

- preservative: *saklayan*

- *pul*: stamp

- to pull or draw: *çekmek*, e.g. *perdeleri çektim* (I drew the curtains)

- *roman*: novel (but not necessarily a romance)

- Roman: *Romalı*

- *sik*: vulgar name for penis

- sick: *hasta*

- *tıraş* (sounds like trash): shaving, e.g. *tıraş kremi* (shaving cream)

- trash or rubbish: *çöp*

Some Tricky Words

False friends aren't the only linguistic trap lying in wait for you in Turkey, where there are many words which sound or look similar to each other but which have different meanings. Just one wrong consonant or vowel can completely change the sense of your sentence – sometimes with amusing or embarrassing results. The best way to avoid this is not to trust your ears and double-check any new words and write them down before you try to use them. The following are just a few examples of the many mistakes made by foreign learners of Turkish – including the author:

- *akraba* means relative or family member, but *ayakkabı* means shoes. Asked why she was going to the UK, a friend explained, '*Ayakkabım hasta*' ('My shoes are ill').

- *ekmek* means bread, but *erkek* means man. Overheard in a bakery, '*Iki taze erkek, lütfen*' ('Two fresh men, please').

- *gökgürültüsü* means thunder (literally 'noisy sky'), but *götgürültüsü* translates as 'noisy bottom'.

- *hayır* means no, but *hiyar* means small cucumber – beware, since this word is also slang for penis.

- *hesap* means bill, but *kasap* means butcher. A friend made this gaffe in a restaurant: '*Kasap lütfen!*' ('Bring me the butcher!').

- *inecek var* means 'someone wants to alight (gef off)', but *inek var* means 'there's a cow' – a number of tourists have made this mistake when asking to get off a bus.

- *öğrenmek* means to learn, but *öğretmek* means to teach, so only the teacher can say, '*Türkçe öğretiyorum*' ('I'm teaching Turkish')

- *omuz* means shoulder, but *domuz* means pig. A doctor was baffled to be told by a patient: '*Domuzum ağrıyor*' ('My pig aches').

FORMS OF ADDRESS

Polite or Informal?

Like many European languages but unlike English, Turkish features two ways of saying 'you' – the formal or polite *siz*, which is also used when addressing more than one person, irrespective of the degree of formality, and the informal *sen* (singular only). English has lost this distinction and has only one word for you, so native English speakers face a dilemma when deciding which form of address to use and when. Call someone *sen* and you

risk offending them; call a friend *siz* and they may think you pompous.

Turkish people are forgiving when foreigners blunder through their language and don't easily take offence. However, theirs is by nature a formal and polite society, therefore it's best use the *siz* form of address if you aren't sure, particularly with older people, officials and any adult you don't know well. You use *sen* with children and friends. Remember, however, that *siz* denotes more than one person, so if you're greeting a group of friends you must always use this form.

Surnames & Titles

Like most people, Turks have a first name (*adı*) and a family name or surname (*soyadı*). Surnames are a relatively new concept, however, having been introduced only in 1934 as part of Atatürk's social reforms. Before this time people were known by their first name, often paired with a nickname to distinguish them from others with the same name. In Turkish villages this tradition carries on and people still have names like 'Fisherman' Ali or 'Fat' Mehmet; you may know a Turk for some time before you learn his surname.

Surnames are used on all official documentation, but it's quite normal in Turkey to address people by their first names with their title added. *Bey* is the equivalent of Mr while *Hanım* means Mrs or Miss. So you address Mustafa Çelik as Mustafa *Bey* rather than Çelik *Bey*. And he will address you as Jane *Hanım* rather than Smith *Hanım*. This is an advantage to foreigners as it saves having to remember a lot of hard-to-pronounce Turkish surnames!

Or you can use *bey* or *hanım* together with their profession. In Turkey it's common to hear a patient addressing a female doctor as *doktor hanım* or a passenger addressing a bus driver as *şoför bey*. The same rule applies when dealing with officialdom. *Memur* means official and *memur bey* or *memur hanım* is the best form of address to use when dealing with any public official.

Children

It's fine to address children by their first names and to use the *sen* form – unless there's a group of them, in which case the plural *siz* applies. Turkish children are brought up to be respectful of adults and may well address you as *beyefendi* or *hanımefendi*. But foreign children relocating to Turkey may be more used to addressing adults by their first names, and you should get them to practise the *siz* form of address with all adults, as well as using the correct titles.

According to Turkey's Interior Ministry General Directorate of Population and Citizenship Affairs, the most popular first names are still those with religious connotations, with Mehmet and Fatma in first place. Yılmaz is the most common Turkish surname.

GREETINGS & GOODBYES

Turks favour the Mediterranean greeting of a handshake and a kiss on both cheeks, although the amount of physical contact depends on how well they know each other and whether or not they're the same sex. Two women almost always kiss, even if it's just a brush of lips to cheek, while two men may embrace if they know each other well. But each greets the opposite sex with far more formality – usually a rather limp handshake or a more distant nod – unless they're family or close friends.

When you're introduced to a Turk, you should shake hands gently (don't squeeze) and say '*memnun oldum*' ('Pleased to meet you'). If the person is much older and the opposite sex, a friendly nod may be more appropriate – some older people aren't used to physical contact with a member of the opposite sex and a Turkish man may baulk at shaking hands with a foreign female.

Most children are happy to kiss and be kissed, unless they're teenage boys. Children will sometimes kiss your hand and press it to their forehead – this is a gesture of respect and older Turks will be utterly charmed if your children do this.

There are a number of greetings (and responses) which you need to know. These include:

- *merhaba* or *selam* – hello or hi (informal);

- *selâmaleyküm* – may God be with you (an Arabic greeting used by older people to which the set response is '*aleykümselâm*');

- *günaydın* – good morning;

- *iyi günler* – good day;

- *iyi akşamlar* – good evening (said after 5pm);

- *iyi geceler* – good night (more usually said on departing in the evening).

Colloquial greetings include '*n'aber?*' ('what's up?') and '*ne var ne yok?*' ('what's happening?'). It's handy to know the right response, which is '*iyidir*' ('it's good') to the former and '*iyilik*' ('good stuff') to the latter.

Enquiring about health is of great cultural importance. In every social situation, you're asked '*nasılsınız?*'('How are you?') and should answer '*iyiyim, teşekkür ederim, siz nasılsınız?*' ('I'm well, thank you, how are you?'). If you're visiting someone's home or business or joining a group of people, you must make the effort to speak to everyone, even if you don't know them. They will greet you with the words '*hoş geldiniz*' ('welcome'), to which you respond '*hoş bulduk*' (literally 'we found nice' but equivalent to 'I feel welcome').

Taking your leave can be a complex affair. With close friends you might say '*görüşmek üzere*' (similar to '*au revoir*') or '*hoşça kalın*' ('goodbye'). A more old-fashioned, but widely used, phrase is '*Allaha ısmarladık*' ('may God go with you'). Many foreigners make the mistake of saying '*güle güle*' for every goodbye, but this is a command to 'go smiling' and should be said only to, and not by, people who are departing. If all this seems too complicated, it's fine to say '*iyi günler*' ('good day') or '*iyi akşamlar*' ('good evening') in lieu of goodbye.

TELEPHONE, LETTERS & EMAIL

In Turkey, it's unthinkable not to have a landline or mobile phone (*cep telefonu*) – preferably both. Text messaging is hugely popular and big businesses now use it to stay in touch with customers. As in the West, the art of writing letters is dying out. Bills and some business letters are still sent by post but many Turks don't trust the postal system (with good reason) and use one of the private courier companies for urgent letters and parcels.

> If you want to send something by post, make sure you send it from a main post office (*PTT*), as post boxes are few and far between and often aren't emptied for days. Include your address as sender (*gönderen*) on the envelope – just in case. Important correspondence should be sent by registered (*kayıtlı*) post.

Telephone

As in many other countries, telephone communication is more often by mobile than a landline (a survey by Euromonitor International in 2006 revealed that there were nearly 50m mobile phone users in Turkey, giving it the sixth-largest subscriber base in the world) and Turks will think you rather odd if you don't have a *cep*.

When the phone rings, everything else stops – it must be answered immediately.

- **If answering**, you say either '*efendim*' or, less formally, '*alo*'. Private callers don't always identify themselves and may expect you to know who they are – presumably from reading the caller ID on your mobile! It's expected that the person who makes the call will hang up, which they sometimes do quite abruptly.

- **If calling**, you say '*iyi günler*' (or an appropriate greeting – see above) and introduce yourself. Businesses usually answer with the name of the company and the words '*hoş geldiniz*' ('welcome'). Automated answering is catching on. It's a good idea to use the *siz* form of address over the phone unless you know the caller well.

Letters

Starting

Formal letters begin with '*Sayın Beyefendi*' (for a male addressee) or '*Sayın Hanımefendi*' (for a female addressee) – with capital letters as shown. If you know the name of the person you're writing to, you should include it, e.g. '*Sayın Mehmet Bey*'. *Sayın* means esteemed or respected. For informal letters you start with '*Sevgili*' ('Dear') followed by the addressee's name, e.g. '*Sevgili Emine*'. If you'd normally use the *siz* form of address with the person you're writing to, you should use the formal beginning (and sign-off – see below).

Addresses

Addresses are usually written as shown below.

Mah. is short for *mahallesi* (district) while *Sok* is short for *sokak* (street). *No* means number and the *D* stands for *daire* (apartment). Sometimes the address will also include the word *kat*, which means floor, e.g. *Kat 2* (2nd floor). Note that there's no ground floor in Turkey – street level is known as the first floor.

Date

When writing the date in full, the correct order is date-month-day-year, e.g. *19 Haziran Salı, 2007* (19th June Tuesday, 2007). The numerical form would be *19/06/07* (not as in the US, 06/19/08).

Name of recipient	*Sayın Ahmet Aydınoğlu*
District	*Cumhuriyet Mah.*
Street name and number and apartment number	*Barış Sok. No: 16 D:12*
Town or village	*Ortaca*
Postcode and province	*48646 MUĞLA*

Cappadocia

Signing off

The formal way to end a letter is with the word *Saygılarımla* ('with my respect'). Informal letters usually end with *Sevgilerimle* ('with love'). The two are dangerously similar so be careful not to use the informal sign-off in a letter to your landlord.

Email

Virtually every business in Turkey has a website and at least one email address, but Turks are often reluctant to use email, preferring to communicate by phone or fax. Even as a social tool, email lags behind text messaging and internet chat rooms. Business emails aren't treated with the same urgency as they are in Europe or the US, and you'll find that messages go unanswered, especially if they aren't in Turkish.

Turks haven't adopted the westerners' casual style of email, so if you're sending an email to someone you don't know, use the same formal address and language as you would in a letter.

Istanbul

6.
THE TURKS AT WORK

One of the most common mistakes foreigners make when coming to Turkey to work or start a business is to assume that they can continue working in the way they did in their home country, particularly if they had a successful business there. Many expatriates underestimate the dramatic differences in business culture between, for example, the Turks and northern Europeans and Americans. This chapter provides information on working for and with the Turks, going into business and business etiquette.

> Working in Turkey usually involves a steep learning curve for foreigners – professionally, linguistically and culturally.

WORK ETHIC

Turks are hard workers. Their family's expectations and their investment in education, along with the spectre of unemployment, all ensure that when a Turk gets the right job, he or she gives it 100 per cent.

In Turkey, work is the only route to improving your position, both financially and socially. There are many rags-to-riches stories of people who have made their fortune through sheer graft – the founders of the Koç and Sabancı dynasties are prime examples. People take pride in their work and devout Muslims regard it as an act of faith, because Islam extols the virtues of honest hard labour. But even those Turks who have little regard for religion feel that success in business or diligence in the workplace brings honour to themselves and their families. Whatever their motivation, Turkish people work longer and take less time off sick than most Europeans.

But Turks also know how to switch off. Holiday entitlements are shorter than in Europe, but leave is always taken. People prefer to keep work and family separate, and they don't allow their job to interfere with family time, and few would use their job as an excuse to get out of social commitments.

Unemployment

Less than a third of Turkey's population was in employment in the last quarter of 2007, according to the *Household Labour Force Survey*. The number of employed people numbered around 23.3m, or just 44 per cent of the population aged 15 or over. Yet the 'official' unemployment rate was only just over 9 per cent. Of those in work, 27 per cent were employed in agriculture, 20 per cent in industry, 6 per cent in construction and 47 per cent in services, which is the fastest-growing sector of the Turkish economy.

WORK PERMITS

Turkey saves its most burdensome tangle of red tape for foreigners wishing to take up employment. Whether you're a would-be employee, a business owner or self-employed, you cannot work in Turkey without a work permit (*calışma izni*) – and these can be as elusive as a flying carpet. The only people exempt from these rules are short-term workers, such as holiday reps, and those from countries with a reciprocal agreement on work permits, e.g. Northern Cyprus.

In order to employ a foreigner, a prospective employer must first obtain approval from the Ministry of Labour and Social Security (Çalışma ve Sosyal Güvenlik Bakanlığı), after which you apply for a work visa. A genuine employer will assist you in this process, but if you want to work for yourself you will have to follow the paper trail yourself. Either way, your application will pass through several government offices, and you'll also require a residence permit (see **Chapter 3**), therefore the entire process can take several months.

There are four types of work permit:

- **Definite work permits** – Initially granted for one year, these can be renewed for three years for work with the same employer, then for a further six years for any employer.

- **Indefinite work permits** – Available to foreigners who have been resident for eight years and worked legally for six years.

- **Independent work permits** – These may be granted to applicants who have had 'uninterrupted' residence for five years, but they're notoriously difficult to get hold of.

- **Exceptional work permits** – A very loose category. Officially, these can be granted to a number of applicants, including spouses of Turks, 'settled' foreigners, nationals of EU member states (in preparation for Turkey's EU membership), embassy staff and 'key personnel'. Applications are assessed individually.

It must be stressed that obtaining a work permit isn't easy. The law protects the rights of Turkish workers, so the onus is on you, or your employer, to prove that there's no suitably qualified Turk who can do a job. Even if you start up your own business, and employ Turkish workers, you still cannot legally work in that business unless you first obtain a work permit. The commitment you make in investing in a business should

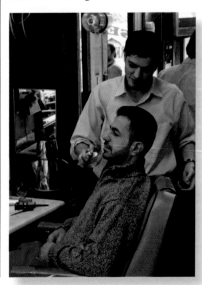

be sufficient to secure you a permit, but often isn't, as many foreign bar owners and hoteliers have discovered.

There's no way to guarantee a successful work permit application, but to give yourself the best possible chance you're advised to employ the services of a lawyer experienced in the jungle of Turkish employment law.

> **Tour operator representatives don't need a work permit, provided they're employed by an overseas company and work for no more than six months in a year. Foreign correspondents, circus performers and sportspeople on temporary assignments are also exempt.**

FINDING A JOB

When a Turk needs work, he starts with his friends or the friends of his friends. Most Turks have a long list of contacts – both social and business – and they never throw a business card away. In Turkey, knowing the right people is the key to finding employment, which means keeping all avenues open. Good jobs go fast, often to acquaintances of the employer, his staff or even his barber.

Networking is one of the first skills you must learn, if you want to find a decent job, i.e. one that's legal and pays more than the minimum wage. Talk to everyone you know, Turks and expatriates, and tell them the kind of work you're looking for. Get your face known – visit prospective employers and give them a copy of your CV. They're more likely to remember a

foreigner, although whether or not they will employ you depends on your skills.

The Expat Network

Employers seeking foreign staff often place job advertisements in the classified sections of expatriate forums and newspapers. Many are of the 'earn $1,000 a week from home' variety, but some merit investigation. The My Merhaba website (💻 www.mymerhaba.com) is a good place to start. Anywhere that expats gather, from language schools to bars and clubs, is likely to have a notice board – keep scanning these and pin up your own advertisement. Just as Turks favour Turks in the job market, so expats are more likely to pass on job tips to their fellow nationals.

Successful foreigners possess something which Turks cannot provide, and this usually means professional or linguistic skills. In the push towards joining the EU, employers want multilingual staff with specific knowledge. Many international companies have branches in Turkey, such as Microsoft, Cadbury Kent and HSBC, most of which are based in Istanbul or Ankara. If you're well qualified, contact some of them before you arrive. Get in touch also with your country's embassy and any relevant non-government organisations (NGOs). They're bombarded with enquiries but you may have something which makes you stand out. If you're lucky, you can set up a job in advance. If not, you need to look at the kind of jobs which may be available to you:

● **Teaching** – Most young Turks want to learn a foreign language (usually English) and some private schools teach in a foreign language (again, usually English), so the demand for teachers is high. But the state insists on qualifications, so if you don't have a degree or, at the very least, a teaching certificate such as TEFL (Teaching English as a Foreign Language), your options will be limited to private language schools. These have a reputation for a fast staff turnover, due to their reluctance to pay more than subsistence wages and to apply for work permits.

- **Tourism** – There's always work available in resorts, where your knowledge of the tourists' language(s) is a great advantage. But much of it is badly paid or illegal – bar and shop work is especially risky, as there are frequent police raids to check for illegal foreign workers. The best place to start is with a tour company based in your own country – most resort representatives are hired at home. Some jobs crop up through the season and go to people who are on the spot. Jobs are seasonal from May to October, so you need alternative employment in the winter months.

- **Property** – The property boom has created an opening for people who can sell to their own nationals, and many estate agencies have foreign staff, while international property companies are moving into the market. Much of this work is based in resort areas. Ensure that you'll be legally employed – estate agency regulations are being tightened up and the government has become reticent about granting work permits to foreigners in this field.

- **Nannying** – English-speaking nannies/teachers are sought after by wealthy Istanbulites (of which there are many) and there are agencies offering work. Some jobs are a ticket to the high life; others mean 18 hours a day of drudgery, dealing with demanding parents and spoilt kids.

Prohibited Jobs

The Turkish government has a list, regularly updated, of jobs and occupations which are prohibited to foreigners, either for security reasons or to protect the interests of Turkish workers. These include many professions, such as law, dentistry and nursing, as well as the civil service. In 2008, this long and often illogical list also included barbers, photographers, drivers, waiters, shoe manufacturers, construction workers and day labourers, household helpers, interpreters and tourist guides. Nor can a foreigner work as a musician or singer in a bar – although many do!

Speaking Turkish

Without the ability to speak reasonable Turkish, work opportunities are severely limited. Even jobs which focus on other foreigners, such as being a tour rep, are much easier if you can communicate with hoteliers and drivers. The better your language skills (and this should include reading and writing), the better your prospects.

Qualifications

Turks like to see as many paper qualifications as possible, for example, an employer advertising a basic

administration position will often demand a degree (*diploma*) of some sort – even if it isn't relevant to the job. If you have qualifications, you should ensure that they're accepted in Turkey and may need to have them certified by a consulate or other authority. You should certainly have them professionally translated into Turkish, along with your CV (*resume*), which must be submitted in both languages and be tailored to the job you're applying for.

Employment Agencies

There are government employment agencies (Türkiye İş Kurumu or İşkur) in most cities but their role is to get the army of unemployed Turks into jobs and finding foreigner's a job is low on their list of priorities. Many Turks prefer to scour job advertisements in newspapers or to log on to one of the recruitment websites, such as Kariyer (💻 www.kariyer.net). Job adverts in English are from employers seeking English-speakers.

Most private recruitment agencies are based in Istanbul, Ankara or Izmir, including international names such as Adecco and Manpower. There aren't, as yet, any dedicated expat employment agencies – the closest is Turkey Joblink (💻 www.turkeyjoblink.com), which is an English-language offshoot of a Turkish employment website that mainly advertises teaching and IT posts.

Selection Process

As the job market gets tighter, so the Western selection method of several interviews, plus aptitude and psychometric testing, is gaining ground – and some companies employ professional recruiters to handle the selection process. At the other end of the scale, a small business owner may be satisfied with a chat over a glass of tea. If you're applying for a teaching post or a job as a nanny, be prepared to be plunged in at the deep end to take a class or entertain children. Turks are always interested in references from Turkish employers or professionals, which is the stage at which 'who you know' becomes of prime importance.

Salary

Turkish salaries (*maaş*) are much lower than those in Europe or the US.

The gross minimum monthly wage is updated twice a year and was set at YTL638 or around €350 in July 2008 – barely enough to cover the rent on a small apartment in Istanbul. Many people (Turks and foreigners) work for cash and earn significantly less than the minimum wage, and some of those in the tourism sector exist on commission and tips. Not surprisingly, a lot of Turks believe that employment is a road to nowhere and that the only way to make their 'fortune' is by running their own business.

Typical net wages in 2007 were €450 per month for an office administrator and €1,175 for a manager, although some workers earn a good deal more, but only in Istanbul. Provincial wages reflect the lower cost of living. Of those jobs typically taken by foreigners, a teacher could earn from €650 per month, with free accommodation, while a holiday rep working for a UK tour company could earn from €500 a month, plus commission on excursion sales.

Salary Payments

Although some employees are paid weekly, most are paid monthly, and new government directives state that they should be paid directly into an employee's bank account. Employers should provide a pay slip (*bordro*) detailing pay and deductions (income tax and social security contributions), but many don't. You sometimes have to remind them to pay **you**. Even if your salary is calculated in foreign currency, your employer can still pay you in YTL converted at that day's official exchange rate.

Many unscrupulous bosses don't register staff for social security, in order to avoid paying contributions – government statistics for 2003 show that over half of employed workers weren't registered to any social security scheme. A Turkish employer should register you with the SSK (Social Security Authority) when you begin a job, otherwise you cannot receive state healthcare. Moreover, if your home country has a social security agreement with Turkey – as do many western European countries, including France, Germany and the UK – your Turkish contributions count towards your national retirement fund, so it's well worth paying them.

> If you suspect you're unregistered, ask for your SSK number – a boss who cannot supply this is almost certainly on the fiddle.

Discrimination

Turkish law prohibits racial and gender discrimination, but as in many other countries, it exists. Many women complain that they're denied promotion or paid less than their male counterparts, and foreigners also face discrimination. While most Turks welcome foreign know-how, some feel threatened by a highly-qualified *yabancı*. Meanwhile, bosses are under social and government pressure to employ their own nationals, therefore if you're in a two-horse race for a desirable job against a Turk, you're unlikely to win.

CONTRACTS

Turkish employment law favours employees over employers. Written contracts (*kontrat*) are required for any employment lasting a year or longer and should state all the relevant conditions, such as wages, working hours and the termination procedure. The maximum duration for a probationary period is two months, while a worker who can secure an indefinite agreement is well set up, as he will be difficult and costly to fire. Predictably, most bosses prefer fixed-term contracts or even no contract at all and they are rare in some fields such as seasonal jobs in tourism. Schools can get around the system by employing teachers only for an academic year. Elsewhere, devious bosses have been known to 'fire' a worker before the end of the year, and then re-employ him.

Contracts are binding on both parties – you must ensure you receive a copy and that you understand it. It will be written in Turkish, therefore an independent translation or taking legal advice is advisable before you sign.

Collective Agreements

General working conditions, such as minimum wage, holiday entitlement, and regulations on sick pay, maternity leave and severance pay are regulated by Turkish Labour Law. Management and unions should employ collective bargaining to resolve employment issues and agree contracts, although the unions' power is limited in Turkey. Only employees who have worked for a year or longer are covered by collective agreements.

STARTING OR BUYING A BUSINESS

Most Turks dream of starting their own business. They aren't short of mentors –

such as the late Vehbi Koç, who began his career in his father's corner shop and built the business into one of Turkey's largest multinational corporations. But for every small business that opens, another one fails – it's estimated that the average lifespan of a small company in Turkey is 12 years. For many would-be entrepreneurs, optimism or a belief in a benign fate count for more than an original idea and a sound business plan.

As in any country, research is the key to a successful business. There are a lot of opportunities in Turkey, where the population is young, increasingly wealthy and keen to jump onto the consumer bandwagon. Many foreigners have built successful businesses based on a thorough understanding of what Turks want. However, just as many have failed through regurgitating the same old formula – witness the number of foreign 'pubs' which come and go in tourist resorts – choosing the wrong location or targeting a limited market.

To be successful in business, you also need a thick skin, as Turks (and other expats) can turn on you when your business acumen threatens to eclipse theirs, and they aren't above copying your ideas and recycling them as their own. Before getting involved in business of any sort, line up a good lawyer, an accountant and a translator, and make sure that your contacts book is full – you'll need all the help you can get.

Starting a Business

Many business start-ups are now funded by foreign money. Turkey makes much of its attractive Foreign Direct Investment (FDI) system, which saw the country ranked as the 13th most desirable location for foreign investors in 2006. Amazingly, setting up a company involves no more bureaucracy than obtaining a work permit or importing a car. Two foreign partners can set up a public limited company (*limitet şirket*) in under a week, with a total capital investment of no more than YTL5,000 (around €2,700), and are free to re-export any profits.

But it isn't all plain sailing. Owning a company doesn't necessarily make it easier for a foreigner to work in Turkey, running costs can be high, and shutting a company down is an expensive and time-consuming process.

The FDI lure is working. At the end of the '90s, there were just over 4,000 companies

fully or partly funded by international capital, which by February 2008 had rocketed to 18,308. Nearly $22bn of investment capital flowed into Turkey in 2007. The most popular sectors for investment are wholesale and retail trade, manufacturing, and property and business activities. European countries provide more than half the overseas investors, with Germany, Britain and the Netherlands leading the way.

Buying a Business

This is risky unless you're absolutely sure of what you're getting involved in, as Turks are great at telling you what you want to hear, not what you need to know. Some have borrowed heavily to keep shaky businesses afloat and are dying for some hapless foreigner to come along and take the entire debt-ridden liability off their hands. Many sellers are genuine but will gloss over the amount of time and work that's involved in running a business in Turkey.

Partnerships

To many foreign investors, setting up or buying with a Turkish partner (*ortak*) is the ideal solution, whereby they

provide the money and ideas, while the partner speaks the language and knows the ropes. A partnership can take the form of a limited company, with the Turk as one of the shareholders, or it can be a small business, such as a shop or café, in which case all paperwork, including the licences (*ruhsat*) and trading documents, will be issued in the partner's name. It is, to all effects, a Turkish business.

Many such partnerships are based on marriage or long acquaintanceship, and some are extremely successful. However, there are also numerous tales of foreigners going into business with Turks, then falling out and losing their entire investment. Partnerships which begin as a romance are especially vulnerable.

> Be very, very careful who you do business with; don't regard partnerships as an easy solution and always obtain independent legal advice.

Loans

Turkey may have loosened the red tape for would-be expatriate entrepreneurs, but you're still expected to put up all the money as the whole idea of FDI is to boost the Turkish economy with an injection of foreign funds. Even if you present a detailed business plan, it's unlikely a bank will agree a loan with only your company as security, and you'll need someone or something (security) to guarantee that it will be repaid. It's difficult for a foreigner to secure any sort of loan, although it may be easier if you have a Turkish

partner, and even if you're successful the interest rates can be eye-wateringly high.

Grants

The FDI system provides a number of incentives to tempt would-be investors. These include exemption from customs duties and certain taxes, bank credit and even free development land. But most incentives target larger businesses which invest large sums of money and provide expert knowledge, as well as employment for Turks. They're geared towards manufacturing and export, rather than tourism and property, which are the sectors primarily attracting expats. The best incentives are in 'priority development regions', which are mainly in the centre and east of the country and not in the comparatively rich and foreigner-friendly coastal districts.

Premises

The majority of business premises (*iş yeri*) are rented, especially shops and offices. Some investors buy commercial properties, such as hotels, which are almost always freehold.

Renting

Renting commercial premises is no different from renting a home, with the same responsibilities, liabilities and rules regarding increasing the rent (see **Rented Property** in **Chapter 3**). Provided you have a contract you're fairly secure. Rents can be surprisingly high, especially in resorts, where landlords sometimes demand payment in euros or dollars, or in a lump sum up front. The better the location, e.g. in a main shopping area or near the beach, the more you pay.

New tenants are often asked for *hava parası* ('air money'), a one-off payment requested by the seller or landlord when premises change hands. It's a charge for the fixtures and fittings and good will – or just the space which the new trader will occupy. Some people have an inflated idea of their premises' worth and ask ridiculous sums for what is literally thin air.

> **Businesses are advertised with the words '*devren satalık*' or '*devren kiralık*' – *devren* refers to a transfer of title. The former suggests the actual property is for sale, although it usually refers to just the business – there will still be rent to pay – while the latter means the premises are available for rent or even as a sub-let, so make sure you know who the real landlord is.**

Buying

The procedure for buying a commercial property is the same as for buying a residence. Ownership is stated on the title deed (*tapu*), therefore foreigners with Turkish partners must be aware that if they buy in their partner's name, he – and not they – will own it outright. Pre-purchase checks should include a careful examination of turnover and profit, all fixtures and fittings, and the licences. Not all 'commercial businesses' keep a record of transactions, some don't possess a current licence and a few have traded illegally for years.

Working from Home

You can set up a business from home, provided you don't disturb or inconvenience your neighbours. An office-based business is fine; a busy restaurant is not – although this doesn't stop villagers from opening temporary pancake cafes in their gardens in summer. You must (in theory) set aside a room in your home from which to run the business, and it's regulated like any other, i.e. you still need all the relevant licences and permits to run it.

Self-employment

Over 30 per cent of Turks are self-employed (*serbest çalışan*), which encompasses everyone from subsistence farmers and fishermen to business owners and freelancers. Anyone can register with the tax authorities as self-employed, which makes you liable for income tax and payments to the self-employed social security scheme, Bağ-Kur. Monthly contributions start at around 40 per cent of the national minimum wage.

As a self-employed foreigner, you still need a work permit – which isn't easy to obtain (see above). There are countless expats working without permits, as writers or artists, selling goods on eBay, designing websites, dealing in property, taking commission on tours and carpet sales, and otherwise making a living. Most know exactly what they're doing, while others are blissfully unaware that, technically, they're working illegally (see **Black Economy** below).

Marketing

The rules of networking which apply to job-hunting also apply to marketing. Turks invest in shiny brochures, flashing websites and huge, unsightly roadside signs to advertise their businesses, but nothing compares to having a good reputation, and as many contacts as possible to spread the word. This is why a Turkish businessman is never too busy to make small talk and sip tea with you – he never knows whn you might come in useful.

BLACK ECONOMY

Tax avoidance and illegal working combine to make Turkey's black economy one of the country's largest obstacles to growth. Estimates put it at between 30 and 50 per cent of gross domestic product (GDP) – far in excess of, for example, Italy or Spain. Research by the Ministry of Finance has revealed that only around half of all income is declared to the tax authorities.

It's almost impossible to avoid the black economy and many expatriates get sucked into it. Under-declaring the value of your house, failing to declare rental income on your villa, paying your cleaner in cash – all are illegal but almost universal activities. Then there's the large army of illegal foreign workers, estimated to number several million, many of whom are badly paid and have no rights or recourse to social funds.

There are serious consequences for those who evade taxes, run an unlicensed business or work illegally – residents may get away with a (first time) warning but non-residents risk being fined and/or deported.

> Many foreigners think they will never get caught but they're easier to catch than Turks. Every summer the tax authorities and police raid resorts, and officials sometimes pose as tourists when looking for casual workers in bars and restaurants. They may also get a helping hand from the public, as expats who do well risk being reported to the authorities – by Turks or their own jealous countrymen.

WORKING WOMEN

Turkey's endemic culture of machismo makes it difficult for women to rise to the top in business and some men would rather see them as mothers and home-makers than as movers and shakers. Women make up about a quarter of the workforce but also account for almost half of the long-term unemployed.

Officially, sexual discrimination is outlawed, but many working women struggle to be taken seriously by (male) bosses who fear they will become pregnant or get married. Female bank workers complain that they're put on counter duty to look pretty, while men do the real work behind the scenes.

A female boss inspires awe and not a little resentment, therefore a foreign female boss really has her work cut out. She will have to work twice as hard to gain the respect of male employees, and this means being 100 per cent serious and dignified at all times. Whatever you do, don't flirt! And don't be surprised if you're sometimes 'mistaken' for a male colleague's personal assistant.

> **Women have a strong position in the professions, where they account for around a third of all public servants, lawyers, doctors and architects, but few are involved in the nation's decision-making. In 2008, 15 years after Tansu Çiller became Turkey's first female Prime Minister, fewer than 10 per cent of MPs were female, and only one woman had made it into the cabinet.**

BUSINESS ETIQUETTE

The Turkish workplace is a formal environment, where old-fashioned courtesy means as much as, if not more than, strategic planning and corporate identity. Westerners can find the pace of work frustratingly slow, but you should resist the temptation to try to shake things up. You need to be sensitive to office politics and business etiquette if you're to gain the trust and approval of clients and co-workers.

Office Politics

Many Turkish businesses are family affairs, and even those that aren't operate like a family, with the boss (*patron*) in the role of father figure. Respect for authority is especially strong and the boss is always right (even if he isn't), and junior staff may stand up when their seniors walk into the room, open doors, fetch drinks and even unconsciously tighten the knot in their ties. The relaxed Western manner of calling your boss by his or her first name is often unacceptable in Turkey, where it's never wise to be too informal with higher-ranking staff.

Roles are reversed when dealing with juniors, who will look up to you and expect your guidance and supervision, and may be uncomfortable if you try to interact with them on their level. Teamwork can be awkward, as team members will insist on deferring to team leaders. Honourable behaviour and discretion are paramount in the workplace. Never criticise someone within earshot of staff or reprimand a junior in front of his peers, which will cause a severe loss of face, for which they may never forgive you.

Appointments

It isn't a good idea to drop in on a Turk at work any more than it is to turn up unannounced at their home. Turks like to be prepared, so make an appointment, preferably by phone, and confirm it by email or fax. (The fax is still popular with Turkish people, who like to have things down on paper rather than on a computer screen.) A letter of introduction from a mutual friend should guarantee that you're seen.

Avoid making appointments around Friday lunchtime – an important time for Muslim prayer – or late in the day during Ramadan, when people's minds are focused on breaking their fast.

Business Cards

In a country devoted to networking, business cards are crucial. They're also extremely useful as they save the embarrassment of trying to remember unfamiliar Turkish names. Turks don't automatically hand out cards, so being offered one is an invitation to stay in contact. Accept it with respect – slipping in into a smart card-holder gives the right message.

Your own cards should be of good quality and feature your details in Turkish on one side. Give them to people you think will be useful – cards are always exchanged at meetings – and also leave one with the receptionist.

Business Gifts

Gifts aren't necessary, although they're always graciously accepted, and many Turks give away promotional items such as calendars and pens. If you want to celebrate closing a deal, something which represents your own culture is the most appropriate choice – a crafted item, illustrated book or elegantly wrapped box of chocolates. All Turks have a sweet tooth, and chocolates are exchanged between businesses and clients during the *Şeker Bayramı* holiday. Don't give a gift which could be construed as too personal, and never give alcohol unless you're absolutely sure that the recipient drinks. If you want to say thank you, it's often better to take clients out for a meal.

Business Hours

Office and business hours are the same as in western Europe – people start between 8.30 and 9am and finish between 5 and 6pm, with no siesta. Everything finishes earlier during the Ramadan fast, so that people can be home by sunset and ready to eat, which creates a mass exodus from offices in the late afternoon. Devout Muslims may take time out of the office to pray, especially on Fridays.

Business Lunches

Some Turks have business lunches but many prefer to entertain in the evening when work is less likely to intrude. Lunch hours are brief – usually an hour at the most – while evening meals are a relaxed and sociable affair and can last for hours. The main object is for you to get to know each other, rather than to discuss business, so don't bring up work unless someone else does first. If you're invited for a meal, your hosts will pay – it's expected that you'll return the invitation and pick up the bill. This can be awkward if you're a female entertaining male clients, when you should have a quiet word with the waiter before he brings the bill.

Dress

This should be smart and professional, both in the office and at a business meal. Men wear a suit and tie, while women wear suits or smart separates. During hot and humid weather, e.g. in Istanbul in high summer, you can forgo the jacket and tie, but never turn up in shorts or 'beach gear'. Turkish women out for the evening often look over-dressed, but only the very young wear short skirts, and you won't be taken seriously if you wear a low-cut or revealing top.

Meetings

A meeting in Turkey is as much about personal contact as it is about the business at hand, and Turks use a meeting to get to know you and decide whether you're someone they feel comfortable doing business with. Negotiations come later, decisions later still – and are probably made in your absence.

First impressions are vital. How you greet business contacts is important and you should always shake hands (though not too firmly), smile and look them in the eye. Women don't always shake hands with men, therefore it's wise to allow the opposite sex to make the first move. You should greet people in order of seniority – if you aren't sure who's who, approach older people first and use the polite *siz* form of address.

> **Turkish names can be a minefield. Turks often use their first name, followed by the Turkish equivalent of Mr or Mrs, e.g. Osman** *Bey* **(Mr Osman) or Fatma** *Hanım* **(Mrs Fatma). If you aren't sure of someone's name, call them sir (***beyefendi***) or madam (***hanımefendi***) – it sounds excessively formal but it's what people expect. Managers (***müdür***) are happy to be addressed as** *müdür bey***.**

Timekeeping

Turks aren't known for their punctuality but are rarely late for business appointments, and even if they are, you shouldn't be – your hosts expect you to behave by European (or American) standards. If you're running late, phone and let them know. In Istanbul's notorious traffic, it's accepted that at least one or two people will arrive late for a meeting.

First Meetings

You won't get much work done, if any, at a first meeting, which is all about building trust and establishing relationships. You may not even meet the boss but rather someone lower down the chain of command, whose job is to assess you. Tea or coffee is followed by (sometimes interminable) small talk and you shouldn't bring up business, however much you want to, until someone else does. Let your hosts (or guests) lead the conversation and be careful how you respond, avoiding any contentious topics (see **Taboos** in **Chapter 4**).

First meetings are make-or-break times, and if a Turk feels there's something strange or suspicious about you, you may never make it to a second meeting.

Language

Unless you're in the tourism business, expect the meeting to be in Turkish. Many business people speak a foreign language, especially English, but don't assume that they do – or that they're willing to use it in a business context. A Turk with limited English won't want to lose face in front of his colleagues, nor will he want to cut Turkish speakers out of the conversation. Always greet people in Turkish and ask politely if they speak your language. If your command of the language is poor, bring along an interpreter.

People are always happy when a foreigner speaks Turkish but they sometimes over-estimate your skills. If the conversation is too fast for you or there are things which you don't understand, let them know, and never pretend that your Turkish is better than it is, as you'll soon be found out. If a meeting is conducted in English, remember that it's your hosts' second language and speak slowly and clearly, avoiding colloquialisms, jargon and technical terms.

Negotiating

There are some important points which you should be aware of when negotiating any kind of business deal in Turkey:

- Agendas aren't always adhered to and meetings can appear to lack structure. There may be frequent interruptions by phone calls (Turks cannot resist answering their mobiles) and other guests, therefore you need to be patient.

- It's rude to interrupt or correct someone. Wait until they finish speaking before putting your point across and be diplomatic with your comments.

- Use visual media to support your presentation, as charts and graphs cut across the language barrier. Important material should be translated into Turkish.

- Don't set deadlines or apply high-pressure tactics, as Turks often find westerners 'pushy' and this will only confirm their suspicions.

> In Turkey, a business negotiation is like a slow dance, both sides offering favours and concessions until a satisfactory compromise is reached. It's a refined form of haggling, as if trying to agree a price for an extremely rare and valuable carpet.

- Money isn't everything and Turks will sometimes turn down a better offer to do business with someone they trust and admire, or who can assist them in other useful areas, such as expanding their overseas contacts.

● Don't expect a quick decision. Most decision-making takes place behind closed doors, usually by someone in authority.

● If you receive an offer (or an offer of an offer), don't presume anything is binding – or invest any money – until a contract is signed.

● If your proposal is rejected, it may be a while before you find out as Turks hate saying 'no' and are masters of evasion. It's unlikely that anyone will be so rude as to say it's a bad idea, but instead they will blame restructuring or cash flow problems. However, if they like you they may leave the door ajar for future negotiation.

Regional Differences

Although honour and respect are national traits, there are cultural differences across Turkey, and these will affect the way people do business. Istanbul is home to an increasing number of brash, hi-tech, European-style companies whose efficiency and reliance on technology seem at odds with old-fashioned manners. A traditional family business in central or eastern Turkey, with its roots in Islamic culture, will be less used to dealing with foreigners, but also more attentive and personal. Resort operations are somewhere in between – foreigners are their bread and butter but many are run by farmers-turned-entrepreneurs, who are still villagers at heart.

Turkey is full of surprises and you can never tell how people will react to you or your ideas, therefore to be successful you must stay flexible and be ready to learn.

EMPLOYING PEOPLE

The difficulty of obtaining work permits for foreigners means that most if not all of your staff will be Turkish. Turkish workers aren't as proactive or independent as their European counterparts and you may need to show them how to do something (several times), rather than just issuing instructions, and they will look to you for leadership. Employing young women involves extra responsibility, as you're responsible for their honour in the workplace – if a young female employee has an affair with a male staff member, her parents will soon be breathing down your neck.

> However tempted you may be, you should never employ an expat friend without applying for a work permit. The penalties for employing illegal workers are far higher than those imposed on 'employees' and could even involve a prison sentence.

Contracts

You must be absolutely certain that someone is vital to your organisation before giving them an indefinite contract – make full use of the two months' probation period. Employees can claim severance pay on dismissal – unless they're fired for unacceptable behaviour – or if they leave to do military service or to have a baby. This is one reason why teenage boys and young women find it difficult to get a

decent job (and children as young as 13 are employed in Turkey). Severance amounts to a month's pay for every year worked for the company and if an employee claims unfair dismissal and wins, you're compelled to re-employ them or pay up to eight months' compensation.

Just as you should seek legal advice before taking a job, it's also wise to do so before taking on a worker.

Domestic Help

Good cleaners or handymen can be worth their weight in gold, as they can always obtain the best prices and know how to get things done. They may adopt you as part of their family, taking care of your house when you're away and even feeding the cat. In return you'll be expected to take a genuine interest in their lives, sympathise with their illnesses and, possibly, lend them money. This is often a mutually beneficial relationship, but you should be wary of getting too close as some Turks become possessive of 'their foreigners', and if you dispense with their services there may be awkward consequences.

Unless they live in, cleaners, gardeners and handymen are almost always paid in cash and blend quietly into the black economy. Some plumbers, electricians and other workmen also expect cash payment, for which they rarely issue a receipt. It's unlikely that they'll report you for playing along, but it's illegal, and if you have a problem with their work you have no recourse. When it's your word against that of a local Turk, you're unlikely to win.

Social Security

Social security is one of the largest expenses for an employer, who must pay a contribution amounting to 19.5 per cent of each employee's gross pay, plus an additional 2 per cent towards the national unemployment fund. The employee pays a total of 15 per cent. As an example, an employee on €350 per month (roughly the gross minimum wage in 2008) costs his boss €425 per month, while he ends up with just under €300 before tax is deducted. This is why so many bosses avoid registering staff for social security, and why a lot of workers prefer to keep quiet about it.

Tax

Employers are also responsible for deducting income tax (*gelir vergisi*) from an employee's salary, and for supplying a monthly payslip and annual tax certificate.

TRADE UNIONS

Trade unions (*işçi sendikası*) aren't powerful in Turkey. Laws were enacted during the 1980 military coup to curb militancy and erode their powers, and today only a small percentage of the workforce is thought to belong to a union. The largest organisation, the Confederation of Turkish Trade Unions (TÜRK-İŞ), claims a membership of only 1.75m workers and in some sectors workers are barred from going on strike. According to the International Confederation of Trade Unions (ICFTU), only around 14 per cent of employees' contracts are negotiated through collective bargaining.

Joining a Union

Joining a union is voluntary but the law doesn't encourage membership. The government won't recognise a union unless over 50 per cent of the total workforce has been persuaded to join. But workers who wish to enrol in a union must have their application notarised and recorded by a lawyer at their own (considerable) expense.

WORKING WEEK

The working week is from Monday to Friday, with banks, offices and government departments closed at the weekend. Sunday is an official day of rest. Most shops open on Saturdays and, sometimes, Sundays, although one-man grocers rarely close. Tourism is notorious for its long hours, especially during summer, and people who work in this sector often put in far more than the prescribed 45 hours a week.

Breaks

Coffee breaks aren't part of the culture, but no excuse is needed for tea, which lubricates the entire day. Almost every small business is linked to a tea kitchen (*çay ocağı*) – many by an intercom

system. Some government offices still employ a *hademe*, whose job is to run errands and ensure a non-stop supply of tea, in addition to traditional 'tea' times at around 10am and 3pm. The afternoon session is usually accompanied by cakes and other snacks and is such an institution that a crisp manufacturer marketed a product called 'Ofis 3-5', especially to fill the afternoon break.

Holidays

Holiday entitlements aren't especially generous and depend on your length of service. A contracted employee with up to five years' service is entitled to 14 days' paid holiday a year, which increases to 26 days after 15 years. In addition, there are five public holidays each year, and two longer breaks to mark the main religious holidays (see below).

Many people take their two-week break in July or August, when schools are closed and there's a mass exodus from Istanbul, heading for the coast.

The religious holidays (*bayram*) are also busy, and it's difficult to get Turks to commit to business during these times of year. As a newcomer, you may have to fit in with other people's holiday plans, which may mean taking your summer holiday outside the main months of July and August. This can be an advantage, as you avoid clogged roads, high prices and oppressive heat – spring and autumn are much pleasanter times to explore Turkey.

Public Holidays

There are five public holidays that are celebrated throughout the country (see box below). All except New Year's Day commemorate significant events in the life of Atatürk, the War of Independence and the formation of the Turkish Republic. They're celebrated with marching bands, folk dancing, sports events and military parades – Victory Day, especially, is an opportunity for the armed forces to show off their formidable arsenal of tanks, jets and warships. Many private-sector businesses stay open on public holidays, though it's customary for them to display the Turkish flag.

There's one more date which, although not a holiday, is special to Turks. Atatürk died on 10th November 1938, and people still stop whatever they're doing to pay their respects in silence at 9.05am, the time of his death.

New Year is a strange festival for foreigners. Influenced by Western television, many Turks have incorporated key elements of Christmas, albeit a week late, into the New Year celebrations. Turkey dinners, gifts, decorations and a 'Christmas tree' are all enjoyed alongside the midnight countdown and firework displays.

Religious Holidays

The two main religious holidays are far more important than public holidays (see **Religious Holidays** in **Chapter 8**). Everyone takes time off to celebrate, and the roads are always busy in advance of the main days – some people take an extra half day off before the main event. The dates are tied to the Muslim lunar calendar, so they move forward by around ten days each year. The dates for 2009 are as follows:

● *Şeker Bayramı* (Sugar Holiday) – 20th-22nd September. This follows

National Public Holidays	
Date	**Holiday**
1st January	**New Year's Day** (*Yılbaşı* – literally 'head of the year')
23rd April	**National Sovereignty & Children's Day** (*Ulusal Egemenlik ve Çocuk Bayramı*)
19th May	**Youth & Sport Day** (*Genç ve Spor Bayramı*)
30th August	**Victory Day** (*Zafer Bayramı*)
29th October	**Republic Day** (*Cumhuriyet Bayramı*)

Ramazan (Ramadan, the month of fasting), which runs from 22nd August to 20th September.

- *Kurban Bayramı* (Feast of the Sacrifice) – 28th November to 1st December.

Christmas & Easter

Christian festivals aren't recognised in Turkey, so it's unlikely you'll get time off work unless you have an understanding boss. In areas with a large expatriate population, however, there are Christmas festivities, although Easter is more low-key.

Leave

There's no formal entitlement to leave for personal events such as moving house or attending funerals. Women are granted paid maternity leave of up to 75 days – half before the birth and half after – and can take further unpaid leave. They also receive paid leave for ante-natal check-ups. In the macho Turkish society, paternity leave doesn't as yet exist.

There's no official allocation for sick leave. If you're ill, your employer will allow you up to week off but you must provide a medical certificate.

Bosphorus bridge, Istanbul

7.
ON THE MOVE

Turks love to travel. This may be a reflection of their nomadic past, but even so, they think nothing of an overnight bus trip to visit relatives or a three-hour drive to an outstanding restaurant. And with most government offices and hospitals situated in larger towns, for many people travel is unavoidable.

Fortunately, there's a good, cheap public transport system, and even small villages are linked by dolmuş (a minibus which is filled to capacity – the word translates as 'stuffed'). But in Turkey the car is king and many prefer to get behind the wheel for any journey, no matter how short. The chances are that you'll be joining them.

To help reduce the surprise – or rather shock – factor of driving in Turkey, this chapter contains useful tips on interpreting road 'rules', driving etiquette and finding somewhere to park, as well as information about getting around on public transport.

> In country areas, drivers are likely to leave their warning triangles in the boot and instead use a pile of rocks to indicate an accident, which is yet another obstacle to be wary of when driving at night.

SAFETY FIRST

On the whole, Turkey is a safe country to travel in, but you should be aware of the following dangers and potential annoyances:

● **Accidents** – The road traffic 'accident' statistics are staggeringly high. The death toll is more than four times higher than that of Italy, a country notorious for its uninhibited driving style. Be aware of the dangers – you're far more at risk when travelling by road than you are from earthquakes or terrorism.

● **Buses** – There are hundreds of bus companies and some of the less well known names aren't so diligent when it comes to maintenance and preventing driver fatigue. Play safe and stick to the large bus companies.

● **Petty theft** – Though rare, this does happen and bus and railway stations are places to be wary. Don't flash your cash and keep your valuables hidden in a money belt.

- **Eastern Turkey** – Roadblocks are common and your journey will be interrupted by many military checks. Night-time driving is sometimes forbidden.

- **Single women** – Most Turks take great pains to put women at their ease. Long-distance bus companies won't seat a woman next to a man she doesn't know, and taxi drivers will also try to segregate single women. You should avoid being too friendly as this could be misconstrued as flirting!

- **Hitchhiking** – This is common (and legal) in rural areas, but women should avoid it. The hitchhiking (*otostop*) call sign isn't a thumbs-up (thumb signs are best avoided in Turkey) but a gentle up-and-down flap of your outstretched hand.

DRIVING

Driving in Turkey is – at best – a challenge, at worst highly dangerous. The unpredictable behaviour of drivers, poor roads and badly maintained vehicles mean that you have to be on your guard at every moment and defensive driving is essential. Pay extra attention to the actions of drivers around you and signal even if no one else does and use your lights and horn to make drivers aware of you. Assume nothing – although assuming that most other drivers are crazy will do you no harm. Above all, keep your cool.

Turkey has a worse road safety record than any country in Europe, with 620,789 accidents in 2005 – that's roughly one for each 10km (6.2mi) of highway. In the same year there was an official average of 12 deaths each day,

and this is an underestimate as police often record only deaths which occur at the site of an accident and not those which result from it.

> If you're new to driving in Turkey, avoid driving: at night, when you share the road with both slow-moving, unlit tractors and speeding drivers who blind you with their full-beam headlamps; during bad weather, when rain and oil turn road surfaces into skating rinks; and on religious holidays (*bayram*), when the whole country is on the road and the accident rate soars even higher than usual.

It isn't all bad news. Turkey is doing its best to tame the *Trafik Canavarı* (Traffic Monster) with speed cameras, stricter law enforcement and public education campaigns, featuring gory pictures of accident scenes. As a result, fatalities have decreased by 50 per cent in parts of the country since the mid-'90s. There are fewer old wrecks on the road and highways are undergoing improvements. Best of all, Turkey has the fewest cars per head of population in Europe and, outside the cities at least, you can cruise along empty roads.

Drivers

Courteous and formal in most situations, Turks often undergo a Jekyll-and-Hyde transformation once behind the wheel. Their sole goal appears to be to get to their destination before anyone else. Taxi drivers are especially aggressive – older cars and those driven by women or with foreign number plates must be overtaken, irrespective of the weather, speed limit or traffic coming in the opposite direction. A favourite driver's insult is '*eşşoğlu eşek*' ('son of a donkey'). This is possibly the only time you'll hear a Turkish woman swear.

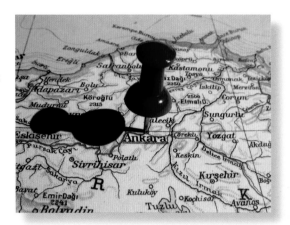

Many drivers lack the necessary skills. There's a driving test but this puts more emphasis on the internal workings of the combustion engine than on safely negotiating the road. Older drivers may have avoided even this, as in the past it was possible to 'buy' a licence.

Another aspect of the Turkish psyche which hinders their driving is their fatalistic attitude. Many believe that accidents aren't the fault of speeding drivers, overloaded lorries or bald tyres, but the will of Allah. You'll see the words '*Allah korusun*' ('may Allah protect me') emblazoned across the back of some vehicles; sadly, the plea isn't always answered.

Among the numerous quirks of Turkish driving, you should be especially wary of the following:

- **Overtaking anywhere** – This includes on the inside lane, on blind bends, and even while you're overtaking another vehicle. Look constantly in your mirror and allow yourself to be overtaken whenever possible.

- **Tailgating** – If the driver behind is too close, which he usually will be, leave plenty of room between you and the vehicle in front in case it suddenly stops – and brake slowly.

- **Driving through red lights** – Approach all junctions with caution, even when the lights are green.

- **Flashing headlamps** – This may mean 'Watch out, there's a police check ahead' but usually means 'Get out of my way!'

- **Tooting their horn** – This is used to greet other drivers or to express annoyance as in, 'Get a move on, slowcoach!'

Turkish Roads

The best roads in Turkey are the motorways, which are toll roads – you take a ticket on joining them and pay as you exit or use a pre-paid card. Unfortunately there are less than 2,000km (1,242mi) of motorways linking a few major cities. The Turkish government is upgrading the rest of its main highways to four-lane dual-carriageways, but many local roads are narrow, unmarked and full of potholes. The further east you go, the worse the roads become.

Roads in towns can be just as difficult to navigate, especially after rain when poor drainage leaves them submerged. Road works are everywhere, and 'new' road surfaces often consist of loose stones peppering your windscreen or red mud congealing on your wheels.

> **Turkey has a lot of radar speed checks, but they're almost always in the same locations and often unmanned after dark. When the *Trafik Polis* go home, they sometimes leave a deterrent behind – a life-size plywood cut out of a police car!**

Road Rules

The Turkish Highway Code is similar to that used in Europe or the US, but strict adherence to it is rare – unless there's a police car in sight. Studies have shown that Turkish drivers believe the rules are there to be bent, if not broken. However, so that you know what you should be doing, among the most important points are:

- Turks drive on the right and give way to traffic approaching from the right.

- Speed limits are 130kph (78mph) on a motorway (*otoyol*); 90kph (56mph) on state highways, also known as D roads (*devlet yolları*), and provincial main roads (*il yolları*); and 50kph (30mph) in built-up areas or as signposted.

- White lines separate traffic lanes. A solid single line means no overtaking – you can overtake only when there's a single broken line or double lines with a broken line on your side of the road.

- When turning left on a busy road, you must first give way to traffic behind you – this explains why cars indicate left and then pull in to the right.

- Seatbelts are compulsory and children under ten must sit in the rear.

- Mobile phones shouldn't be used while on the move (except for hands-free devices).

- The drink-drive limit is 0.5mg per 100ml of blood – lower than in the UK – or zero if you have passengers in the car. You'll be breathalysed after an accident, however minor.

- In case of an accident you must not move the car, even if there's a queue of irate drivers behind you, until the police arrive. This rule was under review in early 2008, but it's best to play safe, or you risk a large fine and may also invalidate your insurance.

- It's compulsory to carry identity papers (e.g. your passport), driving licence and your vehicle documents

Anatolia

when driving. You should also carry two warning triangles, a fire extinguisher and a first-aid kit.

Fines & Penalties

Although Turkey has a penalty points system, it applies only to Turkish driving licences, but on-the-spot fines apply to all drivers. In 2007, these ranged from YTL513 or around €270, plus suspension of your licence, for a first-time conviction for drink-driving to YTL108 (€57) for speeding or driving through a red light and YTL52 (€27) for the national sport of throwing rubbish out of the window.

Fines can be paid on the spot (ask for a receipt!), at a bank or via the internet, and are discounted by 25 per cent if you pay up within 15 days. Interest is added to late payments.

Finding Your Way

Turkish roads are quite well signposted – motorway signs are green, highway signs are blue, local signs are white and those indicating places of interest are brown. People are always happy to give directions, which is fine if your language skills can cope with it, but trying to map-read your way around a large city will make you a target for impatient drivers. It's better to learn the route by taxi first or pay a taxi to lead the way and follow it.

Motorcyclists, Cyclists & Pedestrians

Turks (and foreigners) who cannot afford a car often own a scooter, an elderly moped or a bicycle and may pile the whole family on board. Cyclists often disregard traffic lights – and the need to fit lights to their machines – making these two-wheelers a particular hazard at night. Even if you obey the law, which requires that motorcyclists wear helmets and goggles, and exercise common sense, two wheels make you vulnerable to the carelessness of other road users – most drivers consider cyclists to be almost as irrelevant as pedestrians – and the bad road surfaces will test even an experienced rider. Turkey isn't a place to learn to ride a scooter.

Road safety is taught in schools but pedestrians still dart across roads without looking. Pedestrian crossings (*yaya geçidi*) are marked by black and white stripes and Turkish drivers usually stop only if there's someone in the middle of the road, therefore if you decide to stop check your mirrors first, as the car behind could plough straight into you. As a pedestrian, don't expect traffic to come to a courteous halt as soon as you set foot on a crossing. Traffic lights also allow pedestrians a chance to cross.

Some Important Road Signs

Dikkat – Attention

Dur – Stop

Park yapılmaz/edilmez – No parking

Yol çalışması – Road works

Taşıt giremez – No entry

Tek yön – One-way street

Yol kapalı – Road closed

Hız kontrolü – Speed control area

Roundabouts & Traffic Lights

Roundabouts (*kavşak*) are often combined with traffic lights (*trafik*

ışıkları) at major junctions. You drive round anti-clockwise and give way to traffic as it joins the roundabout. Traffic lights flash a rapid green before turning amber then red. At night they may just flash a continuous amber or red to warn drivers to take care at a junction – it isn't compulsory to stop. Large cities may have 'countdown' lights, where you can expect much revving of engines as the numbers decrease.

Traffic Jams

If you live in a small town or village, you may never encounter queues of traffic, except on market day or when a favourite football team wins. However, in large cities they're inevitable. Traffic jams have many causes, from accidents to bad parking, but often result simply from too much traffic for the road system to cope with. This is especially true of Istanbul, where the bridges across the Bosporus and the roads which run along its shorelines become almost impassable during the lengthy rush hours and at weekends.

> Driving in Istanbul is a particular skill in itself, where you have to be both defensive and assertive at the same time; hesitate for a moment and you'll be engulfed by impatient drivers. Fortunately, Istanbul has a fairly good public transport system.

Parking

The larger the city, the harder it is to find a parking space. That said, Turks can squeeze their vehicles into the smallest of places. Some cities now have parking meters, although it's more usual for the *zabita* (council police) to patrol the streets and charge fees for on-street parking. Almost all towns have areas designated as car parks, which range from rough patches of land to multi-storey or underground car parks, some of which have an attendant who will take your keys and move your car as necessary to maximise the use of space. Some are free (*ücretsiz*) but most charge a small fee (*ücretli*).

Double Parking & Illegal Parking

There's a law against double parking, just as there's a law against leaving your hazard warning lights flashing while you pop into the shops, but everyone does it. If you return to your car to find it boxed in, try sounding your horn continuously. If you don't attract the driver you may well attract the police, who may tow the offending vehicle away.

If you park illegally in cities and busy resorts, you may have your vehicle towed away. The police can tell you the location of the local car pound and you'll have to pay for the tow truck as well as the parking fine (the latter will be at least €27, while the cost of the former varies).

Petrol Stations & Repair Shops

Petrol stations (*benzin istasyonu*) are plentiful in western Turkey, but less so in central and eastern areas, therefore you need to fill up when you can. As in most other countries, three kinds of fuel are available: standard (*süper*), unleaded (*kurşunsuz*) and diesel (*motorin*). There's no longer a state monopoly on petrol sales and you'll see BP and Shell garages alongside *Petrol Ofisi*. Few stations are self service – you sit back while an attendant tops up the tank, cleans the windscreen and brings your change. Some offer a free car wash, tea or coffee and there's always a toilet (take your own paper just in case).

But the service has a sting – Turkish petrol is among the most expensive in the world. At over €1.60 per litre it's on a par with British prices and four times higher than in the US. To combat the high costs many cars have been converted to run on liquid petroleum gas (LPG).

If you have a breakdown or need repairs, the place to go is the *sanayi* – an industrial area on the outskirts of town where you'll find all manner of Mr Fixits. Turkish mechanics have a reputation for being able to solve almost any car problem with a screwdriver and a bit of wire – at least in the short term! Repairs to local models are inexpensive as labour costs are low, but parts are costly for imported cars.

PUBLIC TRANSPORT

Turkish public transport is cheap and surprisingly reliable and unless you

live in an out-of-the-way village, a car is rarely a necessity. Public transport isn't just a great way to get around but also provides an insight into the Turkish psyche.

A few general points apply to most types of transport:

- Smoking is banned on most public transport – unless you're the driver.
- You must carry ID on all journeys.
- Tickets can be booked at airports and stations, and through agents, who often charge a small commission.
- All transport companies have a website and tickets can be booked online – in theory. In practice, many websites are slow and difficult to use, and you may have to register to book online and conduct your transactions in Turkish.
- At holiday times seats fill up fast, especially if there are offers – so book your ticket well in advance.

Taxis

Like New York cabs, Turkish taxis (*taksi*) are yellow. There are around 18,000 in Istanbul alone and every

village has a taxi driver (*taksici*). Scruffy old Fiats are being replaced by smart new people-movers, and these can be hailed on the street, picked up at a rank or called by phone. All have meters, which drivers are required by law to use, although they may have to be persuaded. For longer trips you can negotiate a fare.

Turkish drivers have a reputation for driving like Michael Schumacher, although not quite as skilfully, and most are courteous and helpful, but there are a few rogues. A favourite trick is to switch the meter rate to 'night' (*Gece*) for daytime trips, increasing the fare by 50 per cent – between 6am and midnight, ensure it reads 'daytime' (*Gündüz*). A few drivers prey on tourists and take you via the 'scenic' route, although some are out-of-town drivers whose Turkish pride prevents them from admitting that they don't know the way!

Fares are reasonable and you should expect to pay around €3.50 for a 15-minute journey. Tipping isn't compulsory and most passengers simply round up the fare.

Planes

New low-cost airlines are shaking up domestic air travel, and Atlasjet, Pegasus and Onur Air are proving to be stiff competition for Turkish Airlines. In some cases their fares are half that of the national carrier, but they sometimes fly into secondary airports, such as Istanbul's Sabiha Gökçen – on the Asian side – so you need to factor in the extra time and cost of transfers. In 2008, Turkish Airlines announced that it was launching its own low-cost airline.

Here are a few things you need to know about air travel in Turkey:

- Istanbul is the undisputed hub for domestic journeys and fewer routes connect through Ankara. If you want to fly across the country, e.g. from Bodrum in the south-west to Trabzon on the Black Sea, you may have to change planes at Istanbul.

- Domestic flights can work out more expensive if you book them from outside Turkey. Turkish Airlines has an excellent website, although flights with other companies are best booked through an agent.

- The cheapest fares are off-peak and at night.

- It's difficult to get from the 'tourist' airports to the coastal resorts by public transport, and taxis are expensive, sometimes costing as much as the air fare. Istanbul's Atatürk International is a surprisingly cheap airport to arrive at, from where a metro journey into the city costs just €2.

- The Havaş Bus is a shuttle service which links airports to city centres and nearby resorts. It operates from many airports, including Dalaman, Bodrum

and Antalya, and is timed to connect with domestic flights.

- English is spoken at airports catering to tourists and announcements are also made in English. Smaller airports may only have Turkish-speaking staff.

- Airport food is expensive. For example, a Burger King meal at Dalaman Airport costs more than €11, twice as much as in a town-centre fast-food outlet.

Buses

Cheap fares, frequent departures and a network linking every town in Turkey make bus travel the most popular choice for long-distance journeys. Trips can be very long, for example, it takes 14 hours to travel from Istanbul to Fethiye in the south, but buses are modern and comfortable and it's possible to sleep through overnight trips. The bus experience is a real adventure, shared by people from all walks of life, as you watch Turkey unfold from your seat.

- Bus journeys begin at an *otogar* or bus station. Every town has one, with colourful ticket desks, fast-food vendors, shoe-shine boys and lottery-ticket sellers, and it's worth visiting one just to soak up the atmosphere. The main Büyük Otogar in Istanbul is a city in itself, with more than 150 ticket desks and even its own metro station and mosque.

- Many bus stations are outside the city, but you can buy your ticket (*bilet*) from a central office and take a free bus to the *otogar*.

- There's a huge choice of bus companies, each with its own offices and departure bays (*peron*). The best, in terms of comfort and safety, are

the established names such as Kamil Koç, Ulusoy (🖳 www.ulusoy.com.tr/eng) and Varan (🖳 www.varan.com.tr/english/default.asp). Some companies boast of their comfort and have airline-style seats.

- Prices are reasonable – roughly half the price of a comparable plane trip – and there are discounts for students. Children aged 6 to 12 travel half price and those under six can travel free on a parent's lap.

- The best seats are usually halfway down the bus. You should avoid the seats at the front, which have limited legroom, are too close to the TV screen and are exposed to the lights of oncoming traffic at night. Turks hate draughts and don't want to sit opposite the centre stairs, so if you sit there you may get two seats to yourself.

- Many buses don't have toilets but stop every few hours en route. The rest stops are also a chance to eat, shop and – vital for Turks – make mobile phone calls. Mobiles must be switched off while the bus is moving – supposedly because they interfere with the controls but the ban also prevents disturbances from incessant and loud phone conversations!

> Touts swarm at large bus stations, steering tourists to 'their' bus company. This may not be the best choice for you as it may mean changing buses or even ending up in a different town, waiting for a non-existent service bus. Your fate doesn't concern the tout, who will have pocketed his commission long before you reach your destination.

Trains

Slow, dirty, unreliable and with a limited network, Turkish trains have lost much of their glamour since the days of the (original) Orient Express. However, some of the major lines are being updated to carry high-speed trains, and the advantage over buses is that you have more room, plus access to dining and sleeping cars. Rail travel is also the cheapest way to get around Turkey.

- The main train routes are those linking Istanbul, Ankara and Izmir with each other and with the east. There are no tracks along the Black Sea or the Mediterranean coasts.

- The best trains are the express (*ekspresi*) trains, although 'express' is a relative term. The Ankara Ekspresi is an all-sleeping-car train which takes ten hours to cover the 450km (280mi) between Istanbul and the capital, and it takes nearly two days to get from Istanbul to Van in Turkey's far south-eastern corner – a journey of around 1,600km (1,000mi). Ordinary passenger trains are even slower.

- The operator of all rail services is Turkish State Railways (*Türkiye Cumhuriyeti Devlet Demiryollari or TCDD*). Tickets are sold at stations or by TCDD-approved agents and you cannot reserve seats more than two weeks before the travel date.

- Sleeping cars (*yataklı vagon*) save you the cost of a hotel room and accommodate up to three people; beds are comfortable and some of the newer trains have carriages with showers. The cost for two people travelling one way on the Ankara Ekspresi is around €60.

- Discounts available include 20 per cent for over-60s and 20 per cent for a return (*gidiş-dönüş*) ticket. For frequent travellers, 30-day Train Tour Cards are a good investment. Children under eight travel free.

In November 2007, a one-way journey between Istanbul and Izmir cost the following:

By plane – from €52 with Turkish Airlines;

By bus – from €24 with Kamil Koç;

By ferry and train – from €24 crossing the Sea of Marmara to Bandırma and then taking the an 'express' train.

City & Town Transport

Buses and *dolmuş* minibuses are the main forms of transport in towns, but the choice is wider in the major cities:

- **Istanbul** – There are numerous city buses and some truly antiquated trains. There's also the Tünel, a two-stop underground line, and a tramway, both dating from the 19th century, which ply the sleep hill between the Galata Bridge and Taksim Square. More modern options include a funicular, a cable car and an expanding tram and metro system. The best way to cross the Bosporus is by ferry. For all public transport in Istanbul, you must buy tickets (or, in many cases, tokens) in advance, rather than paying on board. One of the best deals in Istanbul is the Akbil transit pass, which is valid on all local transport and works out 10 per cent cheaper than individual fares.

- **Ankara** – The city has two metro lines, one of which serves the main bus terminal. Discounts are available if you buy more than five tickets.

- **Izmir** – There's an east-west metro line as well as trains between the city centre and the airport. Ferries connect the waterfront to some residential suburbs.

Dolmuş

Where the bus routes end, the minibus (*dolmuş*) takes over. This ubiquitous mode of transport carries people, luggage, even livestock, to every corner of Turkey, no matter how remote. It also provides a good alternative to city buses and taxis. A *dolmuş* is generally a minibus, although in a few places you may still find large saloon cars in service (*taksi dolmuş*), a reminder of the days when American sedans were used. Whatever the vehicle, the service is the same. A *dolmuş* rarely runs to a timetable but leaves when it's full. Fares are set, as on a bus, but stops aren't. You can flag it down anywhere and if there's room, the driver will squeeze you in and you can get off wherever you want.

> Never ask a *dolmuş* driver to change a large-denomination note.

ON FOOT

To be a pedestrian in Turkey requires nerves of steel, lightning reactions and impeccable judgement. Here are a couple of points to be particularly aware of:

- **Crossing the road** – By law, motorists must stop at a pedestrian crossing but often they don't, especially if there are no lights. Only cross if cars have plenty of time to stop. At a crossing controlled by traffic lights, even if you have the green light, make sure that all traffic is going to stop before you step out. If there's a bridge or underpass, it's advisable to use it.

- **On the pavement** – Potholes aren't confined to roads. Many pavements (*kaldırım*) have broken paving stones, bits of pipe sticking up, open manhole covers and other obstacles. Cars are routinely parked on pavements and slippery tiles and high steps down to the road level are additional hazards. Many rural roads have no footpaths at all and you should wear something bright when walking at night.

Belly dancer

8.
THE TURKS AT PLAY

Becoming socially adept in a different culture is perhaps the greatest challenge in your bid to 'fit in' abroad, as you're most likely to do the wrong thing when in company. The Turks are extremely cordial people so you'll find yourself in many – sometimes awkward – group situations.

To help you avoid social gaffes, this chapter contains information on how to dress, what to do (and what not to do) when dining out (and when entertaining), when and what to drink, and where to eat, smoke and dance. It also explains what happens at important family events and on religious holidays, and describes the most popular Turkish sports and cultural activities.

'The world was my oyster but I used the wrong fork.'
Oscar Wilde (English author)

DRESS CODE

Turks dress up, not down. People are judged (or think they're judged) on their appearance, so a scruffy, down-at-heel look suggests you're unwell, impoverished or an eccentric foreigner. Almost everyone, irrespective of income, makes a huge effort to dress well, especially on the main religious holidays or when attending a major social event.

Turks enjoy fashion (*moda*) and like their clothes to have the 'right' label. Areas such as Bağdat Caddesi in Istanbul are as stylish as Paris's Rue du Faubourg Saint Honoré or London's Bond Street – and the fashions on offer range from revealing miniskirts to conservative turbans (a more demure alternative to the headscarf). Away from the capital, people still follow fashion trends, rummaging at the weekly market for 'designer' gear.

Top fashion labels include Boyner, Damat and Vakko. There are many well known fashion designers, including Hussein Chayalan and Rıfat Özbek – both of whom trained in the UK and have won the title of British Designer of the Year.

Although village women dress alike, in layers of loose trousers (*şalvar*), tunic and waistcoat, they express their individuality with their scarf – and there are many ways to tie it. All have special clothes for special events.

It's only in areas where package tourism dominates that shorts and T-shirts are standard wear and beach clothes appear on the street – and even here, the more smartly dressed people are invariably Turkish.

Home

Turks have indoor clothes and outdoor clothes and they may wear a comfortable old tracksuit in the house, but change to go out, even if it's only to the shops. They don't want to be seen in their house clothes, therefore you should avoid surprise visits.

Religious Places

Everyone visiting a mosque, tomb or cemetery dresses with respect; even women who don't usually wear a scarf will cover their heads in a mosque or at a religious event such as a *mevlut* (a gathering to remember the dead). Never enter a mosque in 'holiday clothes'; legs, arms and shoulders must be covered, and women should cover their head, and you must leave your shoes outside.

Social Occasions

If you're invited to a wedding or any major social event, you should always dress well. Turks pull out all the stops, and so should you. Women often invest in a new outfit with matching accessories, while men always wear a suit and tie, and children appear as miniature versions of their parents. Never mind that it costs a week's wages, it's unimportant when set against the respect gained from their peers.

Work

Turkish workers dress smartly, especially in an office, bank or customer-service environment. This means suits and ties for male workers, and suits or smart separates for female staff – many women wear trousers for comfort and decency. The western concept of a 'dress-down' Friday doesn't exist.

Grooming

Cleanliness is next to godliness in Islam, and for many Turks the idea of going out unshaven or with 'bed hair' is as unthinkable as wearing dirty shoes. The hairdresser (*kuaför*) and barber (*berber*) are social hubs, and unisex salons are rare. Grooming is a private affair, and it's imperative that the opposite sex sees only the result and not the work which went into it.

Many men visit the barber every day, where a shave is a self-indulgent experience and includes a head and shoulder massage followed by a splash of refreshing lemon cologne. Women visit the hairdresser regularly, not just for a cut but to have their hair washed and blow-dried. They like big, fluffy hairdos held rock solid with hairspray – think Sue Ellen from *Dallas*.

Hairdressers can be scissor-happy and it's a good idea to go by recommendation. If your language skills are weak, take a picture or show them how many 'fingers' of length you want cut.

> Many barbers use an old-fashioned cut-throat razor and remove excess ear hair with a flick of a lighted flame, which is alarming rather than painful. Another curiosity is threading, whereby beauticians tweak out stubborn hairs with a loop of fine cotton. This is painful.

EATING

Mealtimes are occasions to be savoured rather than pit stops during a busy day, and Turks make time to sit down and eat and don't like to be interrupted. Few people skip breakfast; banks and government offices close for lunch and workmen down tools to eat.

The weather and the region determine what's on the plate. Chilli and spices are popular in the south-east, fish is important along the Black Sea coast and olive oil is a mainstay in the Aegean. Meals are light during summer in the Mediterranean and robust in the central Anatolian winter.

You'll spend a lot of time eating with Turkish people, and knowing what to expect and how to behave will make this an even more enjoyable experience.

Meals

Breakfast

Turks eat breakfast early – around 7am. Typically, it consists of olives, tomatoes, cucumber, fresh white cheese (similar, but in most Turks' opinion superior, to Greek feta), eggs (boiled or fried), yoghurt and preserves, such as local honey and rose-petal jam. The essential ingredient is bread, lots of it – if you're lucky, you'll sample traditional bread, baked on a metal plate (*tava*) over an open fire, or *gözleme* pancakes, which are a feature of restaurants offering a 'village breakfast'. Although the Turkish word for breakfast (*kahvaltı*) translates as 'after coffee', most Turks wash it all down with tea.

Lunch

After such a generous breakfast, a large lunch isn't necessary, and it's the smallest meal of the day. There's usually just one course, e.g. Turkish omelette (*menemen*) or a dish of beans and rice, eaten between 12 and 2pm, either at home or at *lokanta* (local eating place). Most *lokantas* offer a 'takeaway' service, where a boy delivers all the courses, condiments and cutlery to the customer's office.

Dinner

This is the highlight of the day; several hours go into its preparation and the whole family sits down together, usually between 6.30 and 8pm. There are a number of dishes, either served in courses or brought to the table all at once, which include soup, a meat dish, vegetable dishes, a salad, yoghurt, and rice or pasta. Bread is always served. There's often more on standby in the kitchen in case there are last-minute guests.

Due to the size of the main meal, there's often a break before dessert, which consists of fresh fruit, sticky pastries such as *baklava*, and milk-based puddings (a famous one features chicken breast!).

Restaurant meals are served in courses – soup, followed by hot and cold *meze* (see below), then the main course. Diners may take a walk after dinner before going to a pudding shop (*muhallebici*) for dessert and Turkish coffee.

Meze

Meze are appetisers or hors d'oeuvres (in the English, not French, sense) – similar to Spanish *tapas*, which accompany drinks. However, like *tapas*, they've become a meal in themselves. There's a huge variety of hot and cold *meze* on offer at most restaurants, including the following:

- *acılı ezme* – a spicy tomato dip with hot chillies;

- *cacık* – yoghurt 'soup' with cucumber and mint;

- *dolma* – vegetables or vine leaves stuffed with rice or meat. *Dolma* translates as 'stuffed thing'.

- *kısır* – similar to Lebanese *tabbouleh*, bulgur wheat mixed with tomato, onion and handfuls of parsley and mint;

- *patlıcan salatası* – roasted aubergine or eggplant, served cold;

- *sigara böreği* – tubes of deep-fried pastry stuffed with cheese and herbs. The name comes from their resemblance to cigarettes.

Bread

Bread is the 'national food' of Turkey. It's served with every meal, and the average family gets through four loaves a day. Eating bread is a sociable activity and only formal (or tourist) restaurants serve bread rolls on individual plates. Most present it sliced in a basket, while those with a bread oven may serve *lavaş*, a long, puffed-up flatbread similar to pita bread. You take a portion with your fingers, then tear off smaller pieces to eat; Turks never cut bread with a knife. It's acceptable to use your bread to mop up your food.

Bread should always be treated with respect. The custom, should you drop a piece, is to pick it up, kiss it and touch it to your forehead before replacing it on the table.

Seating

The sexes are usually separated in Turkish culture, so couples may be seated side by side but with men next to men and women alongside women. The host sits at the head of the table, while the hostess is closest to the kitchen. An old-fashioned seating arrangement has all the men on one side of the table and all the women on the other. Segregation may be taken to extremes in rural areas, with men eating at the table and women (and children) on the floor, often in another room. This creates problems of what to do with foreign female guests, who are sometimes seated with the men. Always wait to be seated so you don't mistakenly take the wrong place.

Cutlery

Cutlery (silverware) is always used, with knives and forks placed on the right and left of your plate, with soup and dessert spoons above. You use the outermost and topmost implements first. Less exclusive restaurants supply one service and replace cutlery between courses. Always use cutlery if it's provided – even for fruit and cake.

> Turkey's famous *Maraş* 'ice cream' can be eaten only with a knife and fork. Its consistency is firm and chewy, due to a special ingredient called *salep* – the dried root of the wild orchid – which prevents it from melting. The result is so elastic that it's hung on meat hooks for storage.

If you're served seafood, chicken legs or corn on the cob – something which is easier to eat with your hands – wait to see how other diners tackle it. Many people prefer to eat fish with their hands, as it's easier to deal with the bones. Bread is always eaten with the hands. .

In more casual settings, Turks eat with a fork and spoon – or just a spoon and a piece of bread, which is used to push food onto the spoon or to dip into a communal plate. Fast food can be eaten with your fingers.

When you've finished eating, you should indicate this by crossing your knife and fork on your plate.

When to Start

The meal begins once everyone is served and in traditional households young people wait for their elders to start. At a dinner party, your hostess may insist you don't wait for her, especially if she's busy serving a lot of dishes – take your cue from your host. He or she will say '*Afiyet olsun'* which is the equivalent of the French '*Bon appétit*', to which the correct response is '*Elinize sağlık*', which means 'health to your hand'.

Table Manners

Turks keep their hands above the table while eating. They lean across to take things rather than asking other diners to pass them, and will stand up if necessary. If you're seated on the floor, try to keep your feet tucked out of sight and cover your lap with a corner of the tablecloth. Smokers light cigarettes between courses – if you're a non-smoker, you just have to put up with it. Turks will also answer their mobile phones during a meal, although for a long conversation they generally leave the table.

Noises

It's rude to cough or blow your nose loudly at the table. If a cough or a sneeze cannot be avoided, try to do it discreetly – cover your mouth with a napkin. Burping and passing wind are also impolite, when you should apologise quietly or excuse yourself and go outside.

Toasts

Turks toast each other's honour, rather than their health, by saying *Şerefe* or, more politely, *Şerefinize*. There may be many spontaneous toasts throughout the meal, in proportion to the amount of alcohol being consumed, and each demands that you clink your glass with all the other drinkers – even those at the far end of the table. It's considered bad manners to put your glass back down without first taking a sip.

Rakı is the unofficial national drink of Turkey. It's a clear and potent spirit (up to 50 per cent alcohol) with a strong aniseed taste. It's known as lion's milk (*aslan sütü*), a reference to its milky appearance when water or ice are added – and to the fact that it's a drink for strong men!

> '**Listen a hundred times; ponder a thousand times; speak once.'**
>
> Turkish proverb

Conversation

Conversation is often loud and animated. What you talk about depends on how well you know your hosts, but will probably include the weather, family, children, local issues, sport – and your views on Turkey. Take care to give a positive impression. You'll also be asked about your home country – Turks are fascinated by foreign countries and will ask you how much things cost and what people earn. There are certain taboo subjects which you should not raise (see **Taboos** in **Chapter 4)** and if they crop up in conversation you should try to avoid commenting or remain neutral.

hookah water pipe

DRINKING & SMOKING

Alcohol is more widely accepted in Turkey than in many other Muslim countries, and beer, wine and spirits are readily available in western cities and tourist areas. Turks who have contact with foreigners are more likely to drink alcohol. Otherwise, few people drink (least of all women), most restaurants don't serve alcohol and you can buy it only from shops which are licensed to sell the government-owned Tekel brands. Look for the Tekel *Bayii* (vendor) sign. Under-18s aren't permitted to purchase alcohol.

There are those who believe that drinking is becoming less socially acceptable in Turkey. Successive governments have raised taxes on alcohol and a bottle of spirits is now beyond the budget of many people and a can of beer is now cheaper in a British supermarket than in Turkey.

Politics aside, Turkish people don't need to drink in order to have fun – there's no culture of getting drunk, let alone of binge drinking, and major social events, such as weddings, are often 'dry'. Turks don't understand why many foreign cultures revolve around alcohol and they have a low tolerance for drunkenness. If a Turk drinks to excess, he brings shame on his family, while if a foreigner drinks to excess he will gain a reputation that will be difficult to shake off.

> According to a 2003 World Health Survey, in a sample of more than 6,000 Turkish women interviewed, 92 per cent said they'd never tried alcohol.

Smoking

Turks are among the heaviest smokers in the world – some 40 per cent smoke and one in five deaths are estimated to be smoking-related. Such is Turkey's reputation for cigarette consumption that in many countries, a heavy smoker is said to 'smoke like a Turk'. Cigarettes are cheap in comparison to Europe and the US, and there's little social stigma attached to smoking, although young people may avoid lighting up in the presence of elders, out of respect.

The idea of an outright ban on smoking is inconceivable to most Turks, but in 2008 the government passed new legislation to ban it in all indoor public places, including restaurants, bars and cafes. This was an extension to the law already in place to prevent smoking in state buildings and public transport and the new law is expected to come into force in 2009.

CAFES & BARS

Turkey doesn't have a lively bar and café scene, in the way that Europe does. The widest choice of bars is found in Istanbul, Ankara and Izmir – some are traditional, others chic – and in tourist resorts, which overflow with 'English' pubs and cocktail bars. Coffee culture is slowly infiltrating Turkey. Starbucks and Gloria Jeans have opened outlets in Istanbul and Ankara, and many imitations have followed. The modern, alcohol-free environment is fashionable with women and young people. Starbucks and Gloria Jeans serve traditional Turkish coffee alongside their branded cappuccinos and lattes.

Thankfully, there are some uniquely Turkish places where people go to drink and socialise, which include:

- *çay bahçesi* **(tea garden)** – Popular with families and often run by the municipality, they're usually near the mosque, therefore alcohol is off the menu.

- *kahvehane* **(coffee house)** – all-male domains where, despite their name, the drink of choice is tea;

- *meyhane* – Turkey's answer to an American bar or British pub. A *meyhane* can be a slightly seedy male enclave, although those in Istanbul's Beyoğlu district are popular with couples and serve good food.

- *şarap evi* **(wine house)** – a stylish alternative to a *meyhane*.

- *nargile kahvehanesi* **(water-pipe café)** – A fashionable recreation in Ottoman times, the *nargile* (water-pipe or hookah) is enjoying a revival, particularly among students. Some *nargile cafés* (as they're called by young people) are located in attractive courtyards; a few stay open 24 hours and, in a change from the past, welcome women as well as men.

Most cafés open from 9am to 9pm, bars and *meyhaneler* from midday until the early hours, while tea gardens close at sunset and the *kahvehane* shuts when the last customer goes home. Some roadside restaurants and those at airports and bus stations are open 24 hours, while businesses in resorts remain open as long as possible to catch the passing trade. Self-service is rare and even the smallest café has a waiter who takes your order and brings the bill.

RESTAURANTS

Eating out is cheap in comparison to most western countries, and there's an abundance of choice. Istanbul is the place to find world food, including Thai, French and Italian cuisine, and has some five-star restaurants with five-star prices to match. Turkish restaurants in tourist towns may try to imitate foreign dishes, although few succeed.

A simple restaurant is known as a *lokanta* and often serves *sulu yemek:* literally 'wet food', a reference to the trays of soups and stews kept on the go all day. These venues are popular with local people, workers and canny foreigners. Some of the nicest places to eat are outdoors – on a terrace overlooking the Bosporus or in a rural trout restaurant, where you can lounge on cushions over-looking running water.

Wherever you choose to eat, bear in mind the following:

● **Opening hours** – Most restaurants open from 11am until midnight, though some are open for breakfast. In provincial towns, restaurants

may have set hours – 12-2.30pm for lunch, 5.30-8.30pm for dinner – and some workers' restaurants are open at lunchtimes only. In resort areas, many eateries close for the winter.

● **Booking** – Usually necessary only for top city restaurants, or at busy times such as Sundays and on major holidays, when it's best to check, and book, by telephone. Some out-of-the-way restaurants offer a complimentary *servis* bus to pick up customers and return them home.

● **Seating** – The waiter will show you to a table, although you can request a specific place – e.g. on the terrace or near the fire – if there's a table free. Some provincial restaurants are full of men, but there's usually a family room (*aile salon*) where single women will feel more comfortable.

● **Table settings** – Top restaurants have full silver service, but in a *lokanta* the table may be bare except for salt, pepper, lemon juice, dried chillies and paper napkins (cloth napkins are rare). A few restaurants impose a charge (*giriş ücreti*) to cover the cost of bread.

● **Menu** – You may have to ask for the menu (*yemek listesi*). Turks would rather see food than read about it, so *meze*, meat and fish are displayed in a chilled cabinet, while in a *lokanta*, food is kept on hot tables. If there's a menu, it's divided into soup, hot and cold *meze*, main courses (*ana yemek*), salads and desserts. It's advisable to order *meze* and decide on a main course later. There's no pressure to order more food, even if others are having a full meal, and all restaurants provide children's portions.

> Turkish dishes have some highly descriptive names, such as 'ladies' thighs' (*kadın budu* – a plump meatball with rice), 'the priest fainted' (*imam bayıldı* – an aubergine dish lavished with olive oil) and a hat-shaped pastry called 'twisted turban' (*sarığıburma*).

● **Service** – This is attentive, sometimes obsequious but rarely rude. Most waiters are knowledgeable and professional; others are willing but less able, and spend a lot of time tidying tables. There may be several waiters at your table but rarely a waitress – waiting isn't a profession that's popular with women.

● On the rare occasion that you need to summon a waiter, call '*Garson!*' or '*Bakar mısınız!*' ('Come here, please'). If service is slow, it may be due to delays in the kitchen – food is usually cooked to order – or because staff don't want to rush you. Dishes are often served lukewarm as Turks don't especially like piping hot food and some think it's unhealthy.

● If you have a complaint, never rebuke the waiter in the restaurant as this will cause him to lose face. Instead, have a quiet word with the manager (*patron*), who will do his best to ensure that you have good reason to return.

● **Water** – In a basic *lokanta* there will be a jug of tap water (*çeşme suyu*) on the table; in a restaurant you'll be given bottled water (*kapalı su* or 'sealed water') and charged for it. Most Turks prefer bottled water and, given the sometimes dubious quality of tap water, it's a more sensible option.

● **Bill** – You must ask for the bill – say '*Hesap lütfen*'. It will arrive in a glass or a fancy box, folded so that your guests cannot see how much the meal cost. Check to see if a service charge is included – if it is the bill will state '*servis dahil*' and around 10 per cent will be added to the total. If it isn't, and you're happy with the service, you can leave a tip – see **Tipping** in **Chapter 10**.

Fast Food

Turkish fast food is a world away from burgers and fried chicken pieces. Some of the best 'fast food' meals can be   found in small,

unassuming eateries or bought from simple stalls. Many specialise in just one type of food but do it extremely well. When ordering, you can ask for a single portion of food or, if you're hungry, '*bir buçuk porsiyon*', which is half as much again. Some good fast-food options include:

● *pideci* – serves fresh Turkish pizza (*pide*), which is lighter than the Italian version. The boat-shaped *pide* is rolled out and topped with minced meat, cheese or any other topping and cooked in a bread oven. An alternative is *lahmacun*, a thin meat pizza which you roll up and eat with lemon.

● *köfteci* – specialises in meatballs (*köfte*), small and juicy and served sprinkled with cumin and chilli pepper. There are as many different meatballs as there are regions, and Turks will drive great distances for good *köfte*.

● *kebabcı* – home of the revolving *döner* kebab. The kebab originated with Turkish nomads, who speared pieces of meat on their swords to cook over an open fire, although the word refers to almost any dish in which the main ingredient is meat.

● *pastane* – a patisserie selling cakes, biscuits and elaborate gateaux, as well as a variety of *börek*, savoury pastries stuffed with meat and cheese;

● *çorbacı* – soup shops open 24 hours a day. Try chicken, lentil or (if you're brave) tripe soup – the last is said to be a good remedy for a hangover.

On any Turkish street, you're rarely more than five minutes away from food. Some of the best are hot chestnuts, grilled corn, stuffed mussels and, for the adventurous, *kokoreç* (grilled sheep's intestines) and

ciğ köfte (Turkish steak tartare). One of Istanbul's most famous street-food options is a hot fish sandwich sold from a boat by the Galata Bridge.

NIGHTLIFE

Istanbul has a thriving club scene with hundreds of clubs – disco, techno, gay and straight – as well as atmospheric music bars and many lively *meyhaneler* (see **Cafés & Bars** above). Bodrum is where Turkish celebrities take their holidays and is home to Halıkarnas, one of the largest open-air nightclubs in the world. Away from these centres of nocturnal fun, much of Turkey is in bed by midnight, although there are two uniquely Turkish after-hours venues:

● *Türkü bar* – This specialises in Anatolian folk songs played on traditional instruments such as the *saz* (a Turkish lute). The clientele join in with singing and dancing, which is spontaneous and completely unselfconscious.

● *gazino* – a venue for cabaret-style entertainment, and not for gambling. Most are family-friendly places where people go to watch their favourite arabesque singers (see **Icons** in **Chapter 2**) and Oriental (belly) dancers.

Some Turkish nightlife is more seedy than sophisticated. Women should avoid the male-dominated *birahane* (beer hall) and men may wish to steer clear of the *pavyon*, which is a sleazy 'hostess club' where foreign men sometimes fall victim to scams (see Crime in Chapter 10).

Music bars and *gazinoler* open in the evening, but most nightclubs don't get going until 11pm and keep going until 5am – or 2am if they're likely to keep nearby residents awake. Clients must be aged 18 and you may be asked for proof of age. Most clubs have a dress policy, which is stricter for men than for women – *halıkarnas* (nightclubs) asks customers to 'dress for the occasion'. There are doormen (or bouncers) who can and do refuse entry to people they don't like the look of (usually single men who have had a few drinks) and they have a tough reputation, deservedly so as fights occasionally break out in provincial clubs.

Alcohol is expensive – at from €5 a drink – with imported spirits and cocktails costing even more. Some nightclubs have an entry charge, which can be as high as €20, although it usually includes a drink. You can pay for drinks at the bar, but if you're seated at a table your bill will be presented at the end of the evening. Turks don't buy rounds but may split the final bill, although if the night out was your idea you may be expected to pay for everyone! In some clubs, drinks may appear inexpensive but beware of the trimmings. These include any nuts, dried chickpeas, sticks of cucumber and carrots, all of which may arrive un-ordered at your table and aren't complimentary, and will add a sizeable amount to your bill.

FAMILY EVENTS

In Turkey, the family comes first, and most celebrations mark important family events, which include quiet and private occasions and large social gatherings. The most important life events and celebrations are listed below.

Births

The birth of a baby is the most significant occasion in many Turks' lives, especially a first born or a long-awaited grandchild. There's still a slight preference for boys in rural areas but urban parents welcome either sex. Islam's version of a christening is a baby-naming ceremony, in which the *imam* or a relative reads from the Koran and whispers the baby's name three times into the its right ear.

In villages it's traditional for the grandparents to decide on a name, but urban couples prefer to choose their own; as a compromise, a child may have two names. Turkish names are significant. Some are religious, such as Ramazan (for a boy born during the month of fasting), while others are descriptive, such as Birgül ('a rose'). A few are frank and to the point – Yeter ('enough') for the last in a succession of girls or even İmdat ('help') for the last in a line of boys after, presumably, a difficult birth!

The conventional 'lying in' time is 40 days, with mother and baby confined to the house. Visitors are welcome a few days after the birth, when female relatives man the stove and fuss around mother and baby like a flock of hens – there's never a shortage of babysitters.

Remember to say '*Maşallah*' when you go to see a baby, which is a request for Allah's protection – older people believe that if you heap too much admiration on a baby, an evil spirit (*jinn*) may try to steal the child. Customary gifts include gold coins and trinkets, especially those with a *nazar* bead to deflect the evil eye. Baby clothes and accessories are equally welcome.

> **Turks don't bother celebrating birthdays and probably won't acknowledge yours – many older Turks don't even know their date of birth. In the past, villagers registered a birth when it suited them and would sometimes hold back from doing so to delay a son's eligibility for military service.**

Circumcision

This Muslim rite of passage is part of growing up for all Turkish boys – and only boys; there's no female circumcision in Turkey. The ceremony itself is the equivalent of a Jewish *bar mitzvah* or Christian confirmation, though very different from either. Circumcision (*sünnet*) is the surgical removal of the foreskin by a specialist surgeon, which can be performed at any time after birth but is usually done between the ages of around seven and nine.

Traditionally, it's a public event, the operation taking place on a table

surrounded by family and friends, although nowadays many parents prefer to have it done quietly in a clinic or at home, with a party afterwards.

Much tradition surrounds circumcision. The boy wears a white satin suit, with a cape, a feathered cap and a sash emblazoned with the word '*Maşallah*' for protection (see above). He tours the neighbourhood on a horse or, more usually, the bonnet of a car, accompanied by musicians. The circumcision follows, during which he's held by a close male relative or friend, whose role is similar to that of a godfather in a Christian baptism.

Once it's over, the boy reclines on a bed, the centre of attention, which is why boys look forward to their *sünnet* as much as they dread it! Gifts are given to the boy to distract him from the discomfort and also to celebrate the event. Appropriate gifts include gold, sweets and the latest toys, but it's normal to give a boy 'manly' items such as a watch, bicycle or toy gun.

If you're invited to a circumcision party in a village, be prepared to witness the full event, followed by refreshments. In a city setting, it will probably be more like a wedding party, the deed having been done in advance, with everyone dressed up and a banquet of food and drink. You should say '*Hayırlı olsun*' ('congratulations') to the parents and '*Geçmiş olsun*' ('may it [the pain] soon pass') to the boy.

Military Service

A young man's second rite of passage is his military service (*askerlik*), which is compulsory for all men aged between 20 and 40, and lasts for 15 months. It can be deferred, but not avoided, by full-time students; exemptions are made only on grounds of poor health. Men who delay their call-up may have difficulty obtaining a good job, a fiancée or a visa to travel abroad.

The draft isn't without its dangers, therefore the young soldiers visit all their family before they depart, to kiss their elders' hands and receive gifts. Their friends' farewell is less restrained – if you see a convoy of cars zooming around town, horns blaring, roofs draped with a Turkish flag, you can be sure one of the passengers is off to do his *askerlik*.

Soldiers are paid, but very little. If you know a young man who is off to perform his military service, it's a kind gesture to give him some money.

Engagement

As marriage unites two families, family approval is important. In the past, many marriages were arranged and the bride's family would negotiate a price for their girl, which still occur, especially in rural parts of eastern Turkey. A poll in *Hürriyet* newspaper in 1993 suggested that up to 70 per cent of marriages were 'arranged' – although 'introduced' might be a better word, as couples can (and do) say no.

> There's a quaint custom involving the *görücüler*, who's a women who visits the girl's home on behalf of the groom's family to decide if she's suitable bride material. A girl is (usually) free to turn down a suitor she hasn't seen or doesn't wish to see, the polite way being to put salt in the *görücüler*'s coffee!

Engagement (*nişan*) often begins with a formal family meeting, in which the man asks for permission to marry his sweetheart. It's followed by an engagement party – either a low-key family affair or a major celebration, akin to the wedding itself – when the couple exchange rings. The party is a dressy affair, with dancing, refreshments and gifts. As with other family celebrations, gold is a popular gift, as it can be sold in times of hardship. You should congratulate the couple with the word '*Tebrikler*'.

Weddings

A wedding (*düğün*) is a big deal in Turkey, and families spend a great deal of money on them – tribal weddings in south-eastern Turkey have been known to cost as much as €75,000. A wedding puts the whole family 'on show' and one that's talked about for months bestows maximum honour, whereas a small, discreet affair suggests there's something to be ashamed of.

Many weddings take place in September – rural people needed the

Roman Celcus Library, Ephesus

proceeds of the harvest to pay for the event – which could go on for up to nine days. Today, most couples marry over a weekend, and the procedure includes the henna night (see below), a civil ceremony and the wedding party.

Ceremony

All couples must undergo a civil ceremony, which is conducted by a registrar in a government office, or at the wedding party, in front of two witnesses. It's a brief but formal ceremony, and you may notice the couple trying to stamp on each other's feet as they sign the register – it's said that whoever does this first will have the upper hand in the marriage.

Some couples also undergo a religious ceremony at a mosque, but the marriage isn't recognised by law unless they also have a civil union. The age of consent is 18 and in 2006 the average age for marrying was 26 for men and 23 for women.

> ### Henna Night
>
> This women-only event takes place before the wedding, so that friends and family can wish the bride a happy marriage. Henna is daubed onto the attendees' hands, which is difficult to remove and marks you out as an important wedding guest.

Invitations

Joint invitations are sent out by the families. Some are 'open' invitations and there's no need to reply – in a village the event may even be announced over the local loudspeaker system so the entire neighbourhood can attend. If you know that the wedding will be a formal affair, with catering, it's polite to reply in writing or by telephone.

Gifts

The traditional wedding gift is money or gold and all wedding parties include a jewellery ceremony (*takı töreni*), when family and friends push gold bangles onto the bride's arms and pin banknotes onto sashes worn by bride and groom. When pinning on the money, you say '*Mutluluklar*' ('happiness'). Pinning on the money has a competitive edge and at some weddings the names of the givers (and the amount they give) are announced to the assembled company. As a foreigner, you'll be perceived to be rich and if you offer a small-denomination note the locals will think that you're mean!

At a city wedding, the currency of choice is dollars or euros and the couple may receive enough money to buy a car or put a down payment on an apartment – assuming they haven't been given these already by the family! Alternative gifts include household goods – from toasters to coffee sets. Some Western couples circulate a wedding-gift list.

Dress

Turks wear their very best outfits for a wedding. The bride usually wears a white 'meringue' dress (*gelinlik*) with a veil, although in rural areas she may wear a traditional folk costume in poppy red, while the groom always wears a dark suit and tie. Male guests wear suits and female guests cocktail or evening dresses – brand new and extensively accessorised. The men are freshly shaved, and the women, like the bride, spend hours at the hairdresser's and are often highly made up. You must make an effort with your dress, even for a village wedding – dress down and you'll feel distinctly out of place.

> A common congratulation to the happy couple is '*Allah bir yastıkda kocatsın*', which means 'May God let you grow old on one pillow'.

Key Players

Aside from the bride (*gelin*) and groom (*damat*), the following people have important roles at a Turkish wedding:

● **Bride's father** – looks after his daughter prior to handing her over to her husband. It's his task to tie a red ribbon (*bekâret*) around her waist to signify her virginity.

● **Bride's mother** – arranges the henna night (*kına gecesi* – see above).

● *Sağdıç* – a supportive role taken by friends of the couple, this is the

equivalent of the best man and maid (matron) of honour. They may also act as witnesses (*şahit*) at the civil ceremony.

Traditionally, the groom's family was responsible for organising – and paying for – the wedding, although nowadays the cost is often shared but the groom's parents may host a meal for family and friends. It's known as a *bayrak* (flag) ceremony after the tradition of raising a flag to signify the start of the wedding rites.

Procedure

You may be invited to the henna night and the civil ceremony, but the main event is the wedding party (*balo*) which usually happens on a Sunday evening in the village square, at a *düğün salonu* (wedding salon) or in a restaurant. In rural areas, the whole village attends, and much of the expense goes on hiring plastic chairs and a very loud band. Men and women sit separately and

refreshments are frugal – a carton of juice or some Turkish delight – so it's advisable to eat before you go. Sometimes, men fire guns to celebrate the occasion!

At the opposite end of the social scale, a posh Istanbul wedding takes place at a smart hotel, with mixed tables and a lavish spread of food and drink (sometimes including alcohol). Both events are characterised by deafening music and enthusiastic dancing.

> **The couple may tour the neighbourhood before the wedding party in a car decorated with the words 'Evleniyoruz' ('we are married'). Anyone who manages to stop the vehicle can ask for a gift or money.**

A wedding has a momentum of its own – exciting but bewildering for foreigners, and exhausting for the bride and groom. Chatter continues throughout the event, even when the couple are having photographs taken or cutting the cake. The noise of drum and clarinet is overwhelming and the dancing goes on until the early hours, although the bride and groom usually sneak away earlier, and no one will mind if you do also.

FUNERALS

News of a death travels quickly on the grapevine, and it's often announced from the local mosque. People hurry to pay their respects at the family home and it will be appreciated if you visit. Turks express their condolences with the words '*Basınız sağolsun*', which suggests that you hope they escape the same fate. The deceased are buried (never cremated) within a day or two of death, when the body is washed and wrapped in a white shroud before being carried to the mosque – you're expected to stop and stay silent if you see a cortège go past.

A funeral service (*cenaze töreni*) is conducted at a mosque, where the most important act is the discharge. The *imam* asks those attending what they thought of the deceased and they give a positive response. The body is then taken to be interred, usually at a municipal cemetery (*mezarlık*), where the deceased are always laid on their side, facing Mecca. There are no flowers or wreaths, instead of which people give a donation to charity or plant a tree in their loved one's memory.

In villages, only men attend a funeral, while the women mourn together at home, sometimes with loud wailing. Elsewhere, both sexes attend. If you knew the deceased well, your presence will be welcome, although a foreign female attending a male Turk's funeral may raise eyebrows. It's accepted that both sexes attend a foreigner's funeral.

Cremation isn't yet an option in Turkey, although with the large number of aging foreigners, a crematorium is sure to open soon. When foreigners die, they can repatriated or buried, either in a non-Muslim section of a Muslim cemetery, or in one set aside for those of other religions. If you intend to live out your life in Turkey, you should consider your options and make plans in advance.

There are many superstitions involving animals and death. It's said that if a dog howls during the call to prayer, it heralds a death, and if an owl hoots while perching on the roof of a house, one of the inhabitants will die.

Dress

Funeral dress is conservative and reverential, usually dark colours, with men wearing a suit and tie and women covering their heads. Widows don't wear black for an extended period of mourning as they do, for example, in Greece.

Remembrance

The deceased is remembered on the 7th, 40th and 52nd day after death, and there may also be an annual remembrance, which are known as a *mevlut*. Friends and neighbours eat together and celebrate their loved one's life and then the *imam* recites prayers. Dress is conservative, as it is for a funeral, and most women wear a scarf. If you're invited, you should greet the deceased's family with the words '*Allah kabul etsin*' ('may God accept it'). Deep-fried pastries called *lokma* are handed out to neighbours on the day of the *mevlut* and you say the same words on accepting this gift.

RELIGIOUS FESTIVALS

The two main religious festivals are the most important social events in the Turkish year – as significant as Christmas and Easter in the Christian calendar. Schools, government offices and businesses close, families gather and there's a party atmosphere – everyone goes out visiting in their best new clothes.

As these holidays follow the Muslim (lunar) calendar, the dates change from year to year.

Ramadan

Although not a public holiday, Ramadan (*Ramazan*) is a momentous time of year for all Turks – indeed for all Muslims. This is the holy month of fasting, when strict Muslims abstain from food, alcohol, cigarettes and sex between sunrise and sunset. Not everyone observes *Ramazan* strictly, many giving up only smoking and alcohol. There's no requirement for children to fast, or those who are ill, pregnant or travelling.

There are two meals a day during Ramadan. The first (*sahur*) is eaten before dawn – in some areas, troupes of drummers patrol the streets to wake people in time for this meal. The second is the evening meal (*iftar*), which is much anticipated after a day of abstention and is signalled by the firing of cannon. The time of sunset varies across Turkey and is broadcast on television, along with suitably religious programming.

Ramadan Dates

İftar is a feast where women excel themselves with menus of sumptuous food, and bosses take their staff out for elaborate meals. If you're invited to an *iftar*, you should accept, as it's a great honour. Take great care not to be late as everyone will be starving, but don't start eating until given the signal to do so.

There's a party atmosphere in some cities, with food stalls and amusements set up after dark and despite the self-denial, many people gain weight during Ramadan. But the hours leading up to *iftar* can be difficult, as lack of food (and cigarettes) makes people slow and bad-tempered. It's advisable not to make a journey across Istanbul during the hour before sunset when everyone is racing to get home.

> **Foreigners aren't expected to fast but it's respectful not to eat or drink in front of those who are. If you want to know if someone is fasting, ask them, 'Oruç musunuz?' They will probably reply, 'Niyetliyim', which means 'I intend to'.**

Şeker Bayramı

Ramadan ends in a three-day celebration called *Şeker Bayramı* or Sugar Holiday, also known by its Arabic name, *Eid al-Fitr*. As its name suggests, it's an excuse to eat as many sweets and chocolates as possible. On the first day, people visit the mosque and their close family; children kiss the hands of their older relatives and receive sweets and money. The rest of the holiday is a social whirl of visiting, with children touring the neighbourhood, kissing as many hands – and receiving as much money and candy – as possible.

Kurban Bayramı

This is the most important religious holiday of the year and falls 70 days after the end of Ramadan and lasts for four days – or up to nine days if it falls between two weekends. It also precedes the annual Hajj or pilgrimage to Mecca. *Kurban Bayramı* or the Feast of the Sacrifice (*Eid al-Adha* in Arabic) honours Abraham's willingness to sacrifice his only son to God – and his reprieve when God sent a ram as an alternative sacrifice.

Traditionally, all families who could afford to would buy an animal to sacrifice as a thanksgiving – the meat was then divided between the family, their neighbours and the poor. Nowadays some Turks forgo the sacrifice and donate money instead, although in villages people still slaughter animals in their gardens. After the meat is divided up, cooked and eaten, another round of visiting begins and, for children at least, it's very like *Şeker Bayramı*.

Many foreigners are uncomfortable with the idea of animals being sacrificed,

especially in a neighbour's garden. If you're invited to a sacrifice, you'll be expected to watch and also to eat some of the meat. It's rude to turn this offering down, therefore if you're a vegetarian or you cannot face it, it's advisable to keep a low profile on the first day of the holiday.

> **The standard greeting during the two main holidays is '*İyi bayramlar*' or 'Happy holidays'.**

CLUBS

Turks join clubs in order to network, and many clubs and associations are geared towards business. Several international clubs, including the Rotary Club, have branches in Turkey, where some 10 per cent of members are expatriates and meetings are translated into English. Most other clubs conduct all their business in Turkish.

Joining a sports or social club is a good way to meet people. There are private tennis, golf and sports clubs in the major cities and larger resorts, as well as smaller groups organised by individuals with shared interests, such as walking, bird watching and animal welfare, which are usually popular with foreigners. Local Agenda 21 (*Yerli Gündem 21*) initiatives are supported by municipalities and focus on environmental issues and welcome input from foreigners. Some clubs charge a membership fee and many are organised along formal, hierarchical lines – you may find that rules, regulations and minute-taking detract from your enjoyment.

Expatriate clubs are a lifeline for new arrivals and range from established social networks, such as the International Women's Association of Izmir (which offers support and is involved in charitable events) to local special-interest groups, such as the Fethiye Times Gardening Club. Embassies and consulates also organise events for their nationals.

POPULAR CULTURE

The group dynamic is strong in Turkey, where people get together for many activities that westerners often do alone, such as watching football on television, knitting clothes or making food. They also join forces when angry about something, for example, several million took to the streets to defend secularism in early 2007, although mostly they gather for fun. Sunday afternoon is picnic time as beaches and beauty spots are invaded by extended Turkish families (including grandparents and cousins), who arrive by car or tractor, bringing not only mountains of food but also carpets, cushions, barbeques, kettles, gas bottles, cassette players and anything else which might be needed in the few hours they're away from home.

Turkish Baths

The *hamam*, or Turkish bath, combines three essential elements of Turkishness – cleanliness, tradition and sociability. In Ottoman times the *hamam* was the scene of social and commercial negotiation. Women gathered at the *hamam* to see and be seen, and to check out girls as potential marriage partners for their sons, while men met with business associates on the massage stone. A visit to the *hamam* still precedes important events, such as weddings.

The *hamam* experience, which is halfway between a sauna and a Roman bath, is one of self-indulgence. It begins with a spell in the hot room to sweat out the dirt, followed by a scrub down and then a massage. Every town has a Turkish bath, where men and women bathe separately, either naked or wrapped in a small square of cloth. Only tourist baths allow mixed bathing.

An alternative is a visit to a hot spring and there are thermal waters throughout Turkey, many of which are said to have medicinal qualities.

Festivals & Fairs

Festivals are held all over Turkey throughout the year. *Şeker Bayramı* and *Kurban Bayramı* (see above) are celebrated by all, while others have a local significance, such as Diyarbakır's Watermelon Festival and the many 'tourism' fairs at resorts. Festivals may be religious or traditional, commercial or sporting. Among the most interesting festivals are those listed (in chronological order) below:

- **Camel-wrestling (January)** – Selçuk near Ephesus hosts this

unique 'sport', in which male camels wrestle each other to the ground. It's Turkey's answer to the Spanish bullfight, although the camels are rarely hurt.

- *Nevruz* **(March)** – This is the Festival of Spring, celebrated throughout central Asia, but mainly by Kurdish people in Turkey. It goes back many centuries and has its roots in folk tradition, rather than religion.

- **Anzac Day (25th April)** – Australians, New Zealanders and Turks gather at Gallipoli (Gelibolu) on this day to remember the soldiers who lost their lives during the First World War.

- **Grease-wrestling Tournament (July)** – Edirne hosts this annual contest, which is the largest in the grease-wrestling calendar.

> **Grease- or oil-wresting (*yağlı güreş*) is Turkey's national sport. It dates back to ancient Persia, and the Edirne tournament has been an institution for over 600 years. The oil makes it difficult for opponents to grip each other so it's a test of endurance as well as skill. The winner receives his prize from the president of Turkey.**

- **Hacıbektaş Veli (August)** – A three-day festival when Alevi Muslims make a pilgrimage to the birthplace of one of their holiest saints.

- **Izmir Fuar (September)** – This festival and trade fair is the largest and oldest event in Turkey's commercial calendar.

- **Mevlana Festival (December)** – The annual performance of the Whirling Dervishes in Konya (see **Icons** in **Chapter 2**).

Gambling

Islam forbids gambling and Turks think fate is stronger than luck (*şans*), so games of chance aren't as popular as in other countries. Casinos were closed in the '90s, and the government has been trying to crack down on internet gambling, although this is proving more difficult to prohibit.

There is, nevertheless, a state lottery, Milli Piyango, which had a turnover of YTL1.4bn or around €788m in 2007, when the largest prize was the New Year jackpot of YTL25m (€14m). There are a number of games, with the main one, Loto, being drawn on a Saturday. Tickets cost around €7 and are sold by licensed vendors. You have a 20 per cent chance of winning back your stake.

Turkish men enjoy a flutter on the horses, and there are betting shops in most towns, run by the Turkish Jockey Club. These are social bases, like the coffee houses, rather than gambling dens.

Street Life

From dawn to dusk, Turkish streets are a hive of noise and activity. An Englishman builds his terrace at the back of his house to enjoy his privacy, while a Turk builds his at the front so he doesn't miss a minute of the street 'theatre'.

The 'cast' changes through the day. Shopkeepers open their shutters, then stand and gossip; shoe-shine boys wait for customers as the tea boy whisks by, balancing his tray. Various salesmen tote their wares – vegetables, lottery tickets, Turkish flags, or pink plaster copies of Greek statues. A moped speeds past with two men carrying a huge sheet of glass, a group of lads watch intently as a workman changes the bulb in a street light, and an old woman drags a reluctant sheep on the end of a rope. Schoolchildren dodge across the street, screeching like starlings, while the neighbourhood cats scrounge scraps from the fish-monger's cart, inches from a sleeping dog.

As evening falls, families stroll semi-aimlessly in a Mediterranean promenade until the smell of cooking tempts them in from the street. A boy rushes out to buy extra bread from the corner shop, and the old men outside the *kahvehane* set up one last game of *okey* before shuffling off home.

Spectator Sports

There is sport and then there is football, which in Turkey is little short of a religion. All other spectator sports are eclipsed by *futbol*. Every news bulletin has a section on sport, which is almost entirely devoted to football and there are several sports newspapers, such as the aptly-named *Fanatik*, but they, too, focus on soccer. Only when another sports star makes the headlines does football take a brief backseat.

Football (soccer)

If you follow football, you'll never be short of a conversation starter in Turkey, where the lives of most men (and some women) revolve around the 'beautiful game'. Turkish fans are as fervent as those in England, Italy or Spain. Many hours are devoted to anticipating, reliving and analysing each match, and every fan knows better than the managers, coaches or referees. Turkey literally stops for a major game, such as the national team's 2002 World Cup semi-final against Brazil or the European Championship semi-final against Germany in 2008, and decisive matches in the Super League are a national event.

Turks are lucky if they can attend a live match – tickets to watch one of the big Istanbul sides cost from €18 – but entire household schedules are arranged around an important game on television (all important matches are televised). Those involving the national team are aired on public channels, but Super League games are shown only on the subscription channel Lig

TV, when fans gather in clubs to watch them on giant plasma screens.

There are few foreign players in Turkish professional football and there are strict limits on how many foreign players can play for a team. Fans are concerned with what players do on the field, rather than off it, and footballers' wives (and girlfriends) rarely make the gossip columns. When football gets bad press, it's down to the hooligan behaviour of fans. Although Turks are no more violent than many European supporters, they're infamous for intimidating visiting teams. Drums, firecrackers and guns are taken into stadiums, and fans of Fenerbahçe (an Istanbul team) greet rival supporters with a banner reading 'Welcome to Hell'.

There are more than 140 teams in Turkey, but most Turks support one of Istanbul's Big Three – Galatasaray, Fenerbahçe and Beşiktaş – each of which has its own TV channel, retail stores and supporters' club. Local derbies are hotly contested and the teams' flags are as recognisable as Turkey's national flag.

- **Galatasaray** – The most successful team in Turkey, Galatasaray (nickname *Cimbom*) has won the Super League more than 15 times since 1960, along with two European trophies in 2000 – the UEFA Cup, against Arsenal, and the European Super Cup, against Real Madrid. The team colours are red and yellow, and the best known player is Hakan Şükür. Galatasaray runs soccer schools in Turkey, and also fields successful basketball and volleyball divisions. The formidable supporters' federation is called the Ultralions.

- **Fenerbahçe** – Known as the Yellow Canaries because of its blue and yellow strip, Fenerbahçe is based at the Şükrü Saracoğlu Stadium in Kadıköy, one of Europe's top soccer venues. Winner of the most Super League championships up to 2007, Fenerbahçe is Turkey's richest club – its stock value in 2007 was close to $1.1bn. There are branches devoted to other sports, including boxing, basketball and athletics. The squad includes several Brazilians, but goalkeeper Volkan Demirel is the best known player. (Atatürk supported Fenerbahçe.)

- **Beşiktaş** – Although overshadowed by its two rivals, Beşiktaş (nickname the Black Eagles) has an interesting history. Founded in 1903 as the Ottoman Gymnastics Club, it still supports such diverse sports as handball, gymnastics and Paralympic sports. The 32,000-seat BJK İnönü Stadium is the only one in the world with a view of both Europe and Asia, and the team has some illustrious supporters, including President Abdullah Gül.

> **Beşiktaş striker İlhan Mansiz (now retired) is Turkey's answer to David Beckham, as well known for his style off the pitch as for netting the goal which sent Turkey into the 2002 World Cup semi-finals.**

Turkish leagues: The top 18 teams battle it out in the Super League (*Türkcell Süper Lig*) which is almost always won by one of the Big Three. The season runs from August to May, with most matches being played on weekends. Beneath the Super League, a further 130-plus clubs jostle for position in three more leagues. A system of promotion and relegation applies across all four leagues.

National team: Supporters of the national team, known as the *Ay-Yıldızlılar* (Crescent-Stars), had little to be proud of until its glorious (and unexpected) performance in the 2002 World Cup, when Turkey reached the semi-finals and then beat South Korea to clinch third place. This was a huge boost to fans who had almost given up – the team hadn't even managed to qualify during the previous four decades. Supporters were hoping for more glory when Turkey qualified for Euro 2008, and weren't disappointed when they reached the semi-final, where they were beaten by Germany.

Other Sports

Football apart, there are also a few other sports which Turks enjoy – especially those in which their countrymen excel. Motorsports have gained in popularity since Istanbul joined the Formula One circuit and motorcyclist Kenan Sofuoğlu became World Supersport Champion in 2007. Horse racing has enough followers to warrant its own television channel, and Turkey fields a team in the Davis Cup tennis tournament.

The Turks don't know much about cricket, but Turkey has just joined the international rugby federation and there are grants available to promote the sport. Both sports are covered on satellite TV and shown in bars in areas with large tourist and expatriate audiences. Fox Sports shows English premiership matches and the US Super Bowl, while Eurosport broadcasts a wide range of sporting events.

Turks also take a keen interest in traditional sports, such as grease-wresting (see above) and *cirit*, a combat game on horseback. However, two of the most popular spectator sports are based on ball skills and strength:

Basketball: Increasingly popular since 2001, when the national team was runner-up in the European Basketball Championship, held in Istanbul. The players were nicknamed *On İki Dev Adam* (the 12 Giant Men) and three went on to play in America's prestigious NBA league. There are domestic leagues for men and women, and most teams are named after their commercial sponsors, e.g. Efes Pilsen SK and Fenerbahçe Ülkerspor.

Weight-lifting: Turkey has produced some star weight lifters, both male and female, and the sport provides the country's best chance of medals in international competition. Naim Süleymanoğlu and Halil Mutlu both won gold medals in three consecutive Olympics.

Sporting Events

The following events are important in the Turkish sporting calendar:

Athletics – the Istanbul Eurasia Marathon, which crosses the Bosporus from Asia to Europe (October);
Basketball – league play-offs between the top eight teams (September to May);

Football – the local derbies between Istanbul's Big Three (throughout the season) and the match which decides the Super League champions (May);
Grease-wrestling – Edirne tournament (July – see above);
Motor racing – the Istanbul Formula One Grand Prix (spring) and the Turkish leg of the World Rally Championship (summer);
Sailing – the Bodrum Cup, a wooden-boat regatta (October);
Tennis – the Istanbul Cup, Turkey's main tournament (May).

Bodrum

THE ARTS

Turks are closer to their arts, which have their roots in traditional culture, than many nationalities and are proud of their music and dance, theatre and heritage of museums and ancient sites. The more you appreciate this culture, the better you'll understand the Turks. Many cultural events take place in cities and are inaccessible to rural people, who rely on television for their entertainment. However, there are now cinemas in most small towns.

Cinema & Theatre

The glory days of Turkish cinema were the '50s and '60s, when Yeşilçam (Turkey's 'Hollywood') produced hundreds of low-budget, action-romance films. Since then, American imports have dominated screens, although the quality of home-made films is improving. There are several film festivals, the most prestigious being Antalya's Golden Orange Film Festival in the autumn.

There are state theatres in 13 cities, as well as many private theatres. Turkish theatre isn't high-brow and one of the most popular performances features the shadow puppets *Karagöz & Hacivat*, a show which dates back centuries and which, like Punch and Judy, is as much social commentary as children's entertainment. Most theatre is a challenge unless your language skills are good.

When going to see a film or play in Turkey, you should be aware of the following points:

- **Subtitles** – Most imported films are shown in the original language, with Turkish subtitles, although children's films are often dubbed into Turkish. The Istanbul International Film Festival in the spring shows some Turkish movies with foreign subtitles.

- **Noise & late arrivals** – Be prepared for chatting, mobile phones, people arriving late and the rustle of plastic bags to distract you at the cinema. Theatres are quieter and late-comers must wait for a suitable break to take their seats.

- **Interval** – Films are always interrupted so viewers can stock up on popcorn and take a much-needed cigarette break (theatres ban smoking). Films are often halted abruptly, in mid-sentence.

- **Comfort** – Small local cinemas can be cramped and older ones have very hard seats. Air-conditioning is usually turned up high in summer (when you may need a sweater). A pleasant alternative are the open-air cinemas which operate in Istanbul and some resorts on summer evenings.

- **Prices & discounts** – Tickets are inexpensive at small provincial cinemas and expensive in multiplexes at large shopping malls. There are discounts for holders of a student card.

Listings

Listings magazines, such as *Time Out* and *The Guide*, cover events in Istanbul, Ankara and Bodrum. The My Merhaba expat community website also has an exhaustive list of cultural and social activities, mainly in Istanbul, Ankara and Izmir, which is updated weekly (www.mymerhaba.com/en/main/index.asp).

Music & Dance

Turks adore music and dance and live their lives to a background of throbbing oriental pop or lamenting arabesque. Every district has its own radio station, and singing and dancing are staple ingredients of television light-entertainment shows, weddings and private gatherings; while concerts and folk dancing are always on the bill at festivals. Every region has its traditional

attractions are listed as World Heritage Sites by UNESCO. More formal museums include Ankara's Museum of Anatolian Civilisations and Hagia Sophia (Aya Sofya) in Istanbul, formerly a Byzantine basilica but converted by Atatürk in 1935 into a museum of Byzantine and Ottoman history. Some tombs and museums, such as the Mevlana in Konya, are holy places for Muslims and should be treated with respect – take particular care not to walk in front of people who are praying. All mosques can be visited outside prayer times – between 9am and midday is the best time to go.

Istanbul is also a centre for art lovers, with collections ranging across the centuries, from the Museum of Turkish and Islamic arts to the Istanbul Modern. Turkish art is influenced by many factors, including Ottoman designs, Islamic calligraphy and Anatolian folk motifs. There are also collectable treasures to be found in the small galleries in cities and resorts, where local artists exhibit their work.

When visiting a museum or gallery, note the following:

- **Opening hours** – Museums and galleries are generally open from 9 or 10am until 6 or 7pm (open-air sites stay open later in summer), while some close on Mondays and the first day of the main religious holidays.

- **Entrance fees** – Entrance fees are from €2 to €10, usually with discounts for children, students and disabled visitors; some museums

costumes and dances, which children learn (and what they mean) at school.

Turkish 'classical' music is diverse, encompassing Ottoman military (*mehter*), Western classical, folk and religious music. At the Istanbul Music Festival in June, classical music is performed in some of the city's historic buildings. Opera and ballet attract a smaller but devoted audience, and Turkey's state troupes are world-renowned, thanks in part to Atatürk, who was a supporter of Western arts; Istanbul is on the itinerary of many of the world's major concert tours.

Museums & Art Galleries

Turkey is one massive open-air museum, with over 2,500 historical sites, from the much-visited Roman city of Ephesus to the remote ruins of Knidos at the end of the Datça peninsula. In between, there are thousands of mosques, churches, palaces, caravansaries (historic inns along the Silk Road), tombs and caves – some dating back to prehistoric times. Nine of Turkey's cultural-historic have free entrance on selected days. Private guides are available at large archaeological sites – negotiate a fee and remember to add a tip.

- **Information & photography** – Most major museums are well laid out although the exhibits may be poorly labelled, and often only in Turkish. If there's a curator (*müdür*) handy, you can ask for help. Always check before taking photos as flash photography isn't permitted in places where it may damage the exhibits (e.g. the frescoes in Göreme's rock churches) or disturb worshippers.

- **Refreshments** – There are cafés and shops at most museums, although the kebab stand around the corner will probably offer better, cheaper food. Water is invariably expensive, so take your own.

> Try to avoid museums during the height of the tourist season. Ephesus can be unbearable in high summer but magically atmospheric on a quiet November day.

Disabled Facilities

Facilities for disabled people are the exception not the rule and many smaller venues lack disabled access or toilets, therefore it's advisable to check first. In 2007, the Association of Turkish Travel Agents (TÜRSAB) produced a guide entitled *Barrier Free Istanbul*, stating which of the city's transport, shopping and tourist attractions were suitable for disabled visitors, and many, including the Blue Mosque, didn't make the grade. On a more positive note, Turks treat people with disabilities as equals and are never embarrassed to offer help.

Booking

Tickets can be purchased direct from venues, a few of which offer telephone and online booking, although staff are unlikely to speak foreign languages and most websites are in Turkish only (so it's easier to go along in person). There's no need to book for museums or cinemas (unless the film is a premiere) and you can usually buy a ticket on arrival, although you may have to queue.

For concerts, shows and major sports events, it's advisable to use Biletix, an Istanbul-based ticket agency which sells tickets for events across the country. Contact Biletix (☎ 0216-556 9800, 🖳 www.biletix.com/index.htm) or visit one of its ticket outlets. It also has an excellent website, with an English-language option, which allows you to book online. You're required to set up an account and can then purchase tickets via a secure server.

Mount Nemrut

9.
RETAIL THERAPY

Turkish people love to shop. Whether they're popping out for a loaf of bread or browsing for a wedding outfit, it's seen as an excuse to socialise and is rarely done in a rush – and people dress up for a major shopping excursion. Turks are loyal to big-name brands, especially Turkish brands, such as white-goods giant Arçelık. They appreciate and seek out quality – sellers will try to persuade you to buy something by stressing that it's kaliteli (good quality) – and have the uncanny ability to spot the freshest beans or sweetest strawberries in the market. But they also have an eye for a bargain and the negotiating skills to secure a purchase at the right price.

Shopping is one of the most pleasurable activities you'll undertake in Turkey but it can also be one of the most frustrating, especially if your language skills are limited or you're not used to haggling. This chapter explains the aspects of shopping which are peculiar to Turkey, and how to get the best from the retail opportunities on offer.

> Many shops offer a free gift-wrapping service and will package your goods with a flourish of ribbon – but make sure they remove the price sticker first!

CUSTOMER SERVICE

With a natural affinity for trade and a sociable nature, most Turks make excellent shopkeepers. They are patient, obliging and persuasive – some times a little too persuasive. If they don't have a blue shirt in your size, they'll do their best to sell you a larger one or a red one or any one, just as long as you buy something, which is partly because they hate to say 'no'. Assistants sometimes follow you closely around the shop, which can feel intimidating to westerners more used to searching for someone to help or happy to browse anonymously.

It isn't unusual to be offered tea, fruit or sweets and these friendly gestures shouldn't oblige you to buy – although they may ensure you return. Customer service (müşteri hizmetleri) is less personal in larger stores and supermarkets, although check-in staff will still greet you with a friendly 'welcome' and there's always someone on hand to help.

OPENING HOURS

Turkish shops have generous opening hours and shopkeepers regard a siesta as an excuse for laziness by nations who cannot cope with a bit of heat. Shops are frequently open before 9am and rarely close before 7pm, while local convenience stores (see **The Bakkal** below) open earlier and close much later. Every neighbourhood has at least one shop which stays open 24 hours to service the Turks' voracious appetite for bread, sweets and cigarettes.

In tourist areas, many shops, including supermarkets, are open until 10pm and those selling souvenirs, ice cream and beer don't close until all potential customers have disappeared into the bars – or to bed.

Sundays & Public Holidays

You can shop seven days a week. The official day of rest is Sunday, but traders can apply for a licence to open on Sundays and public holidays, and many (especially those involved in property or tourism) do so. The majority of shops close on the first day of major religious holidays, although even then you'll find the inevitable *bakkal* open.

Islam's holy day is Friday but because Turkey is a secular country this is a normal working day. Some shopkeepers close for a short time in order to visit the mosque, which is more common in religious cities, such as Konya. You may walk into a shop on a Friday to find the shopkeeper deep in prayer. Don't interrupt or he will have to start all over again. Just step outside for a few minutes until he has completed his devotions.

If you're planning to visit a particular shop on a Sunday (or Friday), call first as shopkeepers will often open just for you rather than lose a sale.

QUEUING

Turks don't like queuing but it's now accepted practice in government offices and banks, many of which use a numbered ticketing system – this is much easier for foreigners than the raucous scrum which used to pass for a Turkish 'queue'. Elbows still come in handy in markets (and *dolmuş* stations – see **Chapter 7**) as you compete with Turkish women for the best bargains or the most comfortable seat. It's rarely necessary to queue in shops, as the ratio of staff to customers is high, and shopkeepers have a knack of knowing whose turn it is to be served.

> **Prepare to greet and be greeted in shops – commerce relies on good manners and shopkeepers expect you to stop and chat. You often hear them say '*buyurun*', a catch-all phrase which translates as 'here you are' but can equally mean 'can I help you?', 'follow me' or just 'yes?'. There is no standard answer.**

SALES & BARGAINS

There's no official time for sales. Shops usually cut prices to offload goods in winter, late summer and towards the end of the season in tourist resorts – or whenever they need to shift stock. Look for signs saying '*indirim*' (discount) or '*ucuzluk*' (low prices), when prices may be slashed by up to 70 per cent.

There are many ways to achieve a discounted price in Turkey – sales are only one of them – which include:

● **Paying cash** – Displayed prices sometimes assume that the buyer will pay in instalments (*taksit*). Ask for the cash price (*peşin fiyatı*) and you may get a discount, particularly when shopping for furniture or white goods.

- **Buying in bulk** – Buy more than one item and you should get a discount, e.g. three jumpers for the price of two. If you buy all your white goods in one shop, ask for a present (*hediye*) and you may get smaller items thrown in.

- **Buying at source** – Centres of production offer the best prices. For example, Denizli is the hub of the textile industry and by far the best place to purchase sheets, towels and clothing.

Turks use credit cards to spread their payments and some cards offer interest-free credit. But shopkeepers don't like accepting cards for single-payment purchases as they attract a commission charge from banks, which can be as high as 6 per cent that will no doubt be passed on to you!

The Art of Haggling

Haggling or bartering (*pazarlık*) is an essential part of Turkish shopping culture. Though not as widespread – nor as fierce – as in the Far East, it's still widely practised in rural areas and even resorts (traders assume that tourists expect it) and therefore it's a skill which you need to learn.

There are places where you can haggle and places where you cannot. It isn't appropriate to haggle for groceries or household goods in department stores or supermarkets. In smaller shops with fixed prices, it may be better to try for a discount using one of the above methods. But you can, and must, haggle in tourist centres, especially when buying carpets, leather goods and souvenirs. It's also acceptable to haggle in markets, although not for food.

Many foreigners feel uncomfortable haggling, especially newcomers who aren't familiar with prices, therefore it's advisable to do some research first – talk to locals and check out the prices in shops. Once you take the plunge, bear in mind that successful haggling has its own code:

- **Never appear too keen** – you get the best price on items which you show little interest in.

- **If you haven't a clue as to the 'right' price, let the seller name his price first** – assume it will be at least double the true value (you're a 'wealthy' tourist, after all). His reaction to your counter-offer should give you a better idea of what the item is actually worth.

- **Be prepared to walk away** – the seller may follow you; if he doesn't, you know your final offer was too low.

- **Don't haggle for fun** – once you agree on a price, you're (morally) committed to buy.

- **Don't quibble over the last lira** – haggling should be fun and you won't be welcomed back by the shopkeeper.

> If a shopkeeper throws your money to the ground, then picks it up and swipes it across his chin, don't be alarmed or offended – this is a good-luck gesture, known as *siftah*, which celebrates the first customer of the day.

TYPES OF SHOP

Turkey has every kind of shopping experience. Istanbul is home to probably the first 'mall' in the world – the Grand or Covered Bazaar (Kapalı Carşı), which dates back to 1461 and has more than 4,000 shops, selling everything from rare antiques to fake watches. At the other end of the spectrum is the vast, glittering Cevahir Mall, reputed to be the largest in Europe on its opening in 2005, which features such international chains as Top Shop and Zara in 620,000m² (6,674,000ft²) of retail space.

Turkey's commercial heart beats strongest in its small, family-run shops. Many sell a diverse assortment of goods, from saddles to string; others have a narrow field of speciality, such as chickpeas, fake flowers or mothballs. Although a lot of small shops have been put out of business by the malls and supermarkets, many survive due to the quality of their service and the loyalty of their customers.

There are a few shops which are typical of Turkey, and these include:

- *bakırcı* – makes and mends copper jugs, plates and cooking pots. Copperware is now mainly ornamental, as Turks prefer to use plastic and stainless steel, but goods still in daily use can be relined by the *kalaycı* (tinsmith).

- *büfe* – small shop or kiosk selling sweets, cigarettes, newspapers, ice cream, drinks and other accessories of Turkish street life;

- *değirmenci* – sells flour, oats and milled goods, and will grind customers' own grain and cereals;

- *hırdavatçı* – old-fashioned hardware shop and treasure trove for fans of DIY and handicrafts. Goods include paint, string, nails, farm implements, wooden boards for rolling pancakes, olive sieves and much more.

- *kuruyemişçi* – literally a 'dried food seller', with trays of raisins, apricots and nuts;

- *lokumcu* – sells real Turkish delight (*lokum*), spices and coffee;

- *manifaturacı* – a haberdashery/drapery selling fabrics, rugs, buttons and ribbons, socks, underwear and assorted hair ornaments;

- *sobacı* – specialises in wood-burning stoves (*soba*), the number one heating system in Turkey, and all the implements that go with them;

- *yorgancı* – maker of exquisite hand-stitched satin quilts (*yorgan*), where you can also have cushions and seat pads stuffed. Turks take their quilts and cushions to the *yorgancı* to have their contents fluffed up in the *çırçır* (cotton gin).

The Bakkal

Almost every street corner has a *bakkal* (general store), also called a *dükkân* (market). This is the place where Turks go for bread, soft drinks, sweets, cigarettes – and gossip. The *bakkalcı* (grocer) is at the heart of the community and knows everything that's going on; many also act as a *muhtar* or 'village headman', responsible for local administration. In rural communities, he (it's rarely a woman) sells a huge range of goods, from locally made yoghurt to rubber boots. He's good to his customers and allows regulars to operate a tab which is paid weekly or even monthly. As a result, Turks are usually loyal to one *bakkal*.

Some are located at the bottom of an apartment block and operate an unusual delivery service for residents – the customer lowers a basket from her balcony containing a shopping list and the *bakkalcı* fills it and sends it back up. Get to know your *bakkalcı* and use your local shops, which will help you assimilate into the community and encourage you to practise your Turkish.

Markets

Bazaars

Bazaars (*çarşı*) are groups of shops and kiosks – forerunners of the modern shopping centre or mall. Some bazaars are tucked away underground, while others spread out over several streets. A bazaar may consist of only one type of shop, e.g. selling gold and jewellery, or be a kaleidoscope of stores, like the famous Grand Bazaar in Istanbul. It may also sell food. One of the most exotic bazaars is Istanbul's Mısır Çarşısı (Egyptian Bazaar), which is also known as the Spice Market.

> 'The Covered Bazaar of Istanbul is something like the thousand and one nights for Europeans... [It] beams like the magic lantern of Aladdin in tales.'
>
> Julia Pardoe in her 19th-century travel book, *The Beauties of the Bosphorus*.

Food Markets

Food markets are found in every town, most of which are open from 8 or 9am until late afternoon, Mondays to Saturdays. They range from large covered markets to just a few stalls. Those run by the municipality are known as *sabit pazarı* or 'fixed' markets, to differentiate them from the weekly street markets (see below).

Food markets are cheaper than supermarkets – prices are fixed – where you'll find the freshest produce and enjoy excellent service. Fishmongers will skin and fillet your fish (something most supermarkets won't do), and cheese merchants and other vendors encourage you to try before you buy. Once stallholders know you, they will source and save products for you.

Street Markets

Some street markets have a fixed day and location, like the Çarşamba Pazarı (Wednesday market) in Istanbul's Fatih district. Others tour an area, setting up in a different town each day – these are weekly markets or *halk pazarı* (public markets), which adjust their times to the season, opening early (around 8am) and closing by sundown.

Stalls sell a huge range of goods: clothes, shoes, fabric, fruit and vegetables, every kind of kitchenware, watches, sunglasses, CDs, handbags, donkey harnesses and garden tools. Some goods are shoddy and anything with a designer label is fake (bags, watches, jeans and perfume are the usual suspects), but the fun is in the haggling and you can get a good deal.

There are street markets specialising in arts and crafts, and a few are genuine flea markets (*bit pazarı*). Car-boot sales are starting to appear in resort areas, although they're usually organised by foreigners for foreigners. Most Turks turn up their noses at second-hand goods.

Street Traders

Commerce isn't limited to official shops and markets, and there are traders wherever there's a sales opportunity. Village women sit on the edges of a market selling lemons, olives and tomato plants from their gardens, while artisans patrol the crowds offering to sharpen knives or clean shoes. Trucks park up on

market day, piled high with watermelons or heavy steel safes. Lorry-loads of sheep and goats are a common sight in the weeks before *Kurban Bayramı* (the Feast of the Sacrifice), while spring brings farmers with boxes of baby chicks and ducklings. Vans patrol the streets selling rugs and blankets, tomatoes and firewood – many dealers are unlicensed but the authorities often turn a blind eye.

> **Beware of buying and using fake designer goods, as in some countries (e.g. Italy) they will be confiscated and you can be heavily fined if you're caught with them.**

Supermarkets

Twenty years ago, a Turkish supermarket was a shop with one check-out and a couple of trolleys. Now, every town has a Western-style supermarket with piped music, special offers and a discount card. The best known are Migros and Tansaş, while budget chains include Şok and Bim. These retail giants have taken a large portion of the food market, but haven't really changed the way Turks shop.

FOOD & WINE

Food is an important part of Turkish life and most Turks would rather cook a proper meal than sling a TV dinner in the microwave. Lazy cooks will find the choice of 'ready meals' very limited, with frozen food in particular slow to take off and supermarket freezers containing little more than chicken, vegetables and ice cream. People buy much of their food on a daily basis from specialist shops and markets, and buy food in season; new summer cherries or the wild mushrooms, which appear after the first autumn rain, are eagerly anticipated.

Turks aren't especially adventurous and their shopping basket usually contains the same (high quality) ingredients: an abundance of fresh fruit and vegetables; lentils and beans; rice, pasta and bulgur wheat; white cheese (similar to feta) and yoghurt; olives and olive oil. They also have a peculiar passion for packet desserts and chocolate spread.

Foreign food is becoming more readily available and you can find soy sauce, pesto, parmesan cheese, baked beans and tinned pineapple in many supermarkets, while in tourist areas, canny shopkeepers sell bacon, English teabags, Marmite and custard powder – at a price!

Prices

Food isn't cheap in Turkey, especially when set against people's income. As a rule, locally produced food costs the least; produce which is transported a long distance by road costs more, while imported food is expensive. The following is a rough guide to cost:

- **inexpensive** – fresh fruit and vegetables, local bananas, bread, eggs, yoghurt, white cheese, flour, pasta, rice, pulses, tea, olives, chicken, fish (but only by the coast), basic cleaning goods and bottled water;

- **expensive** – milk, butter, beef and lamb, pork products, seafood (e.g. prawns), pineapples and coconuts, cakes and biscuits, ground coffee and instant coffee (always called *Nescafe*), breakfast cereals, wines and spirits, shampoo and pet food.

Weights & Measures

Turkey uses the metric system of litres and kilograms. Unpackaged food is usually sold by the kilo or in multiples of 100g, although you can buy a piece (*parça*) of cheese or several slices (*dilim*) of cooked meat. Supermarkets have machines which weigh and price produce for you, but in markets you ask for an item or a particular weight, e.g. half a kilo (*yarım kilo*) or 250g (*ikiyuzelli gram*).

It can be difficult to buy small amounts, especially in a market – if half a kilo is too much ask for a lira's worth (*bir liralık*).

Meat & Fish

Meat (*et*) is bought from a butcher (*kasap*), who may have whole sheep hanging in his window and an abattoir at the back of the shop – disconcerting if you're used to neat packets of sanitised steak. But the quality is usually excellent, and butchers will trim and prepare meat to your specifications.

Turks eat far more chicken (*tavuk*) than any other meat, mainly because it's cheaper – you can buy portions or a whole bird. Lamb is the next choice, followed by beef. Pork is forbidden by Islam. All meat is prepared by the Muslim *halal* method, whereby the throat of the animal is cut, the blood drained from the carcass and the meat eaten immediately, rather than

being hung and allowed to 'mature'. Prime cuts are expensive – around €9 per kilo – therefore meat is often used for flavour rather than being the centrepiece of a meal, and mince is popular. Very little is wasted – sheep's heads and tripe are saved for soup.

Fish (*balık*) is also popular, although fishmongers are scarce away from large cities and the coast. Fish is a staple on the Black Sea coast where they put anchovies in everything – including ice cream!

Milk & Dairy

As in other Mediterranean countries, it's difficult to find fresh milk, although heat-treated 'long-life' milk is widely available. Milk (*süt*) isn't considered a necessity in a country where tea and coffee are always drunk black, but yoghurt is indispensable and is sold in large plastic tubs. There's a huge range of cheese – the best known are *kaşar peynir*, a mild yellow cheese, and crumbly white *beyaz peynir*, which is sometimes matured in a goat's skin.

Organic Food

The tempting displays of fruit and vegetables at a Turkish market look

---

Metric/Imperial Conversion

Weight

Imperial	Metric	Metric	Imperial
1 UK pint	0.57 litre	1 litre	1.75 UK pints
1 US pint	0.47 litre	1 litre	2.13 US pints
1 UK gallon	4.54 litre	1 litre	0.22 UK gallon
1 US gallon	3.78 litres	1 litre	0.26 US gallon

Capacity

Imperial	Metric	Metric	Imperial
1 UK pint	0.57 litre	1 litre	1.75 UK pints
1 US pint	0.47 litre	1 litre	2.13 US pints
1 UK gallon	4.54 litres	1 litre	0.22 UK gallon
1 US gallon	3.78 litres	1 litre	0.26 US gallon

Note: An American 'cup' = around 250ml or 0.25 litre.

---

as if they should be organic, but many aren't. Pesticide use is widespread, although farmers are now realising the potential profits to be made from organic food – and the savings from not using chemicals – and the market is expanding. Unfortunately, much of what is produced goes straight for export.

Some organic produce is available in the larger supermarkets, but it usually costs around 30 per cent more than a non-organic equivalent. Turks are quite health-conscious and aware of organic foods, so ask your greengrocer (*manav*) if he can supply it – at the very least, he should have bee-pollinated tomatoes and free-range eggs. If you live in a rural area, your best source of organic produce may be your neighbours.

Wine

The vine has been cultivated in Anatolia for thousands of years, yet Turkey has virtually no wine culture. The average Turk drinks less than a litre per year, and consumption isn't encouraged by the heavy taxes on alcohol – a bottle of reasonable Turkish wine costs as much as a kilo of steak, although you can sometimes get a bottle of French or Chilean wine for less. Not all supermarkets sell alcohol, but many small shops carry wine and beer and some are also licensed to sell spirits. Beware of cheap Turkish plonk which has been stored upright on a dusty shelf for a year or more!

CLOTHES

Turkey is one of the world's largest producers of clothing; some is cutting-edge high fashion, some is cheap and tacky – and there's a great deal in between. The big-city malls sell quality labels, such as Quiksilver and Mavi Jeans, and there are international chains such as Marks & Spencer, although many small clothes shops sell mainly Turkish labels. Street markets focus on bargain fashion, a lot of it fake 'designer label' and covered with logos.

Despite Turkey's strong textile industry, there are no retail outlets to compare with the likes of Primark and JC Penney in the UK and Ireland. (Surprisingly, T-shirts made in Turkey can sell for less in UK chain stores than in their country of origin.) There are few second-hand clothes shops, and charity shops barely exist. The best places to hunt for bargains, aside from the markets, are the rag-trade districts, such as Istanbul's Beyazit, opposite the Grand Bazaar, and factory shops (*fabrika satış mağazası*), which offload end-of-line or defective brand-name goods. Big supermarkets also have some good deals on clothing.

Sizes

Turkey uses the continental sizing system. Shirts and T-shirts are often sized as small, medium, large and extra large, while men's underpants are sometimes sized by number. None of the sizes conform to a uniform standard, therefore you need to try things on. Turks tend to be shorter and slighter than westerners, so it can be difficult for Europeans and Americans to find fashionable clothes in the right size. Look for shops specialising in larger sizes (*büyük beden*).

> If you cannot find the right garment 'off the peg', you can have something made. Turkey has many skilled tailors (*terzi*), who will make you a bespoke outfit for the same price (or less) than a similar ready-to-wear item.

Shoes

Fashionable shoes are widely available, but quality footwear is expensive. Sports shoes are popular – you'll see

Continental to UK/US Size Comparison

Women's Clothes

Continental	34	36	38	40	42	44	46	48	50	52
UK		8	10	12	14	16	18	20	22	24	26
US		6	8	10	12	14	16	18	20	22	24

Men's Shirts

Continental	36	37	38	39	40	41	42	43	44	46
UK/US	14	14	15	15	16	16	17	17	18	-

Shoes (Women's and Men's)

Continental	35	36	37	37	38	39	40	41	42	42	43	44
UK		2	3	3	4	4	5	6	7	7	8	9	9
US		4	5	5	6	6	7	8	9	9	10	10	11

Nike trainers everywhere, but sandals and flip-flops (thongs) are regarded as tourist attire. High heels are city shoes – mud, dust and pot-holes make them impractical in rural areas. Most rural Turks live in a pair of shabby slip-ons, which are the practical choice in a country where you take your shoes off on entering someone's home.

Turkish shoe sizes are continental, and many shoes are quite narrow. Men with feet larger than 45 (UK size 12), or women over size 40 (UK size 6-7), may have trouble finding shoes to fit.

Children's Clothes

At their smartest, Turkish children resemble small adults, in neat little suits and colour-coordinated outfits. Quality children's clothes can be as expensive as those worn by their parents, while the outfits at the budget end of the market tend to be in garish colours and cheap fabrics, with a huge emphasis on Barbie and Spiderman. Large supermarkets and discount stores offer the best compromise. Turkish children are smaller than European kids of the same age, so you'll need to double check sizes – and only a few (expensive) shoe shops have the equipment to measure children's feet. There's a limited range of baby clothes, mainly because Turkish families get knitting to welcome a new arrival.

Alterations

Turks don't like to throw things away, so it's easy to have garments repaired and altered. Every small town has at least one tailor, as well as a shoe mender (*ayakkabı tamircisi*) and maybe even an *örücü*, who undertakes intricate hand repairs. Tailors charge from €3 for a simple alteration, although if new clothes require alteration, the shop or stallholder will whisk them away and alter them while you wait, for which there's often no charge.

COLLECTABLES

Turkish newspapers occasionally run campaigns urging readers to collect coupons which they can redeem for goods, such as books, electronic gadgets and toys. But Turks aren't great collectors – unless you count the many (often gaudy) ornaments in their homes. They do, however, like to invest in quality Turkish goods, such as the following:

Carpets & Kilims

Woven from silk or wool, the best carpets are works of art and an excellent investment. The tradition of weaving carpets and *kilims* (flat-weave rugs) dates back centuries, and motifs

have been handed down through the generations, representing a way of life which is slowly disappearing. Turkish carpet dealers are among the most skilled salesmen in the world and will quickly wear you down; never buy a rug in a hurry and be wary of machine-made carpets that may be passed off as 'antiques'. The best way to buy is to go with a Turkish friend (who will know all the tricks) and avoid shops in tourist areas.

If someone offers to take you to his 'uncle's carpet shop', you can be sure he will earn good commission from the dealer – who may or may not be his uncle or any relative. Commission is an accepted part of Turkish commerce but, as in any country, you should beware of the rip-off. Organised tours usually take in at least one carpet/leather/souvenir shop, where tourists may pay as much as 50 per cent over the odds after the salesman, guide and driver have taken their cut.

If you buy carpets or other expensive items you should pay by credit card, which offers some security. If you're paying cash you should take your purchases with you rather than have then sent abroad by the vendor, as it isn't unknown for goods not to arrive.

Gold & Jewellery

Gold is seen as an inflation-proof investment and many Turkish women wear their wealth. Most gold is 18 carat and is sold by weight, with an additional sum calculated for the workmanship – the choice ranges from plain bangles to elaborate pieces of 'bling'. Turkey also has good-quality silver and precious stones, and

there are modern designs alongside traditional Ottoman pieces. Always check for hallmarks, although most jewellers are reputable and easier to do business with than carpet dealers.

Ceramics

Turkey is famous for its tile work. The centre of excellence is Iznik, near Bursa, where exquisite tiles are produced – Iznik tiles cover the interior of the Blue Mosque and are the reason it's 'blue'. Another place for ceramics is the city of Kütahya, in western Turkey, where intricately decorated plates, bowls and vases, as well as tiles, are produced. Prices start at just a few euros.

It's illegal to buy, own or export anything over 100 years old, including carpets, tiles and furniture, and the offence carries a prison sentence. Antique carpets should be sold with a certificate saying that they aren't over 100 years old. At ancient sites you may be offered coins and pieces of pottery, and although many are fakes, it isn't worth the risk.

ONLINE SHOPPING

Shopping is a 'hands-on' experience in Turkey, where people like to see goods rather than read about them in a catalogue. This, along with the unreliability of the postal system, means that mail-order shopping isn't popular. The major exception is online shopping. Turks have fallen for the internet in a big way – the number of users increased by 700 per cent between 2000 and 2007, according to Internet World Stats.

> Buying online in Turkey should be no more risky than in any other country, provided the site uses a secure server (https:// rather than http://) for all financial transactions.

Internet Stores

Shopping sites are useful if you live outside a major city or resort and there are a number of websites where you can buy everything from a watch to a washing machine. Some supermarket chains, such as Migros, offer online shopping in certain areas. In addition, Turkey has its own version of eBay, although the bulk of the sellers are dealers rather than private individuals. Shopping online can be cheaper, but you must factor in the delivery charge and any bank transfer fee. The major drawback for foreigners is that many of the sites are only in Turkish.

Home Delivery

Due to the unpredictability of the postal system, most goods are sent by courier (*kargo*). There are several courier companies with offices throughout Turkey, which are fast and reliable and deliver to central offices or direct to your home. Prices are calculated according to distance and parcel size, and start at around €2. Supermarkets will deliver for free, provided you live nearby and spend a minimum amount (around €50). If you buy furniture or white goods, delivery and 'installation' costs are included in the purchase price.

RETURNING GOODS

Turkish consumer law is being brought into line with European law, which gives the consumer the right to return defective or unsuitable goods to the shop where they were purchased within 30 days, together with proof of purchase (e.g. receipt). Unsuitable goods must be returned in perfect condition and with their original packaging. Some shopkeepers try to wriggle out of their responsibility, but stand your ground, as few will wish to lose you as a customer.

Refunds

You can request a refund, a replacement, a discount in proportion to the defect, or a free-of-charge repair. If you paid with a debit or credit card, the refund should be credited to your card.

Guarantees

White goods and electronic devices carry a two-year guarantee. during which period you're entitled to free repair – including all parts and labour, as well any call-out charges. If smaller electrical items go wrong within a month of purchase, you can return them to the shop and ask for a replacement (see above); any later and you may have to take them to a local service centre.

Manufacturers sometimes offer long-term warranties (up to five years) to tempt you to buy their products, which are a good deal on heavy-use goods such as washing machines (but it isn't worth paying extra for a longer warranty).

Complaints

The government has been promoting consumer rights and there's a fledgling consumer association, unfortunately called TÜ-MER, so the mere mention of consumer law (*tüketici kanunu*) should be enough to persuade an unwilling shopkeeper to provide satisfaction. If not, call in the municipal police (*zabıta*), who monitor local businesses.

TÜ-MER has a council in each district, contactable through the local administration office (*kaymakamlık*). If your loss is greater than $600 (the 2007 limit) or the seller won't comply with the council's verdict, you need to apply to the consumer court (*tüketici mahkemesi*) through the local court house, and may need the help of a legal translator and/or lawyer.

10.
ODDS & ENDS

A country's culture is influenced by many factors and reflected in myriad ways. Among the principal influences are its climate and geography, which are considered here along with various cultural manifestations, including crime, the national flag and anthem, government and international relations, attitudes to pets, tipping and toilets.

> 'Culture is the foundation of the Turkish republic.'
>
> Mustafa Kemal Atatürk

CLIMATE

Turkey's climate is one of extremes; hot sunshine in the west while eastern cities shiver under deep snow, and water shortages in the Mediterranean while the Black Sea is awash with rain. In Turkey, it's said, you can experience all four seasons in one day.

Istanbul is like New York, hot and humid in summer and subject to one or two heavy snowfalls each winter. In central, eastern and south-eastern Anatolia, summers are hot and dusty and winters can be bitterly cold. Temperatures as low as -40°C (-40°F) have been recorded in the east. The milder Black Sea coast is the only place where you need an umbrella all year round. The best weather is on the Aegean and Mediterranean coasts. Here, the winters, while damp and chilly, are mercifully short, but in summer it can reach 50°C (122°F) in mid-July. Turkey has no siesta culture and it's debilitating to work through weeks of unrelenting heat.

NATURAL HAZARDS

There are a few natural hazards that you should be aware of in Turkey.

Earthquakes

Turkey lies across several fault lines, and a major earthquake rocked Izmit, west of Istanbul, in 1999. This was a wake-up call to the authorities, which resulted in improved building standards and earthquake monitoring. The risk of earthquakes is something you need to bear in mind when deciding where to live (see **Accommodation** in **Chapter 3**).

You should be prepared for an earthquake at all times, especially if you live in Istanbul. Have a bag packed with clothes, water, snacks and medicines in a place you can easily find it, keep a torch and shoes by the bed, and ensure you know how to turn off utilities. If a earthquake hits, don't panic and jump off the balcony – this is what many Turks do! Get outside if you can do so safely, otherwise shelter up against (or below) a sturdy piece of furniture until the quake subsides, then leave the house. It's wise to pre-arrange a place for the family to meet.

Forest Fires

Tinder-dry conditions make fire a frequent hazard in summer, when the Mediterranean and Aegean being the worst-affected areas – thousands of hectares are burned every year. Some fires are due to arson (developers sometimes get the blame, as forestry land cannot be built on) but more than half are caused by the Turks' passions for picnics and smoking.

> **Always douse fires thoroughly with water and dispose of cigarette butts carefully – don't throw them out of car windows. There are penalties for lighting fires in some areas and you're required by law to report a forest fire, however small (☎ 177).**

Wildlife

Turkey has snakes, scorpions and hornets, but by far the most persistent pest is the mosquito, which can make life a misery in coastal and river areas. Window screens, bed nets and a good repellent spray are the best defence. There's a small risk of contracting malaria in the south, east of Adana, but mosquitoes are more of an annoyance than a health hazard.

CRIME

Turkey has a low crime rate. Statistics from Interpol for 2002 – the most recent available (Turkstat, the official statistics organisation, doesn't issue crime figures) – give a total of 387,590 crimes reported to the police, or 570 crimes per 100,000 people. This is a fraction of the figures for the UK, Spain or Germany, and while crime is increasing, violent assaults on strangers are a rarity. Foreigners often remark how safe they feel, and many can relate a story of a lost bag or wallet being returned to them with the contents intact. Nevertheless, don't be lulled into a false sense of security – take out insurance, look after your belongings and use the same precautions as you would at home.

Fear of terrorism puts some people off Turkey, but the risk is extremely low. On his excellent website (💻 www.turkeytravelplanner.com), Turkey expert and *Lonely Planet* writer Tom Brosnahan says that the average traveller has a 1 in 9,270,000 chance of being caught up in a terrorist attack.

Most crime is opportunist – bag-snatching, pick-pocketing, and theft from unsecured vehicles and homes. In cities, foreign men are sometimes targeted by con artists – 'friendly' Turks who spike their drinks and steal cash and passports, or take them to a bar where the 'guest' is forced to pay a very large bill. Be careful who you socialise with or accept refreshments from. Women may be victims of unwanted sexual advances, although this has a lot to do with how you dress and behave, and is more of a problem in tourist areas.

Turkey's 'national crime' is fraud. Most Turks do their utmost to avoid revealing their income to the tax authorities and they may encourage you to do the same. This is something to be especially aware of in property transactions (see **Tax Fraud** in **Chapter 3**). You may also be approached by bogus officials trying to impose cash fines (ask for a receipt) or be palmed off with fake banknotes – always check your change.

If you're a victim of crime, you should report it to the police as you will need the report in order to make a claim on your insurance.

FLAG & ANTHEM

The Turkish flag is distinctive – a white crescent and star on a red background. The design was adopted by the Ottomans in the 19th century and standardised by the republic in the '30s, but its origins go far back in history. The legend of the flag is that survivors of battle saw a crescent moon and star reflected in a pool of Turkish blood. Its nickname is '*ay yildiz*' (moon star). Turks revere their flag and wouldn't dream of wearing it emblazoned on a T shirt or using it as a tablecloth or throw.

> The flag is displayed by official bodies and businesses on all secular holidays. When 13 soldiers were killed in a clash with the Kurdish separatist PKK in October 2007, Turks protested with demonstrations and by hanging the flag from every building to honour their soldiers' memory.

The Turkish anthem is the *İstiklâl Marşı* (*Independence March*), written by Mehmet Akif Ersoy, one of the country's best-known poets, and adopted as the anthem in 1921 after a nationwide competition (over 700 poems were submitted to the Grand National Assembly).

The tune was composed by Osman Zeki Üngör, conductor of the Presidential Symphony Orchestra, and is rousing and uplifting, unlike the dirges which represent some countries. All Turks know the words, which are displayed in schoolrooms and government buildings; the full text runs to ten verses but only the first two (see box) are sung.

National Anthem

*(İstiklâl Marşı/*Independence
March)

*Korkma, sönmez bu şafaklarda yüzen
al sancak;
Sönmeden yurdumun üstünde tüten en
son ocak.
O benim milletimin yıldızdır,
parlayacak;
O benimdir, o benim milletimindir
ancak.*

*Çatma, kurban olayım çehreni ey nazlı
hilâl!
Kahraman ırkıma bir gül! Ne bu şiddet
bu celâl?
Sana olmaz dökülen kanlarımız sonar
helâl,
Hakkıdıir, Hakk'a tapan, milletimin
istiklâl!*

Fear not, for the red flag that proudly
ripples in this glorious dawn shall never
fade;
Before the last fiery hearth that
is ablaze within my nation is
extinguished.
For that is the star of my nation, and it
will forever shine;
It is mine, and solely belongs to my
valiant nation.

Frown not, I beseech you, oh thou coy
crescent!
But smile upon my heroic race! Why
the anger, why the rage?
Our blood which we shed for you will
not be blessed otherwise,
For freedom is the absolute right of my
God-worshipping nation!

GEOGRAPHY

Turkey is vast and shares its border with
eight neighbours – Greece and Bulgaria
to the west, Armenia, Azerbaijan and
Georgia to the east and, to the south-east,
Iran, Iraq and Syria. Its diverse geography
includes vast forests, rolling plains,
snow-covered mountains, and a largely
unspoiled coastline.

There are seven regions – Marmara,
Black Sea (*Karadeniz*), Aegean (*Ege*),
Mediterranean (*Akdeniz*), and Central,
East and South-eastern Anatolia (*İç, Doğu*
and *Güneydoğu Anadolu*). The north
shore faces the Black Sea, while the west
and south coasts adjoin the Aegean and
Mediterranean.

The Marmara region takes its name
from the sea which separates Thrace
(European Turkey) from Anatolia (the
much larger Asian part of the country)
and connects the Black Sea to the Aegean
via the Bosporus. This the most densely
inhabited corner of Turkey – a seventh of
the population lives in greater Istanbul.

The Black Sea coast is steep and rocky
and cut off from the rest of the country
by the Pontic Mountains. This area feels
isolated, in terms of both geography and
culture; it's lush and green with tea, cherry
and hazelnut plantations.

The Mediterranean and Aegean coasts
are 'holiday Turkey', a sun-washed
panorama of olive plantations, fertile
valleys and high peaks which drop down
to an impossibly blue sea. These are also
the most important agricultural areas and
home to many of Turkey's ancient sites.

The centre of Turkey consists of a
high plateau, similar to the Central Asian
steppes, which climbs steadily towards
the wild and rugged east where mountain
ranges dominate and provide the source
for two world-famous rivers, the Tigris
(*Dicle*) and the Euphrates (*Fırat*).
The further east you travel, the more
fascinating – and foreign – the country
becomes.

The South-east Anatolian Project (*Güneydoğu Anadolu Projesi* or *GAP*) has done much to bring irrigation to the area, the centrepiece of which is the Atatürk Dam. Built across the Euphrates, it created the world's third-largest expanse of dammed water, covering an area of 817km² (370mi²).

Vital Statistics

Land area: 780,580km² (301,382mi²).

Coastline & borders: 9,843km (6,116mi) in length.

Highest point: Mount Ararat (*Ağrı Dağı*) at 5,166m (16,946ft), said to be the resting place of Noah's Ark.

Lowest point: Mediterranean Sea (*Akdeniz*).

Longest river: Kızıl River (*Kızılırmak*) at 1,150km (715mi).

Largest natural lake: Lake Van (*Van Gölü*) at 3,755km² (1,450mi²).

GOVERNMENT

The Republic of Turkey, which was declared on 29th October 1923, is a parliamentary representative democracy with a multi-party system, with its seat of government in Ankara. Ankara was best known for its long-haired Angora goats when it became a powerbase for Atatürk, who chose it for its remote location in Anatolia's heartland. Culturally, it's still a long way from cosmopolitan Istanbul.

The Constitution

Turkey's written constitution sets out the organisation of the government, the framework of the legal system, and the rights and responsibilities of the state and its citizens. Important elements include equality of the sexes and freedom of religious belief. Some people believe that certain fundamental rights have been open to (mis)interpretation, but Turkey is under increasing pressure from the West – especially in its accession negotiations with the European Union (EU) – to deal with fundamental issues as human rights, freedom of expression and the treatment of ethnic minorities.

The current constitution was ratified in 1982, although in early 2008 the government was working on a new constitution.

The Judiciary

Turkish law is governed by the Civil Code. The judiciary is independent of parliament, and overseen by the Constitutional Court. There are courts covering different areas of the law, such as civil, administrative and criminal, as well as military courts. At a higher level, decisions are made by supreme courts, which include the High Court of Appeals.

Lawyers choose to become attorneys or barristers, prosecutors, judges or notaries. Judges decide all cases and there's no jury system in Turkey, nor is there any bail. Punishment consists of a fine or imprisonment – capital punishment was abolished in 2004.

Parliament

Turkey has no monarch. The president (Abdullah Gül) is the head of state and sovereignty rests with the Turkish people, who elect their own representatives or deputies to the unicameral (single chamber) parliament, called the Grand National Assembly. Everyone over the age of 18 has the right to vote.

A referendum in 2007 decided that all future presidents would be decided by a US-style system – election by public vote to a five-year term of office. The president's role is mainly ceremonial; although he does have the power to delay legislation or force it to a referendum – something Gül's predecessor, Ahmet Necdet Sezer, was notorious for doing.

> **'Abdullah Gül has a frank look and a reassuring smile ... an air of an oriental George Clooney.'**
>
> *La Libre Belgique* (Belgian daily newspaper)

The real power lies with the prime minister and his council of ministers (MPs). The prime ministers is usually the head of the party that receives the most votes in a general election,

and the current incumbent is Recep Tayyip Erdoğan, leader of the Justice & Development Party (AKP – see below).

The Grand National Assembly consists of 550 MPs, representing 85 electoral districts, who serve a four-year term. Seats are allocated by proportional representation to parties that win at least 10 per cent of the votes.

Political Parties

At the dawn of the republic there was just one political party, the Republican People's Party, which led Turkey for 22 years. Multi-party politics didn't arrive until 1950, when the Democratic Party swept into power. With the RPP favouring state control and the Democrats supporting the private sector, the scene was set for a standoff, which has characterised Turkish politics ever since.

By the late '70s, nationalist and religious parties had entered the ring, and as the many parties divided, regrouped and fragmented again, the result was political chaos. The '90s saw a succession of ineffective coalition governments. The last, an unlikely combination of socialists, nationalists and conservatives, led by Bülent Ecevit, lasted until the economic crash of 2001, when interest rates shot up overnight by an incredible 2,500 per cent, businesses folded and unemployment soared. Concern over Ecevit's health led to a general election in 2002 – and a decisive win for the Justice & Development Party.

At the time of writing, there were 22 active parties, 15 of which contested the 2007 general election. The top three parties were:

● Justice & Development Party (*Adalet ve Kalkınma Partisi* or *AKP*) –

conservative and pro-Islam, with 341 seats;

- Republican People's Party (*Cumhuriyet Halk Partisi* or *CHP*) – socialist and staunchly secular, with 98 seats;

- Nationalist Movement Party (*Milliyetçi Hareket Partisi* or *MHP*) – right-wing nationalist, with 71 seats.

> **Like most nationalities, Turks don't generally trust politicians and consider them boring. But they do take an active interest in politics and rarely waste their vote – the turn-out for the 2007 election was 84 per cent. Election times are festive and streets are strung with banners and each candidate's manifesto is broadcast from a dolmuş to the accompaniment of loud music.**

Local Government

Turkey is made up of 81 provinces, each with its own government headed by a governor, linked to the main administration in Ankara. The provinces are divided into districts, which are administered by sub-governors. Each district has a municipal council (*belediye*) that is responsible for matters such as water supply, refuse collection and street lighting. Municipalities work independently from central government and are headed by an elected mayor. Districts with more than one highly populated area may have more than one municipality, which is the case in some of the smaller tourist resorts that have grown out of villages, where contact with the *belediye* is often a foreigner's first experience of Turkish bureaucracy.

On the bottom rung of the administration ladder is the *muhtar* (headman), an elected official who looks after the interests of a village or neighbourhood.

The Economy

Turkey's economy is on an upward track. The *CIA World Factbook* estimated its gross domestic product (GDP) for 2007 at US $668bn, greater than that of Belgium, South Africa or Saudi Arabia. Some of this is due to a shift towards the private sector – many state institutions have been privatised, including petroleum giant Petrol Ofisi. The economy is also benefiting from the growth in its industry and service sectors, which have both overtaken agriculture. Textiles are the top export but automotive products and white goods are catching up. Tourism and foreign investment also help boost the economy.

The launch of the new Turkish lira (YTL) in 2005 revitalised the currency. The euro, dollar and sterling fell in value against the lira throughout 2007 and it's no longer seen as a fiscal joke.

INTERNATIONAL RELATIONS

Turkey is a good neighbour. It has friendly relations with most adjoining countries and has worked hard to establish good connections with Europe and the world. There are some awkward relationships – such as those with Greece and Armenia – but Turkish governments have built on Atatürk's goal to pursue peace and conciliation and this has done much to boost its global profile.

> *Yurtta Sulh, Cihanda Sulh* **(Peace at Home, Peace in the World) is Turkey's national motto, which sums up Atatürk's policy of peaceful coexistence and the avoidance of conflict.**

The European Union

Turkey has a love-hate relationship with Europe. Membership of the EU is one of its prime ambitions and a natural extension of a westward-looking policy which began in Ottoman times. Yet the demands which the EU has been making since formal negotiations began in 2005, and Turkey's apparent reluctance to abide by all the new legislation are impeding its progress towards accession. Issues over the Kurds and, especially, Cyprus (see below) remain serious obstacles on the road to EU membership.

While some member states, such as the UK and Spain, remain supportive, the seemingly anti-Turkish attitude of others, such as France and Austria, has cooled the enthusiasm of many Turks for accession. In a 2006 Eurobarometer poll, only 43 per cent viewed EU membership in a positive light.

Turkey cannot join the EU before 2013, and some observers think it won't happen until much later, if at all. However, in continuing with its reforms and strengthening its ties with the West, Turkey has as much to gain as it does to lose – in many eyes, a lot more.

The Cyprus Problem

This Mediterranean island has been a battleground for centuries but the roots of the current problem began in the '60s, when violence escalated between Muslim Turks and Orthodox Greeks. Cyprus has been divided since 1974, when a Greek military coup prompted Turkey to invade Cyprus to protect its citizens. Greece now controls the south and Turkey the north, although the international community doesn't recognise the Turkish Republic of Northern Cyprus. An attempt by the United Nations' Secretary General Kofi Annan to unify the island in 2004 failed, when Turkish Cypriots voted yes but Greek Cypriots voted no. However, in early 2008, following the election of a new Greek Cypriot leader, Demetris Christofias, the two sides were once again talking and hopes were high for an eventual resolution to the problem.

The World

Its unique global position often places Turkey in the role of mediator – the West considers it a 'safe' Muslim ally, while Arab states regard it as a link with the West. And Turkey's instinct for commerce – most Turks would rather trade than fight – has helped the country to forge strong international links.

The US has long supported Turkey's EU ambitions, wanting Turkey as an ally in view of its Middle Eastern connections – Turkey has close relations with both Israel and Palestine. The Iraq debacle has tested this relationship – many Turks didn't support US intervention in Iraq and the US wasn't happy when Turkey sent troops into Iraq in a purge on PKK terrorists – but the two nations remain on good terms.

Turkey also has strong ties with central Asia. It shares a cultural heritage with many of the former Soviet states and is in a good position to help cement their relationships with the West. A product of this cooperation is the Baku-Tbilisi-Ceyhan pipeline, which opened in 2006 and carries crude oil from Azerbaijan, via Georgia, to Turkey's eastern Mediterranean coast.

International Organisations

Turkey joined the North Atlantic Treaty Organisation (NATO) in 1952 and helps to safeguard its eastern boundary – there's a NATO headquarters in Izmir. It's also a founding member of the UN, the Organisation for Economic Co-operation and Development (OECD), the Organisation for Security and Co-operation in Europe (OSCE), the Organisation of the Islamic Conference (OIC) and the G20 group of industrial nations. Turkey joined the Council of Europe in the year of its foundation and has been an associate member of the EU since 1963 and a member of the EU Customs Union agreement since 1995. It joined the World Trade Organisation (WTO) in the same year.

PETS

Turks generally treat animals like animals – they provide food, catch vermin and guard flocks, but are rarely considered as pets or part of the family. Many Turks are frightened of dogs, and while few are deliberately cruel to animals, most cannot understand westerners' need for four-legged companionship. Traditionally, birds and fish have been the preferred pets. Dogs and cats are gaining in popularity, and some have become 'fashion statements' – Siberian huskies were 'big' in 2006. Dogs and cats aren't usually allowed inside the home and many Turkish women have a horror of cat hair.

There's reluctance to neuter animals and they're often allowed to roam the streets. Dog packs are a problem in resorts out of season and in cities. The municipalities are required by law to

Turkish Van cat

vaccinate, neuter and care for strays, but some resort to culling.

You can import pets – the official limit is one dog, one cat, one bird and ten fish. Dogs and cats should have a certificate of origin and a health certificate issued within 15 days of travel. Repatriating pets can be difficult, especially to the UK, with its strict quarantine rules.

Pet food and accessories are expensive. Veterinary services are improving and all vaccinations are available, although only big-city practices have the skills and facilities for major operations. Kennels and pet-minding services are rare outside expat areas, and pet cemeteries don't exist.

If all this seems rather negative, note that many foreigners have successfully brought their pets to Turkey – and many more have adopted animals after arrival (the author included). There's certainly no need to buy a pet in Turkey; the problem is resisting all the animals who wish to adopt you.

RELIGION

Turkey is a secular state where a 'gentle' form of Islam is practised – at least on the surface. Alcohol is widely available, women are free of dress

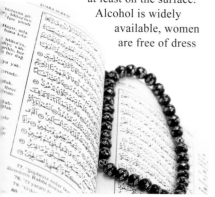

restrictions and you can even buy bacon in some supermarkets. Yet the government is led by an Islamist party, albeit a western-looking, reforming one. Over 99 per cent of the population is Muslim and even if many appear to be lapsed, a large number attend a mosque on Fridays and during the main religious holidays. The most obvious signs of Islam to the visitor are the many mosques and the five-times-daily call to prayer, called the *ezan*.

> The *ezan* is called by the *muezzin*. The opening words '*Allah-u Akbar*' mean 'God is great'.

The word Islam translates as 'submission to God's will' and it isn't just a faith but a way of life. It centres on Allah, who is the 'one God', and on the Koran, which is believed to be the word of Allah as it was revealed to the prophet Mohammed. Muslims are expected to adhere to the 'five pillars of Islam', which are:

● to say the creed: 'There is no god but Allah and Mohammed is his prophet' – knowledge of, and belief in, these words are sufficient to make you a Muslim;

● to pray five times a day;

● to fast during Ramadan (called *Ramazan* in Turkey);

● to give alms and support to the poor;

● to make the pilgrimage to Mecca, known as the Hajj (*Hac*).

The vast majority of Turks are Sunni Muslims, but there are also a large number of Alevis (around a fifth of the population), who believe in a different line of succession from Mohammed. The Alevi religion is closer to Anatolian culture than the stricter Sunni faith. Women don't cover their heads and they worship alongside men in a *cemevi* (meeting house) rather than a mosque. Many Alevis feel discriminated against, as their religion receives no state funding and isn't taught in schools.

Others religions account for a mere 1 per cent of the population. There are Jewish and Christian communities in Istanbul and western Turkey, where you'll find churches and synagogues. The Christian religions include the Armenian and Greek Orthodox churches, as well as the Assyrian Church of the East ,which has its roots in Persia and is now located near Mardin in south-east Turkey.

Some visitors are concerned about religious fundamentalism in Turkey, although while a fundamentalist element does exist, it's less obvious than in many western European countries. You're more likely to see women shrouded in a *burqa* in Birmingham than in Bodrum and the majority of Muslims simply wish to practise their faith (or not) in a forward-thinking country. Those of other faiths will experience no pressure to convert, and provided you respect Islam you're unlikely to feel uncomfortable in Turkey.

The Headscarf

A scrap of cloth is proving to be one of the most controversial issues in modern Turkish politics. Women wearing a Muslim headscarf have been banned from entering government buildings, such as courts, state hospitals and universities, since the '80s. The headscarf (or any religious attire) is seen as a threat to Turkey's principle of secularism, whereby the state must

remain neutral in matters of religion. But this has led to discrimination against scarf-wearing women, who have been denied work and education because of their beliefs, a situation contrary to Turkey's democratic ambitions.

However, in 2007, the country was faced with a new dilemma: both of its leaders were 'new' Islamists with scarf-wearing wives. The government passed an amendment to the constitution in 2008, easing restrictions on the wearing of headscarves in universities. A storm of secularist protest ensued, and the topic is destined to be wrapped in controversy for some time to come.

TIME ZONE

Turkey has only one time zone and is two hours ahead of Greenwich Mean Time (GMT), the same as Athens, Cairo and Pretoria. In common with the rest of Europe and most of the US, Turkey operates daylight-saving time. Clocks go forward an hour on the last Sunday in March and back an hour on the last Sunday in October.

TIPPING

Turks don't usually leave a tip unless they think service has been exceptional. But many workers are badly paid and those in tourist resorts have to stretch their seasonal salary over 12 months. Good tips make a huge difference.

As a rough guide, you should tip as follows: up to 10 per cent in cafés, bars and small eateries; up to 15 per cent in smarter restaurants, but check the bill first in case a service charge has been added. Give around €1 per bag to hotel porters; airport porters usually have a set charge. If you're happy with the service at the hairdresser's, barber's or Turkish bath, split 15 per cent of the cost between staff. With taxi drivers, just round up the fare to the nearest lira. And don't tip *dolmuş* (minibus) drivers.

Turks don't like asking for money and tips should be given discreetly.

Not surprisingly, recipients prefer cash, preferably in local currency, although foreign notes are acceptable (particularly in large wads!) but foreign coins are difficult to change. Many establishments have a tip box, which allows you to deposit your gratuity without revealing the amount, thus avoiding the potential for embarrassment on both sides! The contents are divided between the staff.

TOILETS

There are two types of toilet (*tuvalet*) in Turkey: the type which you sit on and the type which you squat over. The latter can be alarming at first but is more hygienic, since you make no contact with a seat. Doctors also say that the squatting position is better for your bowels, although it's a good idea to ensure the contents of your pockets don't fall out!

Turkish homes often have both types of toilet – a Western-style loo in the bathroom and a separate squat toilet, which may double as a broom cupboard!

> When standard toilets were introduced in petrol stations across Turkey, the management were careful to ensure that they were used correctly, and you may still see signs advising customers not to stand on the seats!

Another peculiarity is the small spout at the back of the seat, operated by a valve to the right of the cistern – or, in the case of squat toilets, the tap and jug. This is for washing your bottom, which must be done with your left hand – Muslims eat with their right hand. Toilet paper is for drying, and is often disposed of in a small bin rather than flushed down the pan to avoid clogging up the (basic) plumbing. Even small hotels use this system, and there's usually a sign to remind you.

Public toilets range from the pristine to the unspeakable. There's generally one near a mosque. 'Men' is '*Bay*' and 'Women' is '*Bayan*'. There's a small charge for using public toilets which may include a few sheets of toilet paper – but always carry some, just in case.

APPENDICES

APPENDIX A: EMBASSIES & CONSULATES

In Turkey

Listed below are the contact details for the embassies and high commissions of the main English-speaking countries in Turkey. A full list of embassies and consulates in Turkey is available from the website of the Ministry of Foreign Affairs (🖥 www.mfa.gov.tr/MFA/Protocol).

Australia: Embassy, Uğur Mumcu Caddesi No: 88, MNG Binası, Kat: 7, Gaziosmanpaşa 06700, Ankara (☎ 0312-459 9500, 🖥 www.turkey.embassy.gov.au).

Canada: Embassy, Cinnah Caddesi No: 58, 06690, Çankaya, Ankara (☎ 0312-409 2700, 🖥 http://geo.international.gc.ca/canada-europa/turkey)

Ireland: Embassy, Uğur Mumcu Caddesi No: 88, MNG Binası, B Blok, Kat: 3, Gaziosmanpaşa 06700, Ankara (☎ 0312-446 6172, ✉ ankaraembassy@dfa.ie).

New Zealand: Embassy, İran Caddesi No: 13, Kat: 4, Kavaklıdere, Ankara (☎ 0312-467 9054, 🖥 www.nzembassy.com/home.cfm?c=40).

South Africa: Embassy, Filistin Sokak No: 27, Gaziosmanpaşa 06700, Ankara (☎ 0312-446 4056, 🖥 www.southafrica.org.tr).

United Kingdom: Embassy, Şehit Ersan Caddesi 46/A, Çankaya, Ankara (☎ 0312-455 3344, 🖥 http://ukinturkey.fco.gov.uk/en).

USA: Embassy, 110 Atatürk Blvd, Kavaklıdere 06100, Ankara (☎ 0312-455 5555, 🖥 http://turkey.usembassy.gov).

Abroad

Listed below are the contact details for Turkish embassies and consulates in the main English-speaking countries. A full list can be found at 🖳 www.turkish-media.com/en/us_tr_embassies.htm.

Australia: Turkish Embassy, 6 Moonah Place, Yarralumla, ACT 2600, Canberra (☎ 02-6234 0000, 🖳 www.turkishembassy.org.au).

Canada: Embassy of the Republic of Turkey, 197 Wurtemburg Street, Ottawa ON, K1N 8L9 (☎ 0613- 789-4044, 🖳 www.turkishembassy.com/II/IIH.htm).

Ireland: Embassy of the Republic of Turkey, 11 Clyde Road, Ballsbridge, Dublin 4 (☎ 01-668 5240, ✉ turkembassy@eircom.net).

New Zealand: Turkey Embassy, Level 8, 15-17 Murphy Street, Thorndon, PO Box 12-248, Wellington (☎ 04-472 1290-2, ✉ turkem@xtra.co.nz).

South Africa: Turkish Embassy, 1067 Church Street, Hatfield, 0028, Pretoria (☎ 012-342-6053-7, 🖳 www.turkishembassy.co.za).

United Kingdom: Turkish Embassy, 43 Belgrave Square, London, SW1X 8PA (☎ 020-7393 0202, 🖳 http://turkishembassylondon.org). Visa information is available from the Consulate General for the Republic of Turkey, Rutland Lodge, Rutland Gardens, Knightsbridge, London SW7 1BW (☎ 020-7591 6900, 🖳 www.turkishconsulate.org.uk).

USA: Embassy of the Republic of Turkey, 2525 Massachusetts Ave., NW, Washington, DC 20008 (☎ 0202-612 6700, 🖳 www.turkishembassy.org).

> **The business hours of embassies vary and they close on their own country's holidays as well as on Turkish public holidays. Always telephone to confirm opening hours before visiting.**

APPENDIX B: FURTHER READING

English-language Newspapers & Magazines

Newspapers

Today's Zaman – daily (⌨ www.todayszaman.com).

Turkish Daily News – daily (⌨ www.turkishdailynews.com.tr).

The New Anatolian – daily (⌨ www.thenewanatolian.com).

Land of Lights – Fethiye local (⌨ www.landoflights.net).

The Post – local serving Marmaris and Fethiye areas.

Voices – Altinkum weekly (⌨ www.voicesnewspaper.com).

Dalyan Times – Dalyan local (⌨ www.naldoken.com/newspaper).

Magazines & Guides

Cornucopia – thrice-yearly collectable glossy featuring all aspects of Turkish culture (⌨ www.cornucopia.net).

Time Out Istanbul – monthly (⌨ www.timeout.com.tr/home.php).

The Guide Istanbul – bi-monthly.

The Guide Ankara/Antalya/Bodrum – annual.

Books

A selection of books about Turkey and Turkish culture is listed below; the publication title is followed by the name of the author and the publisher's name in brackets. Many books are available from booksellers in Turkey and those that aren't are available by mail from websites such as Amazon (⌨ www.amazon.co.uk). Those published by Çitlembik can be obtained through the publisher's website (⌨ www.citlembik.com.tr/index.php?lang=en).

Culture

A Dictionary of Turkish Proverbs, Metin Yurtbaşı (Milet Publishing)

Imagining the Turkish House: Collective Visions of Home, Carel Bertram (University of Texas Press)

Nasreddin Hodja, Alpay Kabacalı (Net Books, Turkey) – available in several languages via the publisher's website (⌨ www.netkitabevi.com/left.htm)

Rumi and the Whirling Dervishes, Shems Friedlander (Parabola)

Sinan Diaryz: A Walking Tour of Mimar Sinan's Monuments, Ann Pierpont (Çitlembik)

The Tulip, Anna Pavord (Bloomsbury)

Turkish Baths: A Light Unto a Tradition and Culture, Yılmazkaya Orhan (Çitlembik)

History

Ancient Turkey: A Traveller's History, Seton Lloyd (University of California Press)

Byzantium: The Surprising Life of a Medieval Empire, Judith Herrin (Allen Lane)

Constantinople – City of the World's Desire, 1452-1924, Philip Mansel (Penguin)

Gallipoli, Alan Moorehead (Aurum Press)

Inside the Seraglio – Private Lives of the Sultans in Istanbul, John Freely (Penguin)

A Modern History of the Kurds, David McDowall (I B Tauris)

Osman's Dream: The Story of the Ottoman Empire 1300-1923, Caroline Finkel (John Murray)

The Ottoman Centuries: The Rise and Fall of the Turkish Empire, Patrick Balfour Kinross (William Morrow)

The Private World of Ottoman Women, Godfrey Goodwin (Saqi)

Subjects of the Sultan: Culture and Daily Life in the Ottoman Empire, Suraiya Faroqhi (I B Tauris)

Sons of the Conquerors: The Rise of the Turkic World, Hugh Pope (Overlook Press)

Storm on Horseback: The Seljuk Warriors of Turkey, John Freely (I B Tauris)

Language

201 Turkish Verbs, Talat Sait Halman (Barron's Educational Series)

English-Turkish/Turkish-English Portable Dictionary, R. Avery (Milet Publishing)

The Rough Guide to Turkish (A Dictionary Phrasebook), Lexus (Rough Guides)

Teach Yourself Turkish, David Pollard & Asuman Çelen Pollard (Hodder & Stoughton)

Turkish Berlitz Phrase Book and Dictionary (Berlitz)

Turkish Grammar, Geoffrey Lewis (Oxford University Press)

Turkish in Three Months (Hugo), Bengisu Rona (Dorling Kindersley)

The Turkish Language Reform: A Catastrophic Success, Geoffrey Lewis (Oxford Linguistics/OUP)

Literature

Berji Kristin: Tales from the Garbage Hills, Latife Tekin (Marion Boyars)

Birds Without Wings, Louis de Bernières (Secker & Warburg)

The Drop That Became the Sea, Yunus Emre (Shambhala)

Istanbul, Orhan Pamuk (Faber & Faber)

Memed, My Hawk, Yaşar Kemal (Harvill Press)

My Name is Red, Orhan Pamuk (Faber & Faber)

On Freedom Street, Yesho Atil (Lynx House)

Poems of Nazim Hikmet, Nazim Hikmet (W W Norton)

Snow, Orhan Pamuk (Faber and Faber)

The Sultan's Seal, Jenny White (Phoenix)

Living Poets of Turkey: An Anthology of Modern Poems Translated with an Introduction, Talet S. Halman (Milet Publishing)

Living & Working in Turkey

Buying in Turkey: A Complete Property Buyer's Guide to Turkey 2007/08, Dominic Whiting (Apogee)

A Handbook for Living in Turkey, Pat Yale (Çitlembik)

Living in Turkey, Stephane Yerasimos (Thames & Hudson)

People

The Alevis in Turkey: The Emergence of a Secular Islamic Tradition, David Shankland (Routledge)

Atatürk – The Rebirth of a Nation, Lord Patrick Kinross (Weidenfeld & Nicolson) – the seminal work on Atatürk; reprints are available.

Atatürk, Andrew Mango, (John Murray)

Crescent and Star: Turkey Between Two Worlds, Stephen Kinzer (Farrar Straus Giroux)

Dervish – The Invention of Modern Turkey, Tim Kelsey (Hamish Hamilton)

The New Turkey: The Quiet Revolution on the Edge of Europe, Chris Morris (Granta)

Portrait of a Turkish Family, İrfan Orga (Eland)

Turkey Unveiled, Hugh Pope and Nicole Pope (Overlook Press)

The Turkish Embassy Letters, Lady Mary Wortley Montagu (Virago)

Turkish Reflections: A Biography of a Place, Mary Lee Settle (Simon & Schuster)

The Turks Today: Turkey After Atatürk, Andrew Mango (John Murray)

Tourist Guides

Aegean Turkey/ Turkey Beyond the Maeander/ Lycian Turkey, George E Bean (John Murray) – in-depth guides to archaeological sites, now out of print but available in second-hand bookshops.

The Companion Guide to Turkey, John Freely (Collins)

Eyewitness Istanbul Pocket Map and Guide (Dorling Kindersley)

From the Bosphorus: A Self-guided Tour, Rhonda Vander Sluis (Çitlembik)

A Guide to Biblical Sites in Greece and Turkey, Clyde E. Fant & Mitchell G. Reddish (Oxford University Press)

Insight Guide to Turkey (APA Publications)

Lonely Planet Istanbul, Virginia Maxwell (Lonely Planet City Guides)

Lonely Planet Turkey, Verity Campbell (Lonely Planet)

The Rough Guide to Turkey – Edition 6, Marc S. Dubin, Rosie Ayliffe, John Gawthrop and Terry Richardson (Rough Guides)

The Rough Guide Map Turkey (Rough Guide Maps)

Time Out Istanbul (Time Out Guides)

Topkapi Palace: Inside and Out, Claire Karaz Ruoff (Çitlembik)

Turkey: Complete Guide with Ottoman Sites, Ancient Ruins and the Best Beach Resorts (Fodor's)

Turkey (Eyewitness Travel Guides), Suzanne Swan (Dorling Kindersley)

Turkey (Lonely Planet Travel Atlas), Tom Brosnahan (Lonely Planet) – better than any map.

The Western Shores of Turkey: Discovering the Aegean and Mediterranean Coasts, John Freely (Tauris Parke)

Travellers' and Expats' Tales

A Fez of the Heart – Travels Around Turkey in Search of a Hat, Jeremy Seal (Picador)

Alexander's Path: From Caria to Cilicia, Freya Stark (Pimlico)

Beyond the Orchard, Azize Ethem (Çitlembik)

From the Steeple to the Minaret: Living Under the Shadow of Two Cultures, Hughette Eyupoğlu (Çitlembik)

Kaptan June & the Turtles, June Haimoff (available from Turkish distributors, including Dalyan Iz, 🖥 www.dalyaniz.com)

Life with a View: A Turkish Quest, Toni Sepeda, (Çitlembik)

South from Ephesus: Travels in Turkey, Brian Sewell (Gibson Square)

Tales from the Expat Harem: Foreign Women in Modern Turkey, Anastasia M. Ashman and Jennifer Eaton Gökmen (Avalon Group)

Turkey: Bright Sun, Strong Tea, Tom Brosnahan (Homer – order though the **Turkey Travel Planner** website – see below)

Uçhısar Unfolding: The Many Faces of a Cappadocian Village, Evelyn Kopp (Çitlembik)

Village in the Meadows, Malcolm Pfunder (Çitlembik)

Miscellaneous

Exploring Turkey (Çitlembik) – for children.

Folk Costumes of Turkey: A Paper Doll Book, Amy Chaple (Çitlembik)

Secrets of the Turkish Kitchen, Angie Mitchell (Çitlembik)

The Sultan's Kitchen: A Turkish Cookbook, Ozcan Ozan (Periplus Editions/Berkeley Books)

Treasury of Turkish Designs, Azade Akaar (Dover)

Turkey (Lonely Planet World Food), Dani Valent, Jim Masters & Perihan Masters (Lonely Planet)

Turkish Carpets: The Language of Motifs and Symbols, Mehmet Ateş (Milet Publishing)

Turkish Delights, Philippa Scott (Thames & Hudson)

Turkish Tiles and Symbols, Mehmet Ateş (Milet Publishing)

APPENDIX C: USEFUL WEBSITES

The following list contains some of the many websites dedicated to Turkey. All are in English or have English-language sections, unless otherwise stated. Note that Turkish websites can be unreliable and links don't always work, therefore you may need to refresh or re-type the address in the address bar.

Culture

Alevi (🖳 www.alevibektasi.org/xalevis1.htm) – facts about Turkey's second-largest faith, Alevi.

All About Turkey (🖳 www.allaboutturkey.com/index.htm) – a wealth of information, compiled by a professional tour guide.

Atatürk.com (🖳 www.ataturk.com) – political but factual website dedicated to the republic's founder.

Hitit Turkey (🖳 www.hitit.co.uk) – 'alternative guide' with easy navigation.

Introduction to Islam (🖳 www.introductiontoislam.org) – understanding the Muslim faith.

Mevlana (🖳 www.mevlana.net) – created by the descendents of the original Whirling Dervish.

Orhan Pamuk (🖳 www.orhanpamuk.net) – dedicated to Turkey's best-selling author.

Turkish Cultural Foundation (🖳 www.turkishculture.org) – from architecture to tapestry, an exhaustive collection of cultural facts.

Turkish Odyssey (🖳 www.turkeyodyssey.com) – a treasure trove of things to do, watch, eat and explore.

Turkish Music (🖳 www.turkishmusicclub.com) – an exhaustive list of musical styles and artists, with samples to download.

Finance, Tax & Business

Akbank (🖳 www.akbank.com/733.aspx) – Turkish bank.

Invest in Turkey (🖳 www.invest.gov.tr/default.aspx) – easy-to-follow information for business investors.

Rental Income Tax Guide (🖳 www.gib.gov.tr/fileadmin/ beyannamerehberi/56_dar_mukellef_ing.pdf) – Information sheet about declaring rental income on holiday property.

Tax Revenue Administration (💻 www.gib.gov.tr/index.php?id=469) – general tax matters explained.

Turkish Central Bank (💻 www.tcmb.gov.tr/yeni/eng) – the authoritative exchange rate.

Turkish-British Chamber of Commerce & Industry (💻 www.tbcci.org/index.php) – document, trade and support services for would-be investors.

Turkish Economy (💻 www.turkisheconomy.org.uk) – invaluable resource on property, tax, banking, insurance, employment and investment from the Office of the First Economic Counsellor at the Turkish Embassy in London.

Türkiye İs Bankası (💻 www.isbank.com.tr/english/english.asp) – Turkish bank.

Work Permits (💻 www.yabancicalismaizni.gov.tr/english/index_eng.htm) –information from the Ministry for Labour and Social Security.

Yapı Kredi Bank (💻 www.yapikredi.com.tr/en-us/mainpage.aspx) – Turkish 'Bank of the Year' in 2007.

Government

Council of Higher Education (💻 www.yok.gov.tr/english/index_en.htm) – complete list of universities.

Ministry of Culture (💻 www.kultur.gov.tr) – stodgy but comprehensive, with a range of language options.

Ministry of Education (💻 www.meb.gov.tr/) – some English content.

Ministry of Foreign Affairs (💻 www.disisleri.gov.tr/mfa) – information on visas and work permits, plus a list of embassies.

Ministry of Health (💻 www.saglik.gov.tr/en) – some English content.

Post & Telecommunications (💻 www.ptt.gov.tr/index_eng.php).

Turkish Statistical Institute (💻 www.turkstat.gov.tr/start.do).

Language

Learning Practical Turkish (💻 www.learningpracticalturkish.com) – an in-depth language guide and lucky dip of Turkish trivia.

Online Turkish (💻 www.onlineturkish.com) – self-study options, plus an index of useful words.

Tömer (💻 www.tomer.ankara.edu.tr/english/index.html) – Ankara University's language centre has been teaching Turkish since the '80s and runs classes in several cities, as well as distance-learning courses.

Turkish Dictionary (💻 www.turkishdictionary.net) – one of the more user-friendly online dictionaries.

Living & Working

Anglo Nannies (🖥 www.anglonannies.com/nannies.asp) – recruitment site for nannies and au pairs.

Ankara City Guide (🖥 www.ankaracityguide.com) – what's on in the capital.

Career in Travel (🖥 www.careerintravel.co.uk/holiday-rep-recruitment.htm) – information about working as a tour company representative.

Emlak.net (🖥 www.emlak.net) – property portal (in Turkish only).

Expat in Turkey (🖥 http://forum.expatinturkey.com) – forum.

Expats of Turkey (🖥 www.expatsofturkey.com) – forum.

Fethiye Times (🖥 www.fethiyetimes.org.uk/cms) – community website for Fethiye residents.

International Women of Istanbul (🖥 www.iwi-tr.org/index2.html) – women's support group.

International Women's Association of Izmir (🖥 www.iwaizmir.com) – women's support group.

Istanbul City Guide (🖥 http://english.istanbul.com/?Vst=2) – well-designed guide to Turkey's premier city.

My Merhaba (🖥 www.mymerhaba.com) – the leading Turkish expatriate website, with a lively and informative forum.

Turkey Central (🖥 www.turkeycentral.com/index.php) – internet directory with maps, guides and a forum.

Turkey Real Estate (🖥 www.turkeyrealestate.co.uk) – reliable property portal based in the UK.

Turkish Living Forum (🖥 www.turkishliving.com/index.php) – more than 5,000 members.

Media

Hürriyet (🖥 www.hurriyet.com.tr/english/turkey) – online news digest.

Sabah (🖥 http://english.sabah.com.tr) – English version of the Turkish daily.

Turkish Press (🖥 www.turkishpress.com) – headlines in English.

Turkish Radio & Television (🖥 www.trt.net.tr/wwwtrt/anasayfa.aspx) – the national broadcaster TRT (in Turkish only); click the menu bar for Voice of Turkey, which will take you to a page with links to more foreign-language radio services. (The direct route to this page is 🖥 www.trt.net.tr/wwwtrt/tsr.aspx.)

Travel

Go to Turkey (💻 www.gototurkey.co.uk) – UK branch of the Turkish tourist board.

Havaş (💻 www.havas.com.tr/en/default.asp) – airport parking and shuttle service.

Lonely Planet (💻 www.lonelyplanet.com/worldguide/turkey)

Turkish Airlines (💻 www.thy.com) – the national carrier.

Turkish State Railways (💻 www.tcdd.gov.tr/tcdding/index.htm) – unwieldy but informative guide to trains, fares – and railway museums.

Turkey Travel Planner (💻 www.turkeytravelplanner.com/index.html) – in-depth travel guide by Tom Brosnahan, long-time Turcophile and Lonely Planet writer.

Wikitravel (💻 http://wikitravel.org/en/Turkey) – community travel guide.

Miscellaneous

Araba.com (💻 http://araba.com) – online car supermarket (in Turkish only).

Binnur's Turkish Cookbook (💻 www.turkishcookbook.com) – recipes from a Turk in exile.

Blog Turkey (💻 www.expat-blog.com/en/directory/middle-east/turkey) – collection of blogs by expats in Turkey.

Earthquake Monitor (💻 www.gezdirici.net/eqmon/index.php?lang=en) – find out where the earth is shaking.

Football in Turkey (💻 www.angelfire.com/nj/sivritepe) – the teams, the fixtures, the results.

Gitti Gidiyor (💻 www.gittigidiyor.com) – Turkey's answer to eBay (in Turkish only).

Hepsi Burada (💻 www.hepsiburada.com/default.aspx?nc=1) – online shopping portal (in Turkish only).

Lycian Way (💻 www.lycianway.com) – trekking in Turkey.

Migros (💻 www.kangarum.com.tr) – online shopping at Migros and other stores (in Turkish only).

Tulumba (💻 www.tulumba.com) – online shopping at the Turkish mega-store.

Wikipedia (💻 http://en.wikipedia.org/wiki/Portal:Turkey) – dedicated portal from the community encyclopaedia.

APPENDIX D: USEFUL WORDS & PHRASES

B elow is a list of words and phrases you may need during your first few days in Turkey. They are, of course, no substitute for learning the language, which you should make your top priority. All verbs are in the polite *siz* form, which is the correct form to use when addressing a stranger. For a guide to pronunciation, see Chapter 5.

Asking for Help

Do you speak English?	*İngilizce biliyor musunuz?*
I don't speak Turkish	*Türkçe bilmiyorum.*
Please could you speak slowly.	*Lütfen, yavaş konuşur musunuz?*
I don't understand.	*Anlamıyorum.*
I need …	*… a (ya)/e (ye) ihtiyacım var.*
I want …	*… istiyorum.*

Communications

Telephone & Internet

phone line	*telefon hattı*
mobile phone	*cep telefonu*
no answer	*cevap yok*
engaged/busy	*meşgul*
internet	*internet*
email	*e-posta*
broadband connection	*ADSL internet bağlantısı*
internet café/wifi spot	*internet kafe/kablosuz bağlantı yeri*

Post

post office	*postane (PTT)*
postcard/letter/parcel	*kartpostal/mektup/paket*
stamps	*pullar*
How much does it cost to send a letter to Europe/North America/ Australia?	*Avrupa'ya/Kuzey Amerika'ya/ Avustralya'ya mektup göndermek için kaç para?*

Media

newspaper/magazine	*gazete/dergi*
Do you sell English newspapers?	*İngilizce gazete satıyor musunuz?*

Courtesy

yes	*evet*
no	*hayır*
excuse me *pardon* (to get past)	*afferdersiniz* (to get attention)
sorry	*özür dilerim* (apology)
	efendim? (incomprehension)
I don't know	*bilmiyorum*
I don't mind	*fark etmez*
please	*lütfen*
thank you	*teşekkür ederim*
you're welcome	*bir şey değil*

Days & Months

Monday	*Pazartesi*
Tuesday	*Salı*
Wednesday	*Çarşamba*
Thursday	*Perşembe*
Friday	*Cuma*
Saturday	*Cumartesi*
Sunday	*Pazar*
January	*Ocak*
February	*Şubat*
March	*Mart*
April	*Nisan*
May	*Mayıs*
June	*Haziran*
July	*Temmuz*
August	*Ağustos*
September	*Eylül*
October	*Ekim*
November	*Kasım*
December	*Aralık*

Driving

car insurance	*araba sigortası*
driving licence	*surucu belgesi*
hire/rental car	*kiralık araba*
How far is it to … ?	*… a (ya)/e (ye) ne kadar uzak?*
Can I park here?	*Buraya park edebilir miyim?*
unleaded petrol (gas)/diesel	*kurşunsuz benzin/mazot*
Fill up the tank please.	*Lütfen depoyu doldurun.*
I need YTL 20/30/40 of petrol (gas).	*20/30/40 liralık benzin ihtiyacım var.*
air/water/oil	*hava/su/yağ*
car wash	*araba yıkıma*
My car has broken down.	*rabam arıza yaptı.*
I've run out of petrol (gas).	*Benzinim bitti.*
My tyre is flat.	*Lasiğim patladı.*
I need a tow truck.	*Çekici araca ihtiyacım var.*

Emergency

Emergency	*Acil durum*
Fire	*Yangın var*
Help	*İmdat*
Police	*Polis*
Stop	*Dur*
Stop thief	*Hırsız var*
Watch out	*Dikkat*

Finding your Way

Where is … ?	*… nerede?*
Where is the toilet?	*Tuvalet nerede?*
Where is the nearest … ?	*En yakın … nerede?*
How do I get to … ?	*… a (ya)/e (ye) nasıl gidebilirim?*
Can I walk there?	*Oraya yürüyebilir miyim?*
How far is … ?	*… ne kadar uzak?*
A map, please.	*Bir harita lütfen.*
I'm lost.	*Yolumu kaybettim.*
left/right/straight ahead	*sol/sağ/düz*
opposite/next to/near	*karşısında/-in bitişiğinde/yakın*
airport	*havalimanı*
bus/plane/taxi/train	*otobüs/uçak/taksi/tren*

bus stop	*otobüs durağı*
taxi rank	*taksi durağı*
train/bus station	*tren istasyonu/otogar*
What time does the ...	*... saat kaçta varıyor/*
arrive/leave?	*kalkıyor?*
one-way/return ticket	*gidiş/gidiş-dönüş bileti*
bank/embassy/consulate	*banka/elçilik/konsolosluk*

Greetings

Hello	*Merhaba*
Goodbye	*Allaha ısmarladık* (said by those leaving)
	Güle güle (said by those staying behind)
Good morning	*Günaydın*
Good afternoon	*Tünaydın*
Good night	*İyi geceler*

Health & Medical Emergencies

I feel ill/I feel dizzy.	*Hastayım./Başım dönüyor.*
I need a doctor/ambulance.	*Doktora/Ambülansa*
ihtiyacım var.	
doctor/nurse/dentist	*doktor/hemşire/diş hekimi*
surgeon/specialist	*operatör/uzman doktor*
hospital/health centre/A&R	*hastane/sağlık ocağı/acil servis*
chemist's/optician's	*eczane/gözlükçü*
prescription	*reçete*

In a Bar or Restaurant

Waiter!	*Garson!*
Menu	*yemek listesi*
bill	*hesap*
well done/medium/rare (for meat)	*iyi pişmiş/orta pişmiş/az pişmiş*
vegetarian	vejetaryen
meat/fish	*et/balık*

Numbers

one	*bir*
two	*iki*
three	*uç*
four	*dört*
five	*beş*
six	*alt*
seven	*yedi*
eight	*sekiz*
nine	*dokuz*
ten	*on*
eleven	*on bir*
twelve	*on iki*
thirteen	*on uç*
fourteen	*on dört*
fifteen	*on beş*
sixteen	*on altı*
seventeen	*on yedi*
eighteen	*on sekiz*
nineteen	*on dokuz*
twenty	*yirmi*
thirty	*otuz*
forty	*kırk*
fifty	*elli*
sixty	*altmış*
seventy	*yetmiş*
eighty	*seksen*
ninety	*doksan*
100	*yüz*
200	*iki yüz*
500	*beş yüz*
1,000	*bin*
million	*milyon*

Paying

How much is it?	*Bu ne kadar?*
The bill, please.	*Hesap lütfen.*
Do you take credit cards?	*Kredi kartı kabul ediyormusunuz?*

Socialising

Pleased to meet you.	*Memnun oldum.*
My name is …	*Adım …*
This is my husband/wife/son/ daughter/colleague/friend.	*Bu benim kocam/hanım/ oğulum/kızım/meslektaşım/ arkadaşım.*
How are you?	*Nasılsınız?*
Very well, thank you.	*Çok iyiyim, teşekkür ederim.*

Shopping

What time do you open/close?	*Saat kaçta açıyorsunuz/ kapatıyorsunuz?*
Who's the last person (in the queue)?	*Kuyrukta en son kim?*
I'm just looking (browsing).	*Sadece bakıyorum.*
I'm looking for …	*… arıyorum.*
Can I try it on?	*Üstümde deneyibilir miyim?*
I need size …	*… beden ihtiyacım var.*
bigger/smaller/longer/shorter	*daha büyük/daha küçük/daha uzun/daha kısa*
A bag, please.	*Bir poşet lütfen.*
How much is this?	*Bu ne kadar?*

APPENDIX E: MAP OF REGIONS & PROVINCES

L isted below are the seven regions (*bölge*) and 81 provinces (*iller*) of Turkey, shown on the map opposite.

Aegean

1. Afyonkarahisar
2. Aydın
3. Denizli
4. İzmir
5. Kütahya
6. Manisa
7. Muğla
8. Uşak

Black Sea

9. Amasya
10. Artvin
11. Bayburt
12. Çorum
13. Giresun
14. Gümüşhane
15. Ordu
16. Rize
17. Samsun
18. Sinop
19. Tokat
20. Trabzon
21. Bartın
22. Bolu
23. Düzce
24. Karabük
25. Kastamonu
26. Zonguldak

Central Anatolia

27. Aksaray
28. Ankara
29. Çankırı
30. Eskişehir
31. Karaman
32. Kayseri
33. Kırıkkale
34. Kırşehir
35. Konya
36. Nevşehir
37. Niğde
38. Sivas
39. Yozgat

East Anatolia

40. Ağrı
41. Ardahan
42. Bingöl
43. Bitlis
44. Elazığ
45. Erzincan
46. Erzurum
47. Hakkâri
48. Iğdır
49. Kars
50. Malatya
51. Muş
52. Tunceli
53. Van

Marmara

54. Balıkesir
55. Bilecik
56. Bursa
57. Çanakkale
58. Edirne
59. İstanbul
60. Kırklareli
61. Kocaeli
62. Sakarya
63. Tekirdağ
64. Yalova

Mediterranean

65. Adana
66. Antalya
67. Burdur
68. Hatay
69. Isparta
70. Kahramanmaraş
71. Mersin
72. Osmaniye

Southeastern Anatolia

73. Adıyaman
74. Batman
75. Diyarbakır
76. Gaziantep
77. Kilis
78. Mardin
79. Şanlıurfa
80. Siirt
81. Şırnak

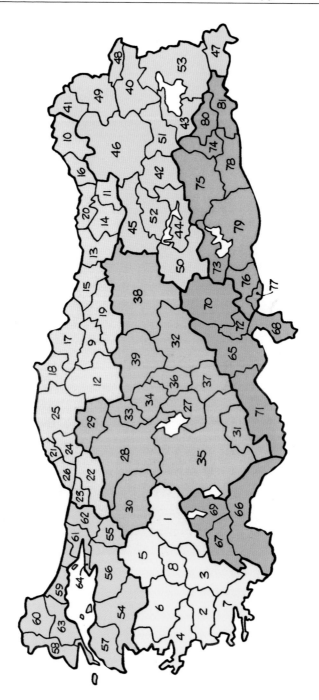

INDEX

Survival Books

Essential reading for anyone planning to live, work, retire or buy a home abroad

Survival Books was established in 1987 and by the mid-'90s was the leading publisher of books for people planning to live, work, buy property or retire abroad.

From the outset, our philosophy has been to provide the most comprehensive and up-to-date information available. Our titles routinely contain up to twice as much information as other books and are updated frequently. All our books contain colour photographs and some are printed in two colours or full colour throughout. They also contain original cartoons, illustrations and maps.

Survival Books are written by people with first-hand experience of the countries and the people they describe, and therefore provide invaluable insights that cannot be obtained from official publications or websites, and information that is more reliable and objective than that provided by the majority of unofficial sites.

Survival Books are designed to be easy – and interesting – to read. They contain a comprehensive list of contents and index and extensive appendices, including useful addresses, further reading, useful websites and glossaries to help you obtain additional information as well as metric conversion tables and other useful reference material.

Our primary goal is to provide you with the essential information necessary for a trouble-free life or property purchase and to save you time, trouble and money.

We believe our books are the best – they are certainly the best-selling. But don't take our word for it – read what reviewers and readers have said about Survival Books at the front of this book.

Order your copies today by phone, fax, post or email from:
Survival Books, PO Box 3780, Yeovil, BA21 5WX, United Kingdom.
Tel: +44 (0)1935-700060, email: sales@survivalbooks.net,
Website: www.survivalbooks.net

Buying a Home Series

B uying a home abroad is not only a major financial transaction but also a potentially life-changing experience; it's therefore essential to get it right. Our Buying a Home guides are required reading for anyone planning to purchase property abroad and are packed with vital information to guide you through the property jungle and help you avoid disasters that can turn a dream home into a nightmare.

The purpose of our Buying a Home guides is to enable you to choose the most favourable location and the most appropriate property for your requirements, and to reduce your risk of making an expensive mistake by making informed decisions and calculated judgements rather than uneducated and hopeful guesses. Most importantly, they will help you save money and will repay your investment many times over.

Buying a Home guides are the most comprehensive and up-to-date source of information available about buying property abroad – whether you're seeking a detached house or an apartment, a holiday or a permanent home (or an investment property), these books will prove invaluable.

For a full list of our current titles, visit our website at
www.survivalbooks.net

Living and Working Series

Our Living and Working guides are essential reading for anyone planning to spend a period abroad – whether it's an extended holiday or permanent migration – and are packed with priceless information designed to help you avoid costly mistakes and save both time and money.

Living and Working guides are the most comprehensive and up-to-date source of practical information available about everyday life abroad. They aren't, however, simply a catalogue of dry facts and figures, but are written in a highly readable style – entertaining, practical and occasionally humorous.

Our aim is to provide you with the comprehensive practical information necessary for a trouble-free life. You may have visited a country as a tourist, but living and working there is a different matter altogether; adjusting to a new environment and culture and making a home in any foreign country can be a traumatic and stressful experience. You need to adapt to new customs and traditions, discover the local way of doing things (such as finding a home, paying bills and obtaining insurance) and learn all over again how to overcome the everyday obstacles of life.

All these subjects and many, many more are covered in depth in our Living and Working guides – don't leave home without them.

The Expats' Best Friend!

Other Survival Books

The Best Places to Buy a Home in France/Spain: Unique guides to where to buy property in Spain and France, containing detailed regional profiles and market reports.

Buying, Selling and Letting Property: The best source of information about buying, selling and letting property in the UK.

Earning Money From Your French Home: Income from property in France, including short- and long-term letting.

Investing in Property Abroad: Everything you need to know and more about buying property abroad for investment and pleasure.

Life in the UK - Test & Study Guide: essential reading for anyone planning to take the 'Life in the UK' test in order to become a permanent resident (settled) in the UK.

Making a Living: Comprehensive guides to self-employment and starting a business in France and Spain.

Renovating & Maintaining Your French Home: The ultimate guide to renovating and maintaining your dream home in France.

Retiring in France/Spain: Everything a prospective retiree needs to know about the two most popular international retirement destinations.

Running Gîtes and B&Bs in France: An essential book for anyone planning to invest in a gîte or bed & breakfast business.

Rural Living in France: An invaluable book for anyone seekingthe 'good life', containing a wealth of practical information about all aspects of French country life.

Shooting Caterpillars in Spain: The hilarious and compelling story of two innocents abroad in the depths of Andalusia in thelate '80s.

For a full list of our current titles, visit our website at www.survivalbooks.net

PHOTO CREDITS

Culture Wise Series

Current Titles:

America
Australia
Canada
England
France
Germany
India
Japan
New Zealand
Spain
Turkey

Coming soon:

Cyprus
Dubai
Greece
Holland
Hong Kong
Ireland
Italy
Switzerland

Culture Wise - The Wisest Way to Travel